BEFORE

EARTH DAY

Before Earth Day

THE ORIGINS OF AMERICAN ENVIRONMENTAL

LAW, 1945–1970 **Karl Boyd Brooks**

 UNIVERSITY PRESS OF KANSAS

Published by the University Press of Kansas (Lawrence, Kansas 66045), which was organized by the Kansas Board of Regents and is operated and funded by Emporia State University, Fort Hays State University, Kansas State University, Pittsburg State University, the University of Kansas, and Wichita State University

© 2009 by the University Press of Kansas

Library of Congress Cataloging-in-Publication Data

Brooks, Karl Boyd.
  Before Earth Day : the origins of American environmental law, 1945–1970 / Karl Boyd Brooks.
     p. cm.
  Includes bibliographical references.
  ISBN 978-0-7006-1627-5 (cloth : alk. paper)
   1. Environmental law—United States. 2. Environmental law—United States—History. I. Title.
  KF3775.B727 2009
  344.7304′6—dc22
                                        2008044077

British Library Cataloguing-in-Publication Data is available.

Printed in the United States of America

10 9 8 7 6 5 4 3 2 1

The paper used in this publication is recycled and contains 30 percent postconsumer waste. It is acid free and meets the minimum requirements of the American National Standard for Permanence of Paper for Printed Library Materials Z39.48-1992.

For Mary

CONTENTS

While actively practicing law in my hometown of Boise, Idaho, between 1983 and 1996, I rarely had time to think about *what* I was doing, or *why*. I was too busy worrying about *how* I was doing to ponder law's *what* or *why*. For nine of those fourteen years, I lawyered in some out-of-the-ordinary ways. I represented 30,000 of my neighbors for six years as a state legislator and then crisscrossed the Gem State for three years on behalf of its biggest grassroots environmental group. Even then, as my legal work brought me every day right up against law's embrace of the natural world, the *how* of politics and advocacy consumed me. The *what* of environmental law, or its *why*? No one paid, elected, or tasked me to worry much about them.

I began studying for a history doctorate in 1996 at the University of Kansas, only one time zone east of my home state but a world away from Idaho's white-hot environmental politics. In the Wheat State, environmental controversy was hardly even "below the fold." Journalistic ignorance and popular indifference hid environmental law from public view. The field lay where it had come to rest by the late 1970s: a specialized province inhabited mostly by public administrators, corporate lawyers, and law teachers. Gaining some personal distance and intellectual perspective on my idled law practice helped me appreciate *what* I had been doing. I had, in fact, spent fourteen years of my young adulthood *making* law. Journalistic jargon classifies elected members of the legislative branch as "lawmakers," so service in the Idaho senate between 1986 and 1992 clearly qualified me. But the more I read and wrote and thought and talked about environmental and legal history during graduate school, the clearer I became about what I—and my colleagues in practice, politics, and public-interest labor—had been doing. All of us had been *making* law. That was the *what* of it.

Nearly as soon as I began writing my dissertation in 1998, under my dear friend Donald Worster's guidance, I realized lawmaking about American nature enlisted more than attorneys, legislators, and lobbyists. Lawyers represent clients, so they make the law, too. Legislators serve at constituents' pleasure, so my neighbors, in their sovereign capacity as voters, made environmental law. Lobbyists and activists speak and write on behalf of their organizations' members: Idaho Conservation League's 3,000 dues-paying members were thus lawmakers. And so were the Idaho Mining Association's corporate founders, and Idaho Power Company's ratepayers, and so on through the infinite directory of organized and unorganized American citizenry.

James Willard Hurst had well understood this many-handed work of making American law. His legal histories in the postwar era broadened our field's focus beyond appellate judges' published opinions, governors' executive messages, and administrative agencies' rules, beyond even the printed texts created by people officially invested in some fashion with lawmaking authority. Willard Hurst showed me how clients, even before they walked into a lawyer's office, while merely being landlords or employees or patients, made law. Those voters who went to the polls in 1986, 1988, and 1990 to mark their ballots for my three Republican opponents in Legislative District 20 were lawmakers, too. Their demands and preferences and prejudices influenced my legislative speeches, bill drafts, and floor votes.

The dissertation that became my first book, *Public Power, Private Dams: The Hells Canyon High Dam Controversy*, impelled me to consider another lawmaker's contributions to postwar administrative law change in the Snake-Columbia Basin of the American Northwest. The Snake River's waters determined whether sugar beets or Chinook salmon, or some of each species, would live or die along the watershed's high desert banks. Those now-rushing, now-silent rivers of the postwar Northwest, whether pounding loud or pooling still, were making and remaking law simply by *doing* and *being*. Americans struggled to remodel their rules about owning, using, and valuing rivers because the waters kept changing—and changing us—as we owned, used, and revalued them. By 1957, when my book about the Hells Canyon controversy closes, the rivers' lawmaking agency had empowered corporations, resisted administrators, perplexed biologists, and divided citizens. Thus divided, citizens had fiercely contested their sovereign right to make new and remake old laws to cope with the rivers' own sovereign, lawmaking power. Historians term the Snake's own power to make change across time as "agency." Lawyers might recognize natural agency as a form of "sovereignty." By whatever label we use to describe the waters' power, it deserved more careful consideration, just as environmental and legal historians study human actors to assess their historical agency.[1]

By trying to explain how natural features and forces interacted with people to make the postwar Northwest's history, I pointed myself toward this book's subject: the origins and emergence of American environmental law. Much of the earlier thinking, reading, and writing that enabled me to write *Public Power, Private Dams* imaginatively outlined the techniques, tools, and evidence I now use to answer the big question at this book's heart. What happened before 1970 to create environmental law? As late as 1967, the evidence indicates that no American legal professional—whether scholar or practitioner—wrote or spoke the simple label, "environmental law." After 1970, not only legal professionals but the lay public recognized something new had emerged. All spoke easily of "environmental law" as that new something. An entirely new legal discipline and way of thinking about law, one of the most stubbornly conservative and gradually evolutionary of human constructs, doesn't just *happen* in three years. This book therefore explores how changes underway before 1970 among the American people and amid the natural world they inhabited transmuted older forms of legal thought and practice into environmental law.

With my first book's manuscript safely in its publisher's hands, I turned to answering this deceptively simple but quite important question. Luckily, the University of Virginia Law School presented me the ideal opportunity to move from wondering about environmental law's emergence to actually offering some tentative first thoughts. Professors Jon Cannon of the Law School and Willis Jenkins of Virginia's Environmental Studies Program invited me, in the summer of 2004, to join a panel of distinguished environmental and legal historians at a conference dedicated to seeing what law and the humanities had to say to one another. My good fortune multiplied when the conference organizers asked me to present some helpful commentary about papers delivered in Charlottesville by the University of Wisconsin Law School's Arthur McEvoy and UVA's own Edmund Russell. In 1986, McEvoy had written *The Fisherman's Problem*, a powerful, provocative study about nature's effects on legal history. Ed Russell had carefully interrogated the American state as war-maker and lawgiver in his 2001 book, *War and Nature*.[2]

My October 2005 Virginia conference comments suggested some ways in which historians could come to grips with the problem of environmental legal change after World War II. And I enjoyed a double helping of good luck when writing up my informal comments for publication by the *Virginia Environmental Law Journal*. The Charlottesville conference gave me the privilege of listening to Georgetown law professor Richard Lazarus's funny, wise talk about how gingerly the United State Supreme Court had handled the new field of environmental law during the 1970s and 1980s. I then enjoyed the pleasure of dining with Lazarus, during which meal he graciously answered my questions about his masterful new book, The Making of Environmental Law.[3]

Lazarus has written a superb legal history, but listening and talking to him convinced me of two things: explaining the origins—the invention, actually—of American environmental law remains very important, and by closely focusing on the period after 1965, Lazarus actually made even more imperative the task of understanding the two prior decades. The book you are now reading contends that the entire quarter-century between 1945 and 1970 composes a unified period of legal creation, one deserving integrated analysis that combines approaches rooted in environmental as well as legal history. Although I do not concur with all of Making of Environmental Law's conclusions, its author's good sense, hard work, and vast experience in teaching, practicing, and studying law immeasurably benefited my work. I wrote this book more quickly and surely because I got a chance to debate hypotheses and compare research with Richard Lazarus at the University of Virginia Law School's innovative conference.[4]

Our encounter vindicated—as if further vindication were needed—the judgment of Thomas Jefferson, the University's founder, who believed spirited conversation among curious people offered the best chance to spread light into corners previously dark. For the privilege of beginning that Jeffersonian conversation about environmental legal history, I thank Art McEvoy, Ed Russell, and Richard Lazarus, who all got me thinking. And I offer my warmest appreciation to Jon Cannon and Willis Jenkins, who invited me to share a table while Mr. Jefferson's community did its work.

McEvoy and Russell proposed in Charlottesville that environmental and legal historians should both closely attend to the American state's two supreme, complementary expressions of sovereign agency: declaring law and making war. Throughout the twentieth century in America, war made both environmental law and environmental history. McEvoy and Russell suggested war-making's exigencies caused the state and its agents, public and private, to transform existing laws. Both contended that old wars have left new legal institutions in their wake. Persuaded by their insights, I begin this history of environmental law's creation at World War II's end. Rules made and enforced by war-fighting institutions continued to reshape America's natural world, and citizens' relationships to it and to each other, long after the global emergency had ended.

President Franklin D. Roosevelt declared his New Deal a "war on want." Indeed, many New Deal institutions facilitated mobilization when real war erupted. I think this was not entirely fortuitous, especially after 1938, when Roosevelt came to believe that a general war in Europe was likely to erupt at almost any time. By focusing on World War II and its aftermath, therefore, we will better appreciate how key features of the New Deal's legal legacy fertilized environmental law's genetic inheritance.

Two quite different American places suggest answers to a question central to tracing environmental law's emergence. How did law and nature respond to war? In the Pacific Northwest and on the High Plains during World War II the national state used law to impress nature into military service. Service for the war-fighting state, a role Edmund Russell has termed "nature as ally," transformed rivers and grasslands. What then happened to law and nature after peace came in 1945?[5]

Wartime and postwar control of natural resources in the Columbia River Basin illuminate environmental law's link to New Deal legal regimes. Six weeks after the Japanese attacked Pearl Harbor, the United States government ordered all private and public electricity providers in Washington, Oregon, Idaho, and Montana to create the Northwest Power Pool. Mobilization for global war accomplished in days what more than forty years of political agitation and trust-busting litigation had not. With a few pen strokes in Portland, Oregon, and publication of a few *Federal Register* pages in Washington, D.C., the national state took control over generating, distributing, and selling all electricity in the region. As hydropower supplied nearly all Northwestern electricity, the federal government thus became the region's watermaster as well as its powerbroker.

In the Northwest during World War II, federal administrative agency discretion—the New Deal's primary legal innovation—supplanted traditional common law and state statutory regimes. Wartime natural-resources managers turned smoothly toward postwar economic and social planning. Broad statutory grants to manage water—the Northwest's principal power source—empowered federal experts to deploy vast administrative discretion largely free from judicial scrutiny or citizen input. Even when political liberalism waned rapidly in the Northwest after 1950, legal institutions and practices established during the New Deal and perfected during World War II influenced the region's economy and shaped its society until the 1970s.[6]

Today, however, the shaky status of a regime based on attempts to control nature through administrative expertise dramatizes environmental law's unstable legacy. No Northwesterner offers much allegiance to federal resource planning. Comprehensive river basin development, a New Deal/Fair Deal mantra, survives only on ancient blueprints and flickering educational films. Judges watch the federal waterpower agencies like hawks. Litigious Native peoples and activist anglers keep the once-mighty agencies on short leashes. The twenty-first-century Northwest epitomizes the decrepitude of environmental law founded upon political expediency and intellectual inconsistency: agencies distrusted, experts ignored, gridlocks over water, power, and fish tightening each day.[7]

However, another wartime legal innovation on the High Plains cautions against writing environmental law's premature obituary. In late summer 1942, the War Department divested ranchers and farmers of some 50,000 acres—nearly half a county—in Kansas' Flint Hills. There, government and industry collaborated to prove the airworthiness of a new generation of heavy bombers. By 1944, the Smoky Hill Bombing Range was absorbing daily poundings from B-29 Super Fortresses built in Wichita for the air war against Japan. Planes tested in Kansas ultimately dropped the two atomic bombs that ended the Pacific War. The national state's war-fighting and lawmaking powers not only transformed Smoky Hill. They tied this pockmarked piece of the High Plains to the damp, green Columbia Basin. Each atomic bomb dropped on Japan by planes tested in Kansas contained radioactive materials created using cheap hydroelectricity that the Northwest Power Pool delivered to the Hanford Works in Washington State.[8]

Kansas' Smoky Hill Bombing Range complicates a straight declension story about environmental law's trajectory after the 1970s. It has become a place covered by a thick residue of environmental law. After national rules shouldered aside common law and Kansas statutes during World War II, environmental law's forms and values still shape the range's management. Amid a state with the nation's smallest proportion of public lands and one of its most environmentally indifferent polities, Smoky Hill stands apart. Defense Department regulations governing the range stress biodiversity over production agriculture. This small space on the vast Great Plains bears thousands of bomb scars. Yet, seen as a legally defined place, Smoky Hill reminds us how legal forms can toughen over time, growing resilient and durable through repetition despite criticisms of their coherence and doubts about their legitimacy.[9]

Taken together, the Columbia Basin and Smoky Hill incite hard thinking about American environmental law's origins and agents. To trace the life of American environmental law requires asking some basic historic questions. What dates mattered? Which places deserve study? What people working within which institutions made and resisted change? Did crises confronted at crossroads form more law, their heat and pressure producing new alloys from simpler materials? Or did environmental law grow incrementally, like a coral reef, as the gradual, almost imperceptible unfolding of doctrines produced a new structure?

My answers to these questions portray environmental law's history as partly declensionist, partly whiggish, and part simply accretive, as one decision settled atop another precedent until something distinctive enough drew people's attention to the emergence of a new field of law.

Environmental and legal historians, as well as legal academics, have often taken the easy way out, ritually intoning that "Environmental law began in or around 1970, shortly after the first Earth Day." McEvoy's older book, *The Fisherman's Problem*, along with Paul Milazzo's new one, *Unlikely Environmentalists: Congress and Clean Water, 1945–1972*, remind us environmental law has a past, too. It did not spring fully formed from Edmund Muskie's furrowed brow along an arc traced by Rachel Carson's golden pen.[10]

My book begins presenting what I believe is a truer, albeit messier, history of environmental law's origins and emergence by addressing the following questions:

1. Why do so many law teachers still date the advent of environmental law to the years 1969–1974?
2. What happened in the twenty-five years before 1969 that stimulated important legal change during the next five years?
3. What traditional legal rules—property, procedure, contract, tort, administrative and municipal law, statutory construction, remedies—underwent decisive change during that period, or even before?

4. How—and how much—did existing legal institutions change these traditional legal fields, and what new institutions appeared to accelerate the pace of change?

5. Which legal rules and institutions persisted, and even resisted change, their inertia impelling development of different responses to long-standing concerns?

6. What mutual, reciprocal influences between 1945 and 1970 drove change through actions by these lawmaking pairs: lawyers and clients, litigants and judges, politicians and constituents, administrators and the regulated, law schools and practitioners?

7. And, to do the fullest justice to a story literally rooted in humans' dependence on nature, what was occurring in the natural world itself that stimulated legal change after 1945?

My answers indicate environmental law began emerging earlier than we think, and well before 1969–1970. Postwar lawmakers largely elaborated administrative and statutory innovations that New Dealers had borrowed from their Progressive Era predecessors. More happened in states and specific local places than previously understood. And despite the new evidence I present, environmental law's history, truly told, requires much more study of individual lawyers, judges, clients, and elected officials responding to specific encounters with natural features and forces at work in specific places.

Over forty years ago, Willard Hurst told legal historians to spend more time watching the lumber market and less time reading appellate opinions if they wanted to know why Wisconsin's pine forests nearly vanished in the second half of the nineteenth century. He pried open what had been, until then, something of a "black box" approach to legal history, one that posited law as a product uniquely grown within a legal system largely impervious to economic, political, and cultural forces. The field of legal history has never been the same.[11]

I have tried to follow Hurst's advice to show how, when, and where American environmental law emerged after World War II. I have imaginatively leaned against the walls in legislative hearing rooms, pulled up a chair to lawyers' conference tables, slipped into administrators' cubicles to look over their desks, and stood just inside corporate boardroom doors. And I have sometimes visited another environmental law forge, a place known somewhat from my past life. I try settling the reader onto metal folding chairs in poorly ventilated high school auditoriums to listen as aspirants for elective office sought to enlist local people to endorse their campaigns.

By visiting these human places, I have tried to describe law being made by being *used*: tested, tossed away, and reinvented. Importantly, I think, this book also visits the riverbanks and freeways, the duck blinds and airsheds where natural features and forces have always been making Americans change their rules. By spending time in all these places, we will begin to better understand the various processes by which the dynamic, unceasing process of legal change created environmental law.

ACKNOWLEDGMENTS

Hanging behind my office desk is a grainy color snapshot, taken in 1977 in Idaho's Sawtooth Wilderness Area, during a particularly cold, wet Fourth of July backpacking trip. I stand with two college-age friends, Steve Edquist and Mitch Anderson, smiling jauntily atop Nahneke Peak's broken granite, as a third Boise pal, Drew Noack, snaps our picture. Sitting on my office desk is a better color picture, taken in 2004, on southern Idaho's Owyhee Desert, just above Battle Creek. During a brief splash of sun that brightened an otherwise cold, wet early June backpacking trip, my children, Jenni and Dylan, smile bravely at me and another longtime Boise bud, Jeff Swanstrum.

Propped against the wall in my home office is an old black-and-white print, taken in Boise's North End on Christmas Eve 1945. Five duck hunters and two wet but noble retrievers pose behind their impressive bag of mallards. My dad, on his eighteenth birthday, three days before he left home to join the United States Army Air Corps, proudly grips his shotgun barrel while, to his left, Army veteran Ernie Day grins broadly behind wire-framed glasses. To these Idaho outdoor inspirations, I offer my sincerest thanks. They, along with dozens of others too numerous to name, have unknowingly helped me write this history of environmental law's emergence after World War II.

No work of history gets written by a busy college professor without generous financial support from his employer. The University of Kansas materially aided my work with a New Faculty General Research Fund grant, a Self Fellows Society Innovation grant, sabbatical leave, and numerous College of Liberal Arts and Sciences travel grants. KU also kindly granted me a year's leave to accept a United States Supreme Court Fellowship in 2001–2002. During that momentous year in Washington, D.C., I began weaving together the threads that became this book.

Nancy Scott Jackson first saw this book's potential and brought me into the University Press of Kansas' fold. Fred Woodward's patience kept me there, despite tribulations and delays that must have taxed even his editorial patience. Kalyani Fernando's and Susan McRory's energy and encouragement finally brought my project through to print. Indexer extraordinaire Mary Brooks has always offered so much more than a busy reader's best friend at the back of the book.

Environmental and legal historians in the Missouri Basin are fortunate to enjoy the proximity and largesse of two neighborhood Presidential Libraries. Materials from the Eisenhower Library in Abilene, Kansas, and Truman Library in Independence, Missouri, enlivened this work as their dedicated archivists brightened my days. I particularly thank Mike Devine and Ray Geselbracht of the Truman Library for inviting me to present early sketches of this work at a 2003 summer teaching seminar and appointing me to chair the 2007 Truman Legacy Conference about postwar environmental history, held in the salubrious surroundings of the president's second favorite place, Key West, Florida.

Like all historians, I depend on libraries' conscientious, thorough professionals. I have been fortunate to work with some of the best, starting with my University of Kansas colleagues who staff Watson and Anschutz Libraries, Spencer Research Library's Kansas Collection, the Robert J. Dole Institute's Archives, and Wheat Law Library in Green Hall. Special thanks go to Wheat's Su Johnson, who made me feel like family by ignoring the boxes I kept accumulating. Farther afield, Denver Public Library staff introduced me to the wonders of its Conservation Collection. The Idaho State Historical Society's Linda Morton-Keithley and Judy Austin opened to my eager gaze the inestimably valuable Bruce Bowler Papers, where Carolyn Bowler shared not only her encyclopedic knowledge of her former father-in-law's legal files, but warm recollections about the man and his time and place.

A work of such breadth (and inadequacy) owes so much to historian friends and colleagues who have read and thoughtfully critiqued early versions. As always, Don Worster gave me the benefit of sharp insights, most of which I have probably not fully appreciated in these pages. The Nature and Culture Seminar, which he founded at the University of Kansas' Hall Center for the Humanities, gave me a last chance to subject my arguments to pungent criticism. Hall Center director Victor Bailey and seminar co-chair Gregory T. Cushman earn my thanks for maintaining this superb ongoing conversation about environmental history. Across the country, at various conferences, Paul Hirt, Sara Dant, Dale Nimz, Adam Rome, Ed Russell, Art McEvoy, and Bill Cronon critiqued various studies that now, much improved, compose part of this work. And Eric Freyfogle, Rob Glicksman, Mark Harvey, Adam Rome, Paul Milazzo, and William Rodgers, Jr., graciously read drafts of multiple chapters while busy with their own writing.

Anything of value reflects their good sense, while its many weaknesses are all my own. Late in every book's writing, as all authors probably know, you begin to doubt the whole enterprise, but two delightful conversations with real environmental law pioneers, Idaho's Scott Reed and Washington's Bill Rodgers, convinced me I was "getting it," at least sort of.

For eight years, I have enjoyed the privilege of trying out ideas about environmental and legal history with hundreds of students at the University of Kansas. Their questions and answers vindicated my conviction about the scholarly value of writing a book to integrate my research interests with varied professional experiences as a practicing lawyer, elected politician, and citizen activist. Thanks to my departmental chairs, especially Bill Woods of the Environmental Studies Program, for annually indulging my fascination with introducing environmental law to undergraduates. Special thanks go to three research students—Alvar Ayala, Michael Martin, and James Roberts—whose energy and results confirm my prediction that they will become valued professionals in their own right.

Early in my fourth career as a historian, KU law professors Francis Heller, Michael Hoeflich, and George Cameron Coggins taught me about studying legal history and environmental law. In their graduate classes, I first glimpsed the possibilities of writing an environmental history of environmental law, though none probably knew I had begun forming such a conceit. During my first two careers as a trial attorney and state legislator, a wonderful cast of Idaho lawyers, judges, politicians, journalists, and administrators encouraged me to think hard about law's intersection with politics. Even, and especially, when we disagreed, they taught me lessons that shape my work still. And every day, as I pursued my third career with the Idaho Conservation League, brave and funny environmental activists reminded me about citizenship's blessings and burdens.

Which brings me back finally to those pictures that surrounded me as I worked. When you are young, ambitious, and busy, you seldom take time to listen—really listen—to older people who have learned a few things about the topic that becomes the heart of a book. I regret not paying more attention to older conservationists, good citizens like Ernie Day and Bruce Bowler. If I have introduced their work and causes to posterity's respectful consideration, then I have partly made up for youthful indifference. I have no regrets for over forty years' worth of trips afield in the company of family and friends. My father and mother, Monte Brooks and Marti Brooks, know this, because they made it all possible. The children in my life—Jenni, Dylan, and Jud—someday will.

My wife, partner, and friend Mary knows how hard I worked to write this book to begin discharging the debt I will forever owe to the lawyers and citizens who always truly subscribed to the principle that we must care, every day in all we do, for the natural world as a public trust.

"TO THINK LIKE AN ENVIRONMENTAL LAWYER"
MAKING AMERICAN ENVIRONMENTAL LAW
THROUGHOUT THE POSTWAR ERA

I

"It is only within the last year or two that the term 'environmental law' has come into common usage. . . . At the same time there is actually very little new law in the field of environmental law."
—Norman J. Landau and Paul D. Rheingold, The Environmental Law Handbook (1971)

"Today both state and federal legislatures have the authority they need to protect the environment. . . . Courts are powerful enough so long as they are enabled to build a common law for the environment, remand dubious proposals to the legislatures, and declare moratoria."
—Joseph L. Sax, Defending the Environment (1970)

"These materials [in our book] are designed to explore traditional questions of law and politics which have assumed heightened significance in a society increasingly influenced by science and technology and increasingly concerned with the quality of its natural environment."
—Louis L. Jaffe and Laurence H. Tribe, Environmental Protection (1971)

Start this search for American environmental law's origins at the drinking fountain outside my office in the quiet university town of Lawrence. The water I drink tastes better because in July 2003 an ambitious project expanded and modernized the city's Kansas River Water Treatment Plant. City engineers in smudged hard hats scuffed through thick dust beneath the humid summer sun to certify that the contractors' work complied with state and federal water-quality laws. Their colleagues in City Hall sent me a pamphlet celebrating the project. The Water We Drink reminded 80,000 Lawrence homeowners, landlords, and renters that "water is one of the most vital elements in our lives, [so] we must have confidence in its safety and quality." To "ensure customer satisfaction by consistently delivering high quality water today and in the future," the Utilities Department announced that its new Water/Wastewater Master Plan would spend over $18 million during the next three years to keep expanding infrastructure and installing newer technology.[1]

I couldn't get to Wichita, 200 miles southwest of Lawrence, that summer, so I missed its annual Arkansas River Festival, "the state's largest party centered on a natural resource." Officials in Kansas' biggest city, halfway between the Arkansas' source in the Colorado Rockies and its confluence with the Mississippi, hoped beer and barbeque would inspire new civic activism to clean the turbid river, officially known only in Kansas as the "Ar-kan-sas." Wichita's mayor and city council president joined nongovernmental organizations to unveil the lime-green T-shirts that "river ambassadors" would sport during the Arkansas Festival. In bold white letters, the ambassadors' uniform asked, "Why isn't the river blue?" and "Are there fish in the river?"[2]

News that same summer told me "river experts and managers" from seven states—stretching nearly two thousand miles from Montana to Missouri—were convening in Atchison, Kansas, for the Missouri River Natural Resources Conference. Project leader Rosemary Hargrove explained why revising the Army Corps of Engineers' *Missouri River Master Operations Manual* was taking such a long time. The *Manual*, which "dictates priorities and policies for the river," was sparking political controversy the breadth of the Missouri Basin. Hargrove pleaded for "better communication" between all the interests that cared about the river, but, she admitted, "We don't have that yet."[3]

Problems with rivers a half-century before, half a continent away, carried this search for environmental law's beginnings to my home state of Idaho, where ordinary people grappled with many of the same environmental challenges Kansans faced in 2003. In January 1954, the Idaho Wildlife Federation's (IWF) annual meeting in Boise resolved to oppose any new power dam in the Hells Canyon of the Snake River, or on the Snake's principal tributaries, the Salmon and Clearwater. Dams proposed by the Army Corps of Engineers for north Idaho's Clearwater River would "be the worst possible example of butchering fish and game on the altar of power," charged Lewiston forester Mort Brigham. Boise lawyer Bruce Bowler, who had been doing the federation's legal work for almost a decade, smoldered as he recounted his November trip to testify against the Clearwater dams. After a 300-mile drive on icy mountain roads to Orofino, Idaho, he found the army's "public fact-finding" hearings were neither. Sounding a little like new Secretary of State John Foster Dulles, Bowler told IWF that the Corps hearings were "undemocratic dupes," contaminated by "arbitrary and unfair procedures" that encouraged "factual misrepresentations." Flawed legal procedures ensured bad environmental decisions, Bowler believed, because government agencies would use biased testimony to act "without consideration of wildlife values involved."[4]

Three months later, in Wenatchee, Washington, the Washington Sportsmen's Council and Oregon Wildlife League resolved to join their Idaho neighbors' fight against new Clearwater dams. New political alliances that ignored state lines to span watersheds encouraged Bruce Bowler to take an unprecedented legal step. His March 1954 Protest on behalf of the Idaho Wildlife Federation urged the Federal Power Commission to block Clearwater dams because Section 10 of the Federal Power Act protected ecological, cultural, esthetic, and recreational values. "Eighty organizations functioning within the State of Idaho . . . which have a total membership of 20,000 persons make this protest on behalf of the public interests involved in the wildlife and its habitat." Citizen-conservationists' first legal intervention in regulatory decisions claimed a new procedural right to participate fully in FPC decisionmaking. IWF's Protest also articulated a novel redefinition of the "public interest" in water. Section 10, Bowler told the commission, precluded "destruction of magnificent natural resources and facilities so affected by said project."[5]

Idaho conservationists' legal innovations paralleled political strategies aimed at linking urban recreationists with small-town wage workers. IWF joined the state AFL-CIO in summer 1954 to launch a two-front campaign for better hunting and stable wood-products employment. IWF and the unions lobbied Idaho's congressional delegation to back bills dedicating a fixed percentage of United States Forest Service timber-sale receipts "to improve wildlife and recreational facilities in our national forests." And the federation tasked Bowler to write a questionnaire, to be printed and sent with union funds, probing all state legislative candidates about their views on restoring the state's Fish and Game Commission's independent nonpolitical status.[6]

The IWF's new Stream Pollution Committee, chaired by Bowler, pressed Idaho legislators in 1957 to toughen the state's new statute controlling dredge mining. And the federation began lobbying the federal government to build water-pollution control muscle to complement state regulations. Resolutions drafted by IWF's Fish Committee in 1958, also chaired by the indefatigable Bowler, urged the Eisenhower Administration and Congress to renew the Federal Water Pollution Control Act and to double appropriations "for municipal aid for sewage treatment." IWF asked the president's new Health, Education, and Welfare Department to appoint "an undersecretary . . . fully devoted to water pollution problems."[7]

Five years before *Silent Spring* appeared in 1962, IWF members, like outdoors enthusiasts elsewhere in the 1950s, were raising alarms about DDT. In late summer 1957, Bowler buttonholed the Boise National Forest supervisor on the street to quiz him about chemical spraying in the mountains north of the city. Meant to kill weeds around newly planted seedlings, the DDT "had resulted in the complete elimination of fish life" in streams downhill from the pine plantations, according to outfitters' reports that reached Bowler. Forest Supervisor K. D. "Ken" Flock immediately wrote to Idaho Fish and Game Department Director Ross Leonard, assuring him that Bowler's questions raised legitimate concerns. Flock and the supervisor of the adjoining Payette National Forest pledged their agency's cooperation should Fish and Game want "to work together . . . to investigate thoroughly to find out what the facts might be."[8]

Idahoans' search for practical solutions to problems already present in the 1950s signals environmental law originated in the years just after World War II. Kansans' use of environmental law in summer 2003 confirms the persistence of an environmental lawmaking process that enlisted millions of Americans during three postwar decades. Many legal professionals—attorneys, judges, and administrators—played an important part in making new law. And much lawmaking occurred purposefully in legislative chambers, courthouses, and agency offices, the traditional venues dedicated to the legal process. Most environmental lawmaking, however, simply happened as people used water, breathed air, and turned soil. American environmental law kept evolving in the opening years of the twenty-first century much as it had been created during the quarter-century following World War II. Less a designed philosophical system than a necessary social product, environmental law emerged daily, fashioned by people who needed rules to help them live sociably, productively, and peaceably in the natural world they did not make.

American environmental law reflects the many rules citizens have imposed on themselves to govern their complex relationships with the natural world. Historian Richard Andrews has broadly framed environmental law-makers' task as one of "managing the environment by managing ourselves." More precisely, environmental law expresses the purpose of those rules humans have adopted to prolong their survival within the nonhuman natural world. Law teacher William H. Rodgers, Jr., defined the field a generation ago as "the law of planetary housekeeping, . . . concerned with protecting the planet and its people from activities that upset the earth and its life-sustaining activities." Even more strictly speaking, Americans have made environmental law since 1945 to ensure a modicum of human health, to guarantee roughly equal political access to natural resources, and to afford nonhuman life forms a basic level of protection against human demands. Leading contemporary legal commentator Richard J. Lazarus recently observed, "Environmental law regulates human activity in order to limit ecological impacts that threaten public health and biodiversity."[9]

Kansans in 2003, like Idahoans in the fifties, demonstrated one way ordinary people made environmental law: by continuously reworking their multiple, dynamic relationships with water. Ecological, economic, political, and cultural imperatives express these relationships. In revising any of their environmental relationships with water, Americans necessarily readjust their social relationships with each other. Law reflects one important, although not exclusive, means they use to order their ever-evolving relationships with water and with their fellow citizens. And human action has contributed one important, although not the only, lawmaking impetus. Incessantly and inevitably, natural features and forces—water flowing downhill, chemistry unfolding molecular structures, microorganisms living and dying—have stimulated legal change. The natural world has exercised sovereignty's prerogative by posing challenges to some humans and presenting opportunities to others. Kansans, like Idahoans a half-century before, were always scooting their chairs over to make room at the table for nonhuman environmental lawmakers, their not-so-silent partners in legal change.[10]

Bold in its creators' aspirations yet modest in restructuring the world their successors have inherited, environmental law and its origins deserve a hard look. Most histories have conventionally dated American environmental law's emergence to the "environmental decade" of the 1970s, triggered by a handful of publicized events that occurred late in the 1960s.[11] During the decade that began with the first Earth Day in April 1970, Congress did enact many new federal environmental laws that have since significantly affected American life. "The years 1969 through 1979 saw the passage of 27 [federal] laws designed to protect the environment, as well as hundreds of administrative regulations," Nancy Kubasek and Gary Silverman have calculated.[12] Between 1969 and 1980, citizen activism and mass-media coverage intensified political pressure on public officials at all governmental levels, who responded by elevating environmental protection into a higher policy priority. However, John Adams's retrospective judgment about the long march to American Independence suggests environmental law originated through a process of legal change operating throughout the entire postwar era. The quarter-century before 1970, as well as the years just before and after Earth Day, must figure into a satisfactory explanation of a social phenomenon so complex in form but limited in substance.

Adams the old revolutionary, writing more than a generation after the thunderous days of 1775–76, believed fighting at Bunker Hill and adoption of the Declaration of Independence ratified more than they initiated. The American Revolution, he concluded, "was effected before the war commenced. The Revolution was in the minds and hearts of the people." Americans made a revolution when they changed their way of thinking, Adams argued, not when their representatives in Philadelphia approved parchment pronouncements. Like American independence and revolution, the most fundamental changes in legal thought and action that created American environmental law had been effected before elected representatives ratified them in formal statutory enactments. Major federal statutes passed in response to the intense political pressure cresting between 1970 and 1976 reflected legal principles already being applied by citizens and legal counsel. Even as scholarly analysis and teaching about environmental law were still in their formative stages, American environmental law had emerged before the first Earth Day, before the first law-school classes in the late 1960s or the first environmental law books of the early 1970s. Its central features had appeared even before 1962, when Rachel Carson's *Silent Spring* galvanized citizens into a new political consciousness of their environmental peril.[13]

Environmental law did not appear in a revolutionary moment of intense national creativity after 1969. A slower, more complicated, evolutionary process of legal change laid down environmental law's foundation before the first Earth Day. By using various lawmaking methods in diverse settings millions of Americans had already established modern environmental law's basic principles by 1970. Environmental law emerged steadily, over more than a quarter-century, in the most ordinary, commonplace ways, its birth less spasmodic than episodic. Its makers were citizens seeking desired outcomes to actual disputes, lawyers representing clients, judges deciding cases, and representatives expressing constituents' views. Recovering environmental law's seed-time in the postwar years puts popular politics and culture into necessary context. The environmental decade accelerated the process of legal change that citizens and their advocates had set in motion before 1970. Like American law as a whole, environmental law developed contextually and sequentially, a series of responses to serve concrete needs and to attain specific goals.[14]

Environmental law teacher John-Mark Stensvaag declared in 1999 his chief purpose for writing textbooks and teaching was getting students to "think like an environmental lawyer." Millions of Americans, among them a few trained environmental lawyers, had already begun to think like environmental lawyers before the first Earth Day. They had been translating their thoughts into actions by making environmental law well before the "environmental decade" opened in 1970. From their thoughts expressed in words and made tangible in deeds, throughout a quarter-century after World War II, emerged a new field of law rooted in the felt necessities of life in the postwar United States.[15]

In jurisdictions from California to Massachusetts, citizens and clients pursuing goals on their own initiative and through their attorneys' advocacy secured recognition of five basic environmental legal doctrines between 1945 and 1970. Citizens established their right to participate in public decisionmaking before governmental agencies altered nature. Courts, especially at the federal level, affirmed their constitutional duty to scrutinize citizen complaints about administrative-agency actions that promised to disorder natural systems. Legislatures circumscribed owners' use of their property within lawmaking's legitimate realm. Political boundaries no longer inherently impeded regulation of human acts that degraded vital natural environments. And national standards, expressed by statute and regulation, slowed the rate of environmental damage by setting baseline relationships between healthy environments and human pollutants. New statutes, regulations, and judicial decisions after 1970 mostly ratified and regularized these broad rules.

The popular impulse indispensable to making these five basic environmental legal principles had been building throughout the postwar years. Americans after 1970 did not invent popular passions for securing a healthy natural environment and ameliorating the consequences of environmental damage. They powerfully amplified demands that activist citizens had been voicing for a quarter-century.[16] Frustrated by traditional legal rules that favored rapid environmental transformation and impeded citizen participation in those changes, clients and lawyers after 1945 innovated new rules and eroded existing precedents.[17] Where they could, activist clients and counsel forced changes in state and local laws. Where local legal cultures had proven too resistant, activists resorted to federal politics.[18]

Law teachers, having always considered nature a worthy topic, should have seen environmental law coming. Unruly nature had always thickly sown their casebooks with legal problems that dim-witted human clients brought to harried attorneys for fumbling solutions. *Hadley v. Baxendale*, my first problem in my first Contracts class on my first day of law school (Fall 1980) posed a classically "natural" legal question: When heavy rains delayed delivery of a new shaft to a mill during the peak of harvest, could the impatient miller or his frustrated farmer-customers sue the dilatory freighter for the lost value of unmilled grain? Disputes like this, arising among people who worked in nature, fill pages of the law texts written to instruct future attorneys.[19]

Law schools' professional presentism, however, impedes historic analysis. Instead of trying to trace environmental law's origins, most legal academics write as if developments before 1970 happened someplace else, in a very different country, somewhat like the Victorian England where mud-spattered Baxendale the carter futilely whipped his heaving horses toward Hadley's fog-shrouded mill. "Environmental problems were addressed primarily by courts, exercising their common law power to decide controversies in litigated cases," according to law teacher John-Mark Stensvaag. "Environmental law's common law roots remain important," another contemporary law school textbook declares, because "they articulate principles that have been highly influential in the development of public law, and they retain considerable vitality in their own right." Despite long experience teaching subjects rife with nature's agency—contracts, property, corporations—law teachers usually reduced older precedents to quaint curiosities instead of contextualizing environmental law by historicizing its connections to their customary classroom subjects.[20]

Law teachers' appreciation of nature's historical agency receded before their foreshortened sense of time. Employed to teach (usually) the law as it is or (occasionally) might be, but rarely the law as it came to be, legal academics privileged the contemporary at the expense of the historic. Their duty to educate future practicing attorneys precluded law professors from showing their students, both in the schools and among the profession, how environmental law unfolded and emerged across comparatively long reaches of American time. The obligatory introductory casebook chapter about environmental law's "sources and origins" typically leaps from common-law classics to Earth Day, offering little that helps the student see how the field developed between 1945 and 1970.[21]

Environmental law textbooks' conclusory, repetitive contention that environmental law began in 1969 or 1970 invites historical interrogation. Stensvaag's 1999 *Materials on Environmental Law* retailed this chestnut as plainly as any. "In 1969," he observed, "scarcely anyone perceived that a separate body of law even existed" and thus "a law school course in the subject of environmental law would have been most unusual." Then seemingly overnight, "this previously unrecognized field" yielded its harvest, the outcome perhaps of spontaneous intellectual generation. "Environmental law—as we now know it—first took shape in those opening months of 1970," Stensvaag asserted. A president and a people ignited "an extraordinary surge of activity" when Richard Nixon signed a congressional bill into federal law and the first Earth Day's celebrants took to the streets in hopeful protest. Since these "two events in early 1970 [that] marked [its] beginning," environmental law "has exploded in scope and importance."[22]

Even a multiauthor 1992 casebook, *Environmental Regulation: Law, Science, and Policy*, which offered a more detailed, leisurely account of its topic's birth, perpetuated the overly simplified "moment of heroic conception" account. Perhaps because a climate scientist and citizen activist helped two law teachers write *Environmental Regulation*, it did remind readers that the "nature and sources of environmental concern" and "the roots of environmental values" shaped "how the legal system has responded to environmental concerns." Even so, the authors asserted environmental law grew "from a sparse set of common law precedents and local ordinances to encompass a vast body of national legislation in the space of a single generation." After 1970, "the federal role in environmental policy changed dramatically" as "within a six-year period, 1970–1976, the United States Congress enacted nearly all of the basic environmental legislation."[23]

Environmental law textbooks' usual accounts of their field's origins have mistaken topicality for novelty. The law teacher's duty is to instruct aspiring professionals how to use rules and methods that have immediate value in practice. Legal academics should of course feature law that became topical because it was instrumental. But written this way, conventional accounts of environmental law's origins unfairly stint the field's historic origins.

Presentism's shiny lure has diverted environmental law teachers' attention from environmental law's rich past, while anthropocentrism's gravitational pull has constrained legal historians' field of vision. The best legal histories agree "we, the people" include more than attorneys and judges, but they still explain American law as solely the people's product. J. Willard Hurst's seminal postwar legal histories first demonstrated the basic principle that law and legal systems reflect all facets of American social life, not just that rarified slice found within the courtroom or attorney's office. Criminals and cops, buyers and sellers, lobbyists and legislators have all shaped the American legal system as they strove to accomplish their varied, often contradictory, and occasionally illegal goals. Hurst's "external" method of writing legal history can help explain environmental law's growth, although its originator only sketched the general outlines of how that should be done.[24]

Hurst, at the apex of his career, pointed the way toward writing an environmental history of environmental law. His masterful 1964 study of North Woods logging in the nineteenth century, *The Legal History of the Wisconsin Lumber Industry*, used trees and forests primarily as historical blackboards on which an array of humans inscribed their greed, hope, and pride. People, Hurst thought, first had to turn trees into wood to make law. To be sure, the law they made reflected many distinctive goals, befitting its multiple agents. Sawyers and timber-cruisers, investors and engineers, builders and developers—not just attorneys and judges—combined to create the law that structured the Upper Midwest's Gilded Age wood-products industry. In Hurst's vivid account of busy people at work, however, forests simply supplied merchantable trees. Complex forest environments, watersheds teeming with macro- and microscopic life, remained mute and inert, their capacities to impel human behavior wholly divorced from human motives. The North Woods served as historic objects par excellence: they lived only to die, proto-commodities ready to be felled, bucked, and sawed. Once toppled by the sawyer and planed by the mill-hand, the forest ceased to influence people and, by extension, the law.[25]

In Hurst's North Woods, lawmaking depended almost exclusively on human acts. People's deeds changed basic legal relationships expressed in such principles as property, contract, agency, tort, and employment. Hurst's legal histories established the value of studying how many kinds of people acting through their varied social organizations made law change over time. His "external" model of historic causation revolutionized legal historiography by revealing the sterility of "internal" legal histories long mired in judges' and scholars' specialized activities. Hurst showed law was the product of society, not simply the preserve of lawyers.[26]

Explaining how and where and why American environmental law emerged in the postwar years encourages reevaluating legal history's tools and methods. Landmarks mapped by other travelers through this legal landscape offer some guidance, but can also mislead the environmental-legal historian. Legal historians since Hurst have seconded his fundamental explanatory principle: a genuine history of law must interpret the civic, commercial, and cultural life of the people who made the law to be used.

Yet Hurst's *Legal History of the Wisconsin Lumber Industry* really did not incorporate those most "external" of historic causes—forces and features of nature. Living forests expressed multitudes of chemical, physical, and biological influences that acted on people, opening some opportunities for choice while foreclosing others. Even after Michigan, Wisconsin, and Minnesota people mined the North Woods by cutting down their biggest trees, forests did not cease to affect humans. Hurst did recognize how the grim specter of cut-over pine barrens influenced the rise of Progressive-era conservation politics. Lost forests stimulated states to invent what would, after 1891, become a new legal relationship: the public forest reserve. By extending Hurst's explanatory model to include natural forces as well as humans' many ways of using law, this environmental history of environmental law tries to offer a more complete but more complex account of its creation. Endless encounters between the American people and natural features and forces have generated numberless opportunities and crises, conflicts and accommodations. Those encounters fertilized the growth of American environmental law.[27]

American environmental historical scholarship should enrich American legal history. Environmental history can infect legal history with a good dose of biology, broadening its vision of agency to incorporate all forces that make legal systems within human culture. An environmental history of environmental law thus extends Hurst's model by expanding the boundaries of agency beyond human society. Environmental law's environmental history encompasses the sovereignty exercised by natural features and forces that operated upon Americans after World War II.

Legal historians' generous definition of the basic term "law" establishes a useful tool environmental historians should use to analyze a problem as complex as environmental law's emergence. Lawrence M. Friedman's *History of American Law* observed simply, "Law is an organized system of social control." An environmental history of American environmental law therefore seeks to explain why distinctive patterns of restraint emerged dedicated to controlling Americans' actions that altered nature. By borrowing legal historians' working definition of law, this environmental history aims to broaden their field of vision. Friedman, like most legal historians, limited his evidence to that generated by people. Historians of the environment, by contrast, show people's actions have rarely occurred in an anthropocentric vacuum, but instead operated amid a complex world inhabited by other life forms. An environmental history of environmental law establishes how, in crucial respects, legal change depended on natural processes other than those summed up by the customary equation "brain + hand = act."[28]

Friedman's authoritative American legal history also considered "law . . . a mirror held up against life." Environmental historians should enlarge this basic principle by showing that "life" encompasses vastly more than our own species' doings. Nothing in Friedman's *History of American Law* impedes application of this principle to an environmental history of environmental law. Friedman himself recognized "a full history of American law would be nothing more or less than a full history of American life." Environmental historians have for some time now tried to reveal more of the past by giving agencies other than human their historical due. The field's achievement now enables environmental historians to accept the imperative task of explaining how American environmental law emerged after World War II. A political, intellectual, and social phenomenon that has exerted considerable force over the American environment in the second half of the twentieth century not only merits the closest scrutiny, it needs little defense.[29]

Environmental historians have started emboldening legal historians to apply their inclusionary instincts to more evidence than just that generated by humans. Arthur McEvoy's important 1986 study of California fish regulation, *The Fisherman's Problem*, began fusing legal and environmental history.

McEvoy's work plainly informed Theodore Steinberg's 1995 *Slide Mountain*, a brace of funny, often mordant, essays about law's uncertain relationship with nature. Richard Lazarus deftly related legal to social change in 2004. Still, his *Making of Environmental Law* emphasized human responses to environmental influences in trying to explain how, when, and where American environmental law emerged as a distinctive field. With this first-rate historical problem yet unsolved, this book—an environmental history of environmental law—borrows and complicates Lazarus's approach, updating an older model of legal history to offer a solution.[30]

Environmental history identifies and illuminates the many ways law binds together nature and the American people. Environmental history tells us more about both nature (the American environment) and culture (the people who have inhabited it). Attentive to natural as well as cultural agents, an environmental history of environmental law tries to explain how this distinctive field, rooted in the relationship between people and nature, emerged over the past half-century. Environmental law, created out of individual and social encounters with the natural world, illustrates important features of American life. A history of its appearance will also expose distinctive aspects of American law.

The quarter-century following World War II especially deserves close study. That decisive generation not only birthed environmental law in America, but those years continue to pose historical problems of the first magnitude about the politics of the environmental movement, the profound economic and geographic changes unleashed by suburbanization, and why Americans changed personal values and social norms. This modest effort to write an environmental history of environmental law tries to explain these twin central problems: how did environmental law appear as a distinctive sphere or field within the American legal system between 1945 and 1980; and what does environmental law's emergence tell us about American life during those years?

I contend natural features and forces themselves exercised historical agency, with environmental law's emergence best understood as a product of dialogue between human society and natural environments. Contingent at best and frequently downright dependent, Americans' environmental law-making reflected distinctive influences exerted by the postwar natural world in which they lived and on which they ultimately had to depend for survival. This environmental-legal history thus accepts Friedman's definitional standard: social control, expressed by organized systems of restraints, is its proper subject. But I contend a proper study of social controls, especially those fashioned by humans living in a world they mostly did not create, must consider both people and nature because both agents shaped the outcome.

This environmental history of environmental law abandons the arbitrary habit of dating the field's birth in 1970. Its more complicated historical account rejects simple "heroic origins" explanations, what might be called the "divine conception" account. It instead asks what the evidence reveals about environmental law's roots and trajectories. By the same token, since historical evidence about law comes from everything reflected in "the mirror of American life," this environmental history of environmental law treats federal statutes and national actions as indicative rather than authoritative. This history goes beyond Washington and behind national movements to identify and explore the many places where American people had to make choices about changing nature and adapting to its constant influence on human life.

This environmental history of American environmental law emphasizes the continuous interplay of human action, natural response, and legal change. It smudges the orderly lines usually demarcating the 1970s from what came before, though the "environmental decade" remains interesting and important, even as historical context diffuses its epochal luster.

Environmental law, even accepting the qualifier "as we now know it," had already appeared in broad but unmistakable outlines before 1970. Law schools and their teachers were cautious about identifying it as a "separate body of law" that warranted its own distinctive semester-long course before then. Nevertheless, clients and their attorneys and citizens and their representatives were, after 1945, pursuing objectives that had, before 1970, established environmental law's most important doctrines.

After that *année zéro* law teachers began condensing into syllabi and casebooks the rules that had been established or at least identified with some confidence. Legal scholars began to systematize the output of various lawmaking actions carried out in various places. Law teachers usually insisted Congress, the president, and federal courts in Washington, D.C., were doing the most noticeable things: proposing and enacting statutes, promulgating regulations, resolving disputes about their meaning. Their initial academic emphasis on federal environmental lawmaking obscured a longer-term development central to the emergence of modern American environmental law: a decisive shift in how people thought about problems involving society and nature. This environmental history of Americans' efforts to devise "an organized system of social control" to handle their complex contact with the natural world after 1945 reveals how clients' new goals and citizens' evolving dreams were, over time, training their advocates and representatives to think like environmental lawyers and lawmakers.

Environmental law appeared in rudimentary form during the immediate postwar years almost everywhere in the United States. Chapters Two through Four show how rising public pressure on natural resources, coupled with intensifying concerns about public health, accelerated the pace and scope of environmental lawmaking in the fifties. Having established some of environmental law's primary features and objectives at the state level by the mid-1950s, citizens came to recognize environmental forces and features spanning state boundaries required more comprehensive regulation. Environmental lawmakers therefore nationalized key features of the emerging system in the early and mid-1960s, a development traced in Chapters Five and Six. Legal professionals contributed their skills and perspectives to environmental lawmaking, and Chapter Seven shows how one practicing lawyer forced the pace of legal change during the postwar decades. Chapter Eight analyzes the work of legal academics just before and after 1970 to show how even the field's intellectual pioneers acknowledged their debts to earlier lawmakers.

The rate of environmental lawmaking attained its zenith in the early 1970s, propelled by a spasmodic surge in public pressure, then subsided to a level more characteristic of other systematized legal fields, such as labor law. The pace of environmental lawmaking at the national level decelerated after the late 1970s as public clamor diminished. Chapter Nine measures the transition from spasm to system, concluding that environmental law's original circumstances rendered it susceptible to traditional economic assumptions and political pressures that have undercut many of its founders' hopes.

During the quarter-century following Ronald Reagan's presidential election in 1980, environmental law has lost media charisma. Its political momentum has lessened. Yet Americans—with and without professional legal training—still encounter natural systems' daily, dynamic sovereignty. Their encounters occur socially, as numbers of people seek both sustenance and pleasure from the natural world. Americans therefore have continued to remodel the complex, unstable environmental legal system they have assembled piecemeal over six decades. Their work appears unending because the edifice rests atop unstable foundations. Kansans' one characteristic summer of lawmaking, at the dawn of the twenty-first century, reveals how environmental law's roots, deeply sunk into the postwar era's cultural soil, have constrained the field's capacity to adapt to new challenges. Kansans' political strife and unremitting economic demands highlight the unstable legacy bequeathed by more than a half-century of environmental lawmaking.

Lawmaking about nature moved across broad ranges of American history and life during the three decades after World War II. Draining vast watersheds of culture, economics, science, and politics, legal change resembled the Arkansas and Missouri Rivers pouring off the Continental Divide across the Great Plains. Like these great American rivers that embrace my adopted state of Kansas, American environmental law sprang from many sources across long time spans before coming together. Environmental law, like waters running from the Rockies toward midcontinent, gained energy by moving through time across space. Sometimes environmental law emerged with a rush, barreling headlong and carving new channels across the legal landscape after flowing steadily between familiar banks. Yet at many other times since 1945, American environmental law has emerged steadily, slowly, incrementally, gathering force as it grew in volume. By emphasizing the flood of environmental lawmaking that crested in the 1970s, most histories have unfairly diminished the significance of the upstream gathering. This work seeks to treat environmental law's headwaters with respect. The Americans, like Boise lawyer Bert Bowler, who first tried to use law to live better along the headwaters deserve no less.

2

The first *Missouri Conservationist* that was published after V-J Day
saluted Americans' new beliefs about nature's purposes. For
nearly two decades before 1945, global conflict had followed
national economic collapse. Readers of the state Conservation
Department's monthly journal had just tried to survive the per-
ils of want and war. Peace now promised an end to Missourians' privation and bloodshed, Charles Callison mused from
Department headquarters in Jefferson City. "A drastic reappraisal of values . . . should point the way toward more intelligent living." The *Missouri Conservationist's* editor believed
"nothing strips a man's thinking down to fundamentals like
fighting a war." Americans, he hoped in November 1945, had
learned enough about suffering and victory to treat "wild creatures and the environment in which they live [as] essential to
the very health and morale of the nation."

Callison's optimism ran a close race with his boss's concern
about postwar prosperity. Rotund, bespectacled E. Sydney
Stephens chaired the Missouri Conservation Commission, five
private citizens appointed by the governor and confirmed by
the legislature, who set broad policy guiding the Department.
In 1936, this mid-Missouri lawyer had orchestrated citizens'
ratification of the constitutional amendment that turned the
Conservation Department from political football into scientific
enterprise. As Commission chair, Stephens backslapped
enough politicians in Jefferson City and quaffed enough cock-
tails with St. Louis businessmen to know their ambitious plans
for postwar economic expansion would challenge conserva-

tionists' aspirations. He smelled trouble ahead for field sports traditionalists, who pursued quarry dependent on clean, flowing water, untainted
croplands, and productive marshes. Stephens cautioned Callison to advise
Missouri's hunters and anglers, whose license fees paid his salary, to seek
new alliances "with millions who never fire a gun or bait a hook." Their
shared passion for higher-quality outdoor experiences had to unite them in a
new movement founded on the conviction that "the real importance of
wildlife resources . . . is in the recreation and pleasure they give."[1]

Changing popular priorities in the nation's heartland began to stimulate
robust postwar debate among conservationists about the legal system. Before
1945, Missourians had accepted widespread environmental damage—air and
water polluted, rivers dammed, and marshes drained—as either the price
paid for progress or the toll taken by wartime mobilization. As long as the nation had struggled to end the Great Depression and then win World War II,
federal and state laws protecting environmental quality had been ineffectual.
What few restraints they imposed on private profit-making or public projects
had been dismissed, to general public acclaim, as irrelevant or ignored as in-
convenient to broader public purposes. By autumn 1945, however, crisis had
abated. Peace beckoned, and perhaps prosperity as well. In concert with millions of other Americans, Missourians' private pursuits and collective actions
began to spark energetic, creative environmental lawmaking.

Until their next war erupted in 1950 in Korea, Americans lobbied governments at all levels to remodel older rules about property and power. They
built new political coalitions. The national movement, often spearheaded by
outdoor recreationists, secured new laws to achieve new goals. The quest for
private prosperity and public security did not cease to motivate most Americans, but millions did deploy their sovereignty to insist on new measures securing quality and beauty, health and comfort. Once in place, new rules
generated their own momentum for further change. Tensions, inevitable in
a federal system that divided governmental power between national and
state governments, prompted multiple approaches to common environmental problems. Clashes among governmental branches, guaranteed by both
the federal and state constitutions' tripartite governmental machinery, fueled more environmental lawmaking as statutes spawned rules, rules provoked lawsuits, and lawsuits triggered more politicking, which, of course,
yielded more statutes.

Conservationists initiated some of the most influential postwar legal

changes. As soon as World War II ended, they sought and got new legal procedures to critique, slow, or even stop government water projects that would
disorder waterways' ecological health. Congressional enactment of the 1946
Fish and Wildlife Coordination Act (FWCA), and conservationists' exploitation of its commands using new procedures established by the 1946 Administrative Procedure Act (APA), illuminate central features of environmental
law's postwar emergence. Legal principles established and political practices pioneered between 1945 and 1950 would endure despite the Cold War's
chill. Novel innovations in legal practice and political argument provided
models that guided the next spurt of environmental lawmaking during the
later 1950s. By the middle 1960s, ambitious new environmental laws were
largely securing legal and political beachheads first seized by early postwar
conservationists.

Ira N. Gabrielson had begun his twenty-year career in government service
as an Iowa conservation department wildlife biologist. He capped it when Interior Secretary Harold Ickes appointed him Director of the United States
Fish and Wildlife Service shortly before World War II. As the nation's most
powerful conservation manager, respected as both a solid administrator and
shrewd publicist, "Gabe" Gabrielson keynoted the National Audubon Society's November 1945 annual conference. Pondering postwar possibilities, he
urged Society members to take pride in their well-deserved reputation among
government employees as "nuisances." Gabrielson urged the Audubons to
strengthen their often touchy relationships with bird hunters and sports anglers by intensifying their activism. He advised them to scrutinize proposed
federal water construction projects for both scientific and political reasons. If
President Truman persuaded the Democratic Congress to fund all the dams,
canals, and levees that hopeful boosters sought, Gabrielson feared wildlife
habitat would suffer grievously. He acknowledged that the Society's emphasis on bird-watching often caused its members to clash with bird hunters
about managing federal wildlife refuges. Yet he believed Audubon activists
shared with field sports enthusiasts a common conviction that "wildlife and
fishery problems . . . are resources of basic importance to the people."[2]

A month after Gabrielson tried to incite the Audubons, Sydney Stephens
drawled a couple of provocative questions, asking the nation's largest annual gathering of conservation activists and managers, "Where are We and
What Time Is It?" Stephens saw America at the brink of ecological crisis as
1946 began, but believed crisis presented conservationists an unprecedented

political opportunity to reach millions of new listeners. If Congress approved billions of dollars to raise new dams, "it is certain that wildlife will suffer at the hands of these projects." Too often in the past, Stephens jibed, hunters and anglers had played the supplicant, meekly begging public dam-builders and private polluters to change their wanton ways. He mocked his mostly male audience by noting one of their legendary heroes, Progressive Era cartoonist J. N. "Ding" Darling, had dismissed conservationists' usual hand-wringing as the ineffectual whining "of a sissy, with ruffled pantalettes, a May basket in her hand and a yellow ribbon in her hair."

Now, Stephens yelled across the smoky New York ballroom, they had to demand "radical changes" in laws. Conservationists should re-frame dam-building's threatened ecological crisis as a political opportunity. Citizens, rightly alarmed by accelerating federal plans to remodel entire river basins, needed to pioneer new political efforts. Instead of begging, conservationists had to make new laws to counter new threats. Lawmaking took serious political work, so the Missourian urged his audience to enlist allies with different agendas into a common cause. Lost or degraded aquatic environments inconvenienced not just anglers and hunters, the savvy street-level organizer maintained. Everyone needed clean water, abundant recreation, and wild places in which to pursue either serenity or adventure, or perhaps both on alternating days. "The people as a whole," Stephens insisted, had to be brought to "realize what most dams will do to their natural resources, and to their way of living."[3]

Environmental organizing after World War II fused a new coalition: veterans eager to enjoy their freedom afield aligned with civilians prosperous enough to pursue their pastimes. Millions of Americans were buying hunting, fishing, and boating licenses, and trunkfuls of new gear to shoot, angle, paddle, and putter. Leaders of an emerging postwar national conservation coalition rallied new activists to the cause of environmental law reform. They targeted key problems—water quality, recreation, and agriculture—and proposed legal solutions. Conservation activists rarely confronted head on American materialism, industrial capitalism, or the booming quest for "security" expressed in consumption and acquisition of goods and services. Instead, they tried to ameliorate or mitigate profit-making's environmental effects. Their preferred response to postwar ecological crisis was managing prosperity by enacting more government regulation to restrain both state sanctioned and privately caused environmental damage.

Environmental lawmaking just after World War II revolved continuously around Congress's most famous conservationist, Representative A. Willis Robertson who, from his home in Lexington, served Virginia's broad Shenandoah Valley. Little remembered outside the Old Dominion today, except perhaps for fathering his evangelist son Pat, Robertson authored or cosponsored all three leading postwar federal environmental statutes: the 1946 FWCA; 1947 Federal Insecticide, Fungicide, and Rodenticide Act (FIFRA); and the 1948 Federal Water Pollution Control Act (FWPCA). And the conservative Democrat strongly endorsed passage of the 1946 APA, which indirectly promoted even more, and more consequential, environmental lawmaking.

A West Virginia native and son of a struggling Baptist preacher, young Robertson came to manhood at the foot of the Blue Ridge Mountains, where his father's ministerial ramblings ended. Early twentieth-century Baptists did not number among Virginia's "First Families," who educated their promising sons at the state university in Charlottesville. Robertson had to scratch together enough money to earn his college and law degrees at a denominational school in Richmond. Scarcely had he returned to Rockbridge County to practice law in his beloved Shenandoah Valley than World War I Army service beckoned. Already politically ambitious, Robertson never shipped out for Europe but also never forgot the thousands of veterans whose support he sought. Widely respected for his intelligence and patriotism, Robertson earned the sobriquet "Major" despite never attaining that regular rank. Veterans' votes propelled him successively, and quickly, into office as a county prosecutor, state senator, and in 1932, a member of the United States House of Representatives. Seventy years later, longtime aide Robert McNeil, chuckling, recalled how field sports and religion had boosted his boss's career. "He'd fished or prayed with everyone in Virginia who mattered."

As a young legislator in the 1920s, Robertson parlayed his passion for the outdoors and political acumen into securing the chairmanship of Virginia's first Game and Inland Fisheries Commission. He got the office courtesy of the newly installed "Byrd machine," although throughout his long political career kept the machine at some distance. After beginning the first of what would become three full terms in the United States Senate in 1949, Robertson helped perpetuate Harry Flood Byrd's "system," its grip sustained by state laws that kept African Americans and many poor whites from voting. He faithfully united with other southern senators in steadfastly opposing

1950s school desegregation and 1960s federal civil rights bills. Even then, his lifelong passion for conservation shaped his unique way of maintaining Virginia's "old order." McNeil recalled Robertson would often answer morning quorum calls on the Senate floor as senatorial maneuvering intensified over the 1964 Civil Rights and 1965 Voting Rights Acts, before disappearing with Mississippi Senator John Stennis to shoot Virginia quail in nearby Culpepper County. Their bird hunt would end as evening quorum calls on Capitol Hill paused that day's filibuster.

His fine head topped by hair of congressional grey, his suits cut courthouse conservative, his demeanor pleasant but formal, Robertson overcame what McNeil recalled as "an awfully squeaky voice" by perfecting outdoors storytelling, both on the stump and among Capitol colleagues. Over his daily afternoon bourbon-and-branch cocktail in some Senate office, and on dozens of podiums at hunting and fishing clubs across the country during the 1940s, Robertson's stories featured people who appreciated nature. His people used the outdoor world—woods, farms, fields, streams—to nurture their spirits, to fill their larders, to test their skills. Almost alone among congressional conservationists during the postwar years, he tried carefully to use writing and speaking to develop "conservationism" into a political philosophy. Robertson, who had been both a law enforcer and a lawmaker, insisted that Americans should properly use rules to harness their habits and instincts. Laws had to "preserve" what was healthy about the natural world, leaving a "legacy" for future citizens.

Hiking along the Shenandoah, fishing the Chesapeake for days at a time, these idylls inspired Robertson's deep skepticism about water control superintended by officious administrators who served industrialists' needs. "Dams were a hot button to him," McNeil recalled. First as a legislator and state agency regulator, then from Congress, he battled Virginia's paper industry over plans to dam the James River above Richmond. Robertson suspected the city's claimed need for more reliable drinking water camouflaged papermakers' desire to use the river as a sewer. He argued papermakers wanted dams so they could flush water downstream to dilute black liquor and sulphites spewing from the Westvaco mill complexes above the capital city. Even after he stopped walking point for conservationists in the 1950s, Senator Robertson still welcomed the political heat he earned by speaking out at public meetings and testifying in administrative and congressional hearings against the controversial River Bend Dam on the Potomac above

Washington, D.C. His disdain for Army Corps of Engineers planners laced his remarks. His abiding love for the woods and fields of historic Loudoun County testified to his deep attachment to lands he believed had been hallowed by the Civil War heroes whose portraits lined his Senate office.

By 1966, Robertson's alliance with the disintegrating Byrd machine dramatized his inability to keep up with Virginia's "new men." Suburban expansion in northern Virginia, making millionaires of builders, developers, and bankers, outpaced his capacity to manage political change. Faced with a serious primary challenge, Robertson desperately tried to hold onto these new powerbrokers by, somewhat pathetically and haltingly, "asking their fathers to ask them to help him," according to McNeil. As the national conservation movement he had done so much in the 1940s to inspire spread and matured, Robertson gradually stopped trying to articulate his own definition of conservationism. He never really embraced environmentalism of the 1960s variety, stimulated by Silent Spring, Santa Barbara, and strontium. A man of Aldo Leopold's time, a conservationist who strode through the fields balancing a shotgun on his shoulder and carrying a box of flies in his vest pocket, Robertson "would not have understood," McNeil mused almost forty years later, "modern enviros, who feared that every industry that polluted was hurting their health."[4]

Robertson entered the House of Representatives in the New Deal cohort that swelled Franklin D. Roosevelt's most supportive Congress between 1933 and 1935. Loyal as he was to FDR, and throughout his life to the Democrats' national leaders, Robertson quickly moved to secure an independent congressional base for conservation advocacy and lawmaking. He persuaded his House colleagues to create a Select Committee on Wildlife Conservation in 1933, which he chaired until moving to the Senate. By his third term in 1937, the Virginia congressman had teamed with Nevada Senator Key Pittman to sponsor a federal excise tax on sporting ammunition and guns. Their "Pittman-Robertson Act" would soon supply not only state conservation agencies' most important source of federal funding. Its very existence offered solid, perennial evidence of conservationists' willingness to restrain themselves in the most invasive way imaginable: by opening their wallets to the government. The rare tax that citizens actually enjoyed paying, Pittman-Robertson enabled state conservation agencies after World War II to sponsor ecological research, acquire valuable habitat, and safeguard viable populations of game animals, upland birds, and waterfowl.

Even after resigning from the House late in the summer of 1946 to fight a frantic, successful "white primary" election for a Virginia Senate seat, Robertson still made time to write letters and give speeches around the country promoting a new federal excise tax on sport fishing equipment. He told *Missouri Conservationist* readers in November 1946 they needed to dig into their wallets "to fund research, improvement of existing [fishing] facilities, and for acquisition and development of new public fishing waters." By 1950, Robertson's idea had become law, when one of his former House colleagues, Michigan's John Dingell, assumed leadership of the campaign to enact what became known as the "Dingell-Johnson Act."[5]

Shortly after the Tokyo Bay peace treaty in late summer 1945 ended the Pacific War, Representative Robertson signaled that conservationists intended to stimulate national debate about nature's place in the postwar world. He scripted a year's worth of hearings before his House Select Committee on Conservation in order to build public pressure to reform national law. Biological scientists, conservation writers, wildlife managers, and field sports activists detailed damage done to American ecosystems by fifteen years of Depression cutbacks in research and publication, New Deal public works pump-priming, and wartime mobilization. After mostly federal managers testified in 1945, the committee widened its focus in early spring 1946. Worried critics detailed how industrial production, compounded by lax law enforcement, had caused widespread ecological disturbances in the nation's waters, forests, and grasslands. Until summer 1946, state and local conservation officials, civilian and federal scientists, and outdoors journalists dominated the witness table.

Committee chair Robertson authorized the National Research Council (NRC) to pay The Wildlife Society, a respected conservation organization, to assemble scientific studies and grassroots viewpoints for a special report, *Some Wildlife Jobs Awaiting Attention*. Published under the Select Conservation Committee's auspices in January 1946, the NRC-Wildlife Society report argued "the improved standards of living, the augmented security we all crave, are dependent on the proper rehabilitation and management of our basic natural resources." Citizens at the grassroots and state-based conservation professionals would have to press for legal reform against federal indifference. They should expect and even welcome agency hostility. "Unfortunately," the report advised the congressmen, "most leaders in high places, whether in the Army, Navy, or civil government, show little appreciation of these problems." To force "prompt and drastic change," the House Conservation Committee concluded, "it should be the responsibility of each informed and interested citizen, and especially of scientific and conservation organizations, to bring the national and local needs in the field to the attention of lawmakers."[6]

War's supreme effort obligated Americans, Robertson argued in the Select Committee's final report, to refit patriotism as peacetime conservation activism. "During the war years," he wrote, "when our hearts were full of patriotism and love for the gallant men and women of our armed forces on far-flung battlefields, fighting to save our democracy, we promised them that they would come back . . . to an America where they could relax and forget in a measure the awful strain of war; . . . where they could enjoy once more the blessed privilege of communing with nature, of hunting and fishing." Now, "in this busy and hectic period of reconversion," the Virginian pleaded, "let us not forget those promises. Unselfish and constructive efforts to preserve our natural resources will help preserve our American way of life."[7]

Robertson knew the 79th Congress had already approved the conceptual outlines of President Truman's ambitious postwar water development strategy. If fully funded, the president's plan aimed to plant new federal dams throughout the Missouri, Columbia, and Mississippi watersheds. Robertson deemed Truman's initiative a national conservation crisis. Government plans required close scrutiny. Bad plans dictated determined resistance. "Over 600 reservoir projects alone have been proposed for construction by the Federal Government," he warned in the Select Conservation Committee's final report, and "these developments will have important effects on the fish and wildlife resources of the Nation." Faced with such a colossal challenge, conservationists had to sharpen their confrontational tone, Robertson believed. "Your committee," he concluded, "cannot stress too strongly that the fish and game resources of this country will be facing critical times in the years immediately ahead. Your committee has stressed in previous reports the fact that we hold in trust our renewable resources. In the past we have abused that trust. We have not stopped to consider the plight of future generations when those resources are exhausted by our greed and carelessness." Indicating how conservationists planned to use water quality to widen their movement beyond field sports recreationists, the Select Committee's report targeted "pollution control" as the most critical "pressing problem still unresolved."[8]

Robertson rallied citizens in both his home state and across the country to demand legal change. A keen, ambitious politician as well as a passionate hunter and angler, he knew Izaak Walton League (IWL) leaders, befitting their generally prosperous membership, often held positions of influence in their communities. For example, John Gwathmey both chaired Richmond's IWL chapter and edited the outdoors section of Virginia's largest newspaper, the *Richmond Times-Dispatch*. Another Robertson confidant in Richmond, M.D. "Mack" Hart, directed Virginia's conservation commission. Hart, like many state agency conservation managers, regularly used his post to communicate agency plans to League leaders and to solicit their views about habitat protection and wildlife conservation.

Gwathmey, Hart, and Robertson corresponded frequently about both local and national conservation politics during the war years. In January 1945, the congressman assured his former Conservation Commission colleague that peacetime promised opportunities to enlist new allies. "I hope to see the day," Robertson wrote Hart, "that vital information concerning a conservation program can occasionally be printed in some newspaper other than the sheet dealing with baseball, football, horse racing and prize fighting." He urged Hart to use his visibility and influence in Virginia to challenge the political prejudice that "protection of habitat is a sporting proposition for a limited number of so-called sportsmen." Hart enthusiastically endorsed Robertson's call for a broad movement dedicated to conserving Virginia's aquatic and upland habitats. "Every citizen of the state, young and old," he assured the congressman, "are [sic] potential beneficiaries as well as those who hunt."[9]

Although Gwathmey lamented to Robertson the "apathy of the general public toward wildlife conservation," the congressman believed postwar conservation organizing and advocacy would invigorate democracy by inspiring Americans to see the virtues of free government.[10] At the 1947 IWL national convention, Robertson told listeners "the work of the Izaak Walton League, and that of all conservationists engaged in a similar program, is now definitely linked to the preservation of our democracy." He challenged America's most influential citizens' conservation group to lead the effort to build a broad, national movement. He assured "Ikes" their "work in behalf of conservation . . . is at last being seen by the rank and file of the American people in its true perspective. It has always been something more than a plan to provide better hunting and fishing and an exhilarating sport for a limited few."

Every American, Robertson maintained, shared the Ikes' traditional goals of clean water, healthy forests, and productive farms. But traditions needed modernizing, as did tactics. The movement needed to enlist citizens not traditionally steeped in the older conservation heritage of field sports. Robertson urged his audience of anglers and hunters to seek new allies. He suggested outdoors enthusiasts seek common cause with rural people whose lands were threatened with inundation by huge reservoirs, urban dwellers whose health depended on clean rivers and estuaries, and biological scientists whose accelerating research into aquatic ecology supplied new arguments against dams. Linking outdoor recreation to the quality of life enjoyed by all citizens, Robertson insisted "our conservation activities in behalf of pure waters have been definitely related to the subject of health as well as to that of fishing." Farmers as well as urban consumers needed healthy watersheds with adequate forest cover, for "our efforts in behalf of the prevention of soil erosion have included the basic concept that land too badly eroded to support wildlife would likewise furnish no adequate living for mankind."[11]

Like other postwar conservationists, Robertson believed outdoors enthusiasts marched in the vanguard of a quest for "the good life." In a nervous, pushy era—what he termed "the age of gross materialism and fear over another global war which may end civilization as we know it" —people who recreated afield had a duty to lead their neighbors to value nature's restorative powers. "Every true sportsman appreciates the perfection of things not built by man. Every true sportsman finds in the undestroyed and unpolluted outdoors a comfort," Robertson observed. As cultural pioneers, the hunters, hikers, and anglers in the IWL "can bring an antidote for millions who are discouraged, unhappy, discontented and brooding over the future."[12]

A year earlier, before a gathering of Wisconsin conservation activists, the Virginian had meditated on this link between protecting nature and defending free government. "In all recorded history I never read of a dictator who loved to either hunt or fish in the sense in which we use those terms," Robertson mused. "In all of recorded history I have never read of a revolution that overthrew an existing form of government which was supported by those who had found peace and contentment." To "the millions who are bowing down to the Golden Calf and seeking happiness in the acquisition and possession of material things," he offered an environmental alternative: "Over and above all else, I want all of our people to be interested in the out-of-doors and to experience the peace and contentment that comes [sic] from personal contact with Nature as God created it."[13]

By challenging the Izaak Walton League to seize postwar political opportunities, Robertson hoped to arouse an organization that had sustained its legacy of citizen activism during wartime's privations. As soon as the war ended, Executive Director Kenneth A. Reid identified safeguarding water quality as a strategic goal. The IWL quickly resumed its conservation advocacy, vigorously alerting governmental officials to its members' demands for strong new water pollution controls. Reid's office wrote to all state chapters in early 1946, urging them to "SHOOT THE WORKS!" by lobbying their congressional delegations to pass a bill empowering the federal government to enjoin polluters that violated new water quality regulations. Since the New Deal, Reid assured Robertson that summer, Ikes had pushed the federal government to assume responsibility for abating and preventing pollution. Acting as the spearhead of a national alliance of "all other conservation organizations," the League wanted Congress to enact legislation before it adjourned in late summer. The Virginian agreed with Reid, though he predicted states-rights senators would ultimately block expansion of national clean water regulatory power. In his own state, the League's Richmond chapter president had been corresponding with him throughout 1945 and 1946 about water issues. Among "a few burning questions" facing both Congress and Virginia's new governor, John Gwathmey wrote Robertson, was "the ever-increasing flood of polluted waters."[14]

Among the IWL's most outspoken members in the postwar years was its Western representative, William Voigt, Jr. From his Denver office, Voigt recruited new Ikes, spoke to community groups, and authored numerous guest columns for newspapers in the region. As an organizer, spokesman, and writer, Voigt advocated Western water and public land law reform, and stressed the need for stronger federal laws to control water pollution.

In 1948, the year after he heard Robertson's keynote address to the national IWL convention, Voigt carried the Virginian's plea for a broad new national conservation movement across the continent. His lunch speech informed the influential Denver Rotary Club "the country is passing from one era to another, from a time when its once-deemed inexhaustible resources could be dealt out lavishly . . . to an age when our future as a nation depends squarely upon the way in which we conserve such resources as are left." Voigt countered the common charge that Ikes cared only about enhancing their fishing and shooting privileges. "The slogan of our group is 'Defender of Soils, Woods, Waters and Wildlife,'" he reminded his business-men listeners. "Please note that we mention wildlife last. This is as it should be. . . . We have learned through the years that conservation means more than game and fish."[15]

Across the country, grassroots activists and state conservation adminis-trators adapted Robertson's congressional critique to confront their most urgent challenge: federal water development plans that menaced home wa-tersheds. I. T. Bode, Missouri Conservation Department director, encour-aged key agency staff to pass along research that Conservation Commission chair Sydney Stephens could use in his speeches. IWL executive director Reid pressed Voigt in Denver to keep innovating tactics that linked conserva-tion activists in the League's Midwestern heartland to the fast-changing West. Government manager or citizen activist, their vivid imagery increas-ingly presented waterways as both nurseries for non-human life and refuges for anxious city-dwellers. They publicized new ecological research showing watersheds composed fragile webs of soil, vegetation, water, fish, and ani-mals. They conceded America's rivers could still support many human de-mands, but nevertheless insisted new laws must enforce real limits on water's capacity to absorb waste and generate electricity.

In the watersheds targeted by the Truman Administration, state wildlife managers and citizen conservationists feared postwar dam-building would compound damage already done to fish and wildlife habitat during the New Deal and World War II. Conservation Department director Bode advised Mis-souri's anglers and hunters in September 1945 that the "growing public in-terest" in dams compelled his agency to wade into the national debate about water. "Certain principles must be upheld in any program adopted," he wrote. "It is the [Conservation] Commission's duty under the [Missouri] Constitution to study as thoroughly as possible and to report to the people what in its opinion will be the effects upon wildlife and forest resources, be they beneficial or detrimental, and where detrimental, to do all within its au-thority to overcome threatened harm."

New Deal and wartime imperatives, the Missouri biologist conceded, had permitted only "desultory" assessments of ecological impacts. "The ten-dency in the past has been to proceed with all the other planning and con-struction on these water projects and then when they are all finished to bring in wildlife and forestry as an afterthought, giving to these latter the crumbs that are left if public indignation forces the issue." But Bode insisted "the values of hunting and fishing and other recreation are real, and no project should be authorized until it has been shown by unbiased judgment that there is more to be gained than lost. We think there has been much distorted conclusion with regard to benefits to be derived." Over 25 million Americans recreated outdoors. Field sports alone generated over $2 billion annually in economic activity. "It does not seem unreasonable," Bode wrote in the Conservation Department's monthly magazine, "to insist that this interest is of sufficient importance to receive proportionate attention in connection with any water development project."[16]

Truman's planners, encouraged by the president himself, envisioned transforming his home state's principal watersheds. Federal agencies proposed to dam the Missouri, Gasconade, Current, White, and Buffalo Rivers. To the state's chief fisheries biologist, this rush to remake Missouri's rivers into managed systems exacerbated past errors by committing new ones. "All too often in the past," G. B. Herndon wrote in the Conservation Department's magazine in spring 1946, "recreation has been a mere by-product incidental to industrial water development." Despite glowing claims about reservoir recreation, "increased hunting and fishing opportunities do not parallel increased water area in flood control or industrial development."[17]

Grassroots activists joined state government leaders in criticizing federal dam plans flowing off Interior Department and Corps of Engineers mimeo machines. "The Army Engineers Corps and the Bureau of Reclamation are both scouring the country like a swarm of locusts trying to find every possible site for a dam," complained IWL executive director Reid. "I could name hundreds of cases all over the country," he warned the Senate Agriculture Committee in summer 1946, "where the destruction is going to be terrific. . . . I just want to put in a word of warning here. Unless we do something to curb the unbridled dam-building proclivities of two of our Government agencies, you are going to destroy the salmon runs on the Pacific Coast." Most "Ikes" lived in Reid's Midwest or the Northeast. His testimony on behalf of Northwestern fisheries indicated how national environmental challenges were stimulating national expansion of conservation activism in the postwar period.[18]

Willis Robertson calculated that conservationists needed a positive goal to sustain their critical campaigns. By late 1945, he decided new law had to force federal dam-builders to redeem "promises" the nation had made to citizens during wartime. To ensure local people and scientific experts had a real chance to understand and weigh ecological values menaced by big, new dams, the Virginian wanted federal environmental law to enforce limits on government power. He introduced the Fish and Wildlife Coordination Act early in 1946 to ride the publicity wave generated by his Select Conservation Committee's hearings. FWCA would require government dam-builders and promoters to submit their projects to scientific appraisal and citizen scrutiny. "The purpose of this bill," Robertson explained, "is, when [federal agencies] plan a project, to let the Congress know, before we appropriate the funds, all that is involved, including what that project is going to do to a great national resource." He had canvassed leading state conservation managers, importuned dozens of the country's activists, and solicited advice from federal and state biological scientists. All endorsed his measure.[19]

The Corps of Engineers objected strenuously, its Chief Engineer Lieutenant General R. A. Wheeler assuring the Senate Agriculture Committee, "I do not think there is any necessity for it." Secretary of War Robert Patterson, Wheeler's civilian superior, warned the committee that the Coordination Act "would burden orderly pre-construction and maintenance duties of the Corps of Engineers."[20]

Confronted by claims for wartime obedience, Robertson dissented. Conservationists had been good citizens during the war. Now they needed to display a new form of citizenship by confronting powerful forces that threatened national safety. As all Americans had faced down fascists and militarists, now conservationists had to defend environmental health. Environmental limits, enforced by new law, would help scientists and local people interrogate dam boosters. Legal duties would force the bureaucrats to justify their concrete dreams. A nation at last at peace, Robertson insisted, no longer needed unquestioned military control over rivers. "In wartime," he testified, "I have always taken the position that the military must be unhampered by civilian control, but in peacetime, gentlemen, I say I do not want the military to be in control."

The World War I veteran, still known to constituents as "Major Robertson," looked across the Senate Agriculture Committee witness table at General Wheeler on a steamy summer morning in July 1946. Measuring his words carefully, he announced that conservationists intended to be more disobedient in the postwar period. "I believe I am justified in telling the Army engineers—and it is no reflection on you—that in the future the peacetime purposes of conserving wildlife resources must be considered by you, along with the other peacetime agencies of the Government, in formulating your plans."[21]

The Corps of Engineers' powerful senatorial friends, John Overton (D-Louisiana) and Kenneth McKellar (D-Tennessee), had quietly sidetracked the Coordination Act after its unanimous passage by the House in May. The Rivers and Harbors and Appropriations Committee chairmen hoped to kill House Bill 6097 as the 79th Congress rushed to adjourn for the 1946 elections.[22] By challenging their authority, as well as the Corps' power, Robertson was jeopardizing his own political career. He had just begun plotting to win the Virginia Senate seat recently opened by the death of his mentor, Carter Glass. Just days later, his home state backers would ask the Virginia Democratic convention to nominate him to contest the special election due for November. Winning the party's nod was tantamount to election, for Virginia in the 1940s was a one-party Democratic stronghold.[23] Yet Robertson was determined to rally the emerging national conservation alliance around the issue of dams and water policy. He favored new law to give local views some influence over national water policymaking. And he insisted only binding legal rules would ensure biological science got equal consideration with economics, engineering, and "orderly" administration of federal agencies.

General Wheeler probably believed "the Army Engineers had been doing everything necessary," Robertson admitted. "He is a great engineer and a great soldier, and he may think that everything necessary has been done, but I think 48 state game departments and all the conservation agencies of this country do not think so." As a young state legislator from the Blue Ridge, he had chaired Virginia's fish and game commission. Invoking this heritage of local service and field-bred knowledge, Robertson urged the Senate Agriculture Committee to approve his Wildlife Coordination Act as testament to the new values awakening in peacetime. "With all due deference to the distinguished Chief of Army Engineers," he announced in his earnest, somewhat squeaky, tones, "I think if they work for ten years they could not do a better job than the 48 state game departments and all the conservation agencies of this country and all the other departments that have cooperated in bringing this bill to you in its present form."[24]

Robertson's firm stance persuaded the Agriculture Committee to defy both the Army Engineers and the cloakroom pork-barrelers. The Coordination Act passed the full Senate on 29 July and again earned House approval the next day. Congress's adjournment shifted the conservation drama down Pennsylvania Avenue to the White House. For two tense weeks, Robertson had to deploy his national coalition to overcome lingering resistance by administrative dam-builders. Loyal to party leaders, aware of public works' capacity to influence elections, he knew it would be difficult to persuade a reluctant Truman to approve the FWCA. "All the private wildlife agencies and millions of sportsmen are interested in my bill, H.R. 6097, to require a proper consideration of wildlife interests," he wrote the president on 25 July. "The conservation world is anxiously watching for the President's signature to H.R. 6097," Ding Darling wrote Truman's press secretary from Iowa. The old Progressive called FWCA "the most important conservation measure that has passed Congress for a number of years." From Columbia, Missouri Conservation Commission chair Sydney Stephens wired the president on 31 July, "The bill has the approval of most if not all wildlife conservation groups, agencies, and related interests. It is definitely in the public interest."[25]

Sophisticated, effective lobbying emphasized conservation's political potential in what promised to be a difficult election year for the new president. Some New Dealers in the administration worried the Coordination Act would impose "an unnecessary burden" on hydropower development. Federal Power Commission (FPC) chairman Leland Olds, a public power enthusiast, urged a Truman veto because designing dams to conserve ecosystems "would have an unduly hampering effect on full conservation, control, and use of the nation's water resources." On the other hand, new Interior Secretary Julius Krug reminded the president of "the wide-spread interest in wildlife of the hunting public, which represents an extremely large cross-section of humanity." He believed Interior's Fish and Wildlife Service, which would manage the Coordination Act's mandatory environmental review process, could cooperate with state agencies because "wildlife resources, although national in scope, are in the last instance enjoyed locally."[26]

Interior's backing persuaded the War Department to soften its initial advice that Truman veto the Coordination Act. Although the Army Engineers sill feared biological surveys "would affect adversely the operations of this Department in carrying out its commitments," War Secretary Patterson concluded "the undesirable features of the measure may be corrected by future legislation or by executive action." After weighing conflicting advice from

Interior, FPC, and the Army Engineers, Truman's Budget Director recommended he sign H.R. 6097. "It seems to me," James E. Webb wrote the president on 12 August, "that approval of this measure will not only be beneficial in the coordination of private, county, state, and Federal programs in the conservation of wildlife, but should not materially interfere, from the standpoint of costs or otherwise, with construction projects under the jurisdiction of other departments or agencies."[27]

Truman, desperate to gain any electoral advantages in a tough midterm election cycle, signed FWCA on 14 August. From his Lexington home, Robertson paused during his own hard senatorial campaign to wire thanks to the president, assuring him, "I shall let 18 million sportsmen know of your interest in their problems by signing H.R. 6097." To emphasize conservation's growing political punch, Sports Afield's capital correspondent Michael Hudoba assured presidential aide Matthew Connelly favorable news about Truman's bill signing would help the partisan cause. "Sports Afield," the journalist bragged, "reaches the largest number of fishermen, hunters and recreationists as well as the most interested reader group on the subject of H.R. 6097." Two days after he signed Robertson's bill, the president and a gaggle of aides and confidantes sailed from Washington for three weeks of strategizing and poker in the Caribbean. Over bourbon and cards, Truman and his comrades tried to foresee the outcome of the first national elections held in the new world promised by peace and prosperity.[28]

Against politicians and their local corporate boosters who projected big new water control structures throughout the nation, Willis Robertson and conservationists had won a small, portentous victory. Enactment of the federal Wildlife Coordination Act between 1945 and 1946 not only energized citizen activism, it began requiring Congress to spend public funds to underwrite dam-builders' and promoters' scientific critics and political opponents. Moderate in tone but radical in its objectives, FWCA required federal agencies to prepare "biological surveys," forerunners of mandatory environmental impact assessments. Rudimentary by the standards imposed in the 1969 National Environmental Policy Act (NEPA), the Coordination Act's biological surveys nevertheless triggered scientific and political pressures that enabled later environmental lawmaking to destabilize the legal system that privileged dams over ecology. "The first important post–World War II measure on sport fisheries and wildlife," according to Congressional Quarterly, FWCA incited federal and academic wildlife scientists, local sports and recreation groups, and state conservation agencies to battle new dams, canals, desert irrigation systems, and coastal construction projects.[29]

The Coordination Act also directed the Interior Department to assess water pollution's environmental impacts, setting in motion administrative study and congressional politics that soon produced the first national water quality law, the 1948 Federal Water Pollution Control Act. The same Congress that passed the Fish and Wildlife Coordination Act also enacted the 1946 Administrative Procedure Act. Robertson, FWCA's chief sponsor, took a much more limited part in deliberations about the APA, but endorsed its basic presumption that legally requiring citizen participation in public policymaking not only helped the federal government make better choices, but upheld essential democratic rights. Like the APA's drafters, members of Congress who wrote the Coordination Act and their activist allies across the nation believed agency personnel required regular doses of outside scrutiny, public criticism, and occasional judicial oversight.

Some historians have underestimated postwar Americans' new passion for environmental quality. "In the years immediately following World War II," contended Hal K. Rothman in 1998, "the issue of 'conservation,' as it was then called, had receded far from the consciousness of American society. In 1945 conservation as a political force had descended to its weakest level in the twentieth century. None of the leading organizations had political standing or significant influence on policymaking or national leadership." In Rothman's estimate, "genteel" white, middle-class, male recreation enthusiasts "lacked a national vision as well as a clearly expressed stance." Engulfed by a tide of consumption and anesthetized by prosperity, "few Americans challenged the dominant ethos of the postwar world, and fewer still were in a position to do anything about the changes in U.S. society." This old-fashioned belief in postwar consensus overstates the American public's passivity in the face of environmental challenges.[30]

Recent social and cultural studies of postwar America have punctured older stereotypes of bland unity, suggesting a better appreciation of postwar environmental politics' sharper edge. Some historians have perceived this new, more contentious tone. "By the end of World War II," Samuel Hays wrote in 1987, "multipurpose river development . . . ran headlong into conflict with newer environmental interests that began to emphasize the importance of free-flowing streams unmodified by large engineering structures." He sensed, without carefully exploring, how a new political alliance united recreationists with scientists. "The stress on habitat," Hays believed, "also brought those interested in fish and game into closer cooperation with a new breed of wildlife enthusiasts who emphasized appreciation of wildlife rather than hunting and fishing." He recently recommended closer study of the environmental values that first emerged during the postwar push for the Coordination Act, believing they incited political action that influenced environmental lawmaking. "Environmental interests emerged so distinctively in the years just after World War II, when in earlier years people had remained rather passive in the face of environmental change [because] one of the most significant elements of the enhanced environmental culture of the last half of the twentieth [introduced] the notion that rivers had many uses other than development."[31]

The national alliance between biologists and recreationists, by seeking legal traction to slow the pace of environmental transformation in the nation's waterways, invigorated new values. Conservation activists urged citizens to reconsider their rivers and wetlands as complex, vibrant biotic systems as well as pollution sinks, transport corridors, and power sources. Conservation rhetoric stretched customary definitions of natural resources to encompass new definitions of national strength that included environmental quality, esthetic pleasure, and recreational opportunity. And conservationists campaigned successfully for new laws, and new interpretations of older laws, to limit governmental and business power to set the nation's environmental agenda. The new laws promoted scientific research, invigorated local people's capacity to resist environmental damage, and challenged powerful institutions that had dominated policymaking for half a century.

The 1946 elections proved conservationists were quickly learning to play smart politics. Robertson won election to the Senate. Re-election of his key House supporters on H.R. 6097, in both parties and from all regions, seemingly vindicated conservationists' conviction that politically active citizens, regardless of party label, backed environmental law reform. Just before the November voting, both to protest the Truman administration's dam-building offensives on the Missouri and Columbia Rivers and to mobilize grassroots activism, Gabe Gabrielson quit the Fish and Wildlife Service to become president of the Wildlife Management Institute. Out of government, he became a more visible activist and more influential critic of the national state he had so long served. Gabrielson's turn to citizen activism dramatized conservationists' new lawmaking strategy. In the past, they had usually relied on public officials to define and defend "the public interest." In the postwar years, however, their growing political influence gave them a new tool to secure their goals. Organized citizens began demanding change rather than passively accepting whatever benefits public policy might bestow.

Gabrielson helped transform the Wildlife Management Institute, originally founded by Aldo Leopold to host an annual conclave of state game biologists and managers, into one of environmental activists' leading forums. Until the mid-1960s, first as chairman of the Citizens Committee on Natural Resources and then as president of its successor, the Natural Resources Council of America, Gabrielson's speeches, articles, and correspondence traced the leading edge of environmental lawmaking. [32]

The welcome task of authoring a new entry on "Wildlife Conservation and Management" for Encyclopedia Britannica's first postwar edition encouraged Gabrielson to speculate about conservationists' growing political clout. He began by noting how quickly the topic "had grown from the status of an interest for a limited number of people to an integral part of a national program for the management of renewable resources, inseparably connected with the sane and sensible management of lands and waters and of the forest products, crops, and other valuables that are taken from them each year." For half a century, conservation activists and experts had tried to buffer industrialism and urbanization by limiting the numbers of birds, animals, and fish that could be killed for sport. "But the combination of land development and increasing human population makes other measures necessary," he argued. "Fundamentally," Gabrielson's Britannica entry concluded, "it is sound management to maintain the biological community as a whole, as it is healthiest when composed of all the forms natural to it." For outdoors enthusiasts, the postwar presented an opportunity, perhaps even an imperative, to expand their traditional campaigns for stricter game laws. "Belatedly it was recognized," the longtime game warden conceded, "that protective laws alone can maintain wildlife populations only where the environment remains undisturbed."[33]

Gabe Gabrielson's and Sydney Stephens's speechmaking promoted this new environmental ethic nationwide. Charles Callison's Missouri Conservationist columns percolated it throughout Middle America. William Voigt, Jr., and Kenneth Reid labored to plant conservation from East to West across the grassroots. Willis Robertson's campaign for the Wildlife Coordination Act stimulated citizen activism, inspiring hopes for more change. Political activism in turn promoted federal and state lawmaking. Peace and prosperity—the postwar's shimmering promise—encouraged more Americans to question the price American nature had paid during the New Deal's pump-priming public works binge and World War II's production blitz. Between 1945 and 1948, outspoken activists and ambitious politicians sounded more alarms about dirty water and dying species. They accepted fewer assurances that government agencies and private business would repair the damage "after the emergency." Concluding that two very big emergencies—the Great Depression and the war—had given way to, and perhaps even accelerated, a new environmental crisis, conservationists encouraged state and federal lawmakers to enact new environmental laws. Within three years after the war ended, new rules regulated farm chemical use, limited federal agency dam-building, began restricting pollutants that fouled water and air, and promoted scientific research into ecosystems. Legal change, far from the preserve of professionals, was actually stimulating citizens to use their own lawmaking powers.

Less than three years after V-J Day, the new conservation coalition had attained its top postwar legal priorities. Later legal reforms built atop these postwar foundations. Conservationists also unintentionally began to create the conditions to make even more far-reaching environmental law when they used science and local knowledge to challenge federal agencies' discretionary power to dam rivers or license chemicals. Few conservationists perceived the legal significance at the time of their skepticism about administrative power. They mostly hoped for short-range political victories, perhaps a dam project defeated in a congressional committee or an objectionable feature of a new highway modified by an engineering department. Yet by demanding a regular method for citizens' input to shape federal and state agency decisions, conservationist pressure helped enact the most important environmental law hardly anyone has ever heard of, the 1946 Administrative Procedure Act.

Enactment of the 1946 Fish and Wildlife Coordination Act (FWCA), 1946 Administrative Procedure Act (APA), 1947 Federal Insecticide, Fungicide and Rodenticide Act (FIFRA), as well as the 1947 California Air Pollution Control Act (Cal APCA) and 1948 Federal Water Pollution Control Act (FWPCA)—and a host of lesser-known state law counterparts—make the postwar years central to understanding environmental law's emergence. These new laws did not block all dams or clean every polluted river. Prairies were still poisoned and bureaucratic domains entrenched. It would be fatuous to contend these new restraints, even combined with complementary state law changes, signaled that Americans were radically re-evaluating material benefits and political liberties conferred by their governments' embrace of market capitalism and mass prosperity. Nevertheless, legal histories should better appreciate how later, more celebrated, changes extended these initial advances. Postwar lawmaking neither replaced unrestrained environmental transformation with managed change, nor fundamentally challenged power's disposition within the economy and polity. Conservationists' critique, coupled with their new political sophistication and rhetorical ferocity, did teach citizens how to use law to contest their adversaries' plans. By resisting consensus, by protesting, by deploying their new political power and scientific knowledge to force legal change, postwar activists illuminated important struggles that lay ahead.

The first five years of peacetime incited a transformation in conservation ideology and methods. Leaders pioneered ideas, rhetoric, and techniques that coalesced over the next two decades into a distinctive environmental philosophy. Sweeping federal plans to dam and channel thousands of miles of free-flowing rivers triggered a clash of ideas over water policy's environmental consequences. Conservationists, their critical edge muted by the war's emphasis on industrial mobilization, sharpened their dissent. Heirs to a movement rooted for a half-century in field sports, postwar conservationists enlisted reform allies among a wider public by emphasizing dam-building's threat to healthy aquatic environments. By fanning doubts about damming rivers and draining wetlands, organized local activists and state government officials incited the creative tension that began making American environmental law.

3

Shortly after Congress adjourned for midterm elections in late summer 1946, personal and political motives sent House of Representatives Merchant Marine and Fisheries Committee chair Schuyler Otis Bland across the continent. Fact-finding in Portland, Oregon, "Queen City of the Columbia," offered the venerable Virginia Democrat a breezy haven from the capital's semitropical swelter. His three-member subcommittee hearing also allowed him to highlight environmental lawmaking's bipartisanship. Democrats, facing a restless electorate after sixteen years in power, could show voters they appreciated the minority party's contributions while still emphasizing their own leadership.

Bland's Republican colleague Homer Angell used the hometown hearing to pursue his own delicate balancing act across party lines. His Portland district wanted more cheap federal hydroelectricity from federal agencies dominated by Democrats, but Angell also needed to conciliate Republican Oregon's state agency conservation managers, who resented federal management of Columbia Basin water and fish. Henry Jackson, Bland's rising young Democratic colleague, also enjoyed the hearing's local and national benefits. Its publicity would boost his first crucial reelection campaign, highlighting for his hydroelectric-dependent Seattle constituents how fast their new congressman was becoming a big wheel in public power policy.[1]

Bland's subcommittee came to the Northwest to learn how the great New Deal dams—Bonneville and Grand Coulee—

were affecting Columbia Basin migratory fish survival, but environmental law, as much as environmental research, preoccupied witnesses. A bevy of biologists and engineers testified that a decade of scientific study still left the issue of fish versus kilowatts uncertain, though none doubted the region's economic dependence on the dams. When local conservation activists challenged formal testimony about ecology and technology, the hearing previewed the lawmaking potential that Schuyler Bland had just helped Willis Robertson, his Virginia colleague on the House Wildlife Conservation Committee, implant into federal administrative law. Congress hoped that new procedures would resolve specific administrative disputes that in turn were already generating broad, unexpected legal changes. New laws enacted to encourage consensus were actually provoking deep tension within the legal system. New conflicts were already rewriting some basic rules that had long structured Americans' relationships with the natural world.[2]

Americans who struggled to accomplish divergent goals within the postwar administrative state began constructing environmental law's foundation. The Fish and Wildlife Coordination Act (FWCA) and Administrative Procedure Act (APA) took effect just as Bland convened his August 1946 hearing. The new statutes encouraged new groups to use new administrative law methods to bring new claims into the legal system. Passed just weeks apart by the 79th Congress and signed, despite some misgivings by President Truman, both statutes, worked in tandem by citizens and governments, ignited productive collisions about how law should regulate people and nature. Each dispute that impelled citizens to use existing rules helped make new ones as administrative law laid another course atop environmental law's rising postwar foundation.[3]

The APA stimulated perennial postwar environmental lawmaking by refereeing the confrontations that the Coordination Act triggered. Citizens and congressmen who sponsored the APA expressed no particular concern for environmental quality. They wanted to curb discretionary power that federal administrative agencies had accumulated during the New Deal and World War II. Responsible in constitutional theory to the president and delegated only enough authority to discharge Congress's statutory directives, executive branch agencies had actually assumed life-and-death powers over nature. They made their own form of law in administrative rules and adjudicatory decisions. Federal agencies' regulations now shaped every facet of the complex, dynamic relationship between citizens and the nonhuman world. Administrative law decreed when foods were safe to eat, where roads should slice forests, how birds could be shot and bees poisoned. Administrative law helped sustain what Cold War publicists liked to call "the American way of life."[4]

The Fish and Wildlife Coordination Act's sponsors had explicitly intended to empower ordinary people and dissident scientists to defend nature and their new law promoted stricter scrutiny of administrative lawmaking. The FWCA mandated federal dam-building agencies prepare "biological surveys" to help citizens and Congress assess water management plans' ecological impacts. The statute's sponsors intended critical ecological science to originate outside the federal agencies. Congress deemed state wildlife agencies at least as knowledgeable about dams' environmental effects as were the Army Corps of Engineers and Interior Department's Reclamation Bureau. The Coordination Act essentially armed dissidents in state agencies and local communities with scientific arguments that were paid for with tax dollars. New biological surveys sparked new legal and political challenges against administrators whose construction projects menaced the natural world. While the APA's and FWCA's sponsors never consciously coordinated their lawmaking, unintended combined effects began establishing new rules to referee early environmental law battles.[5]

When linked by activist citizens, jealous state managers, and assertive federal judges, FWCA and APA began destabilizing federal administrative law. Under the Coordination Act, federal agencies had to first solicit and then consider ecological science before firing up bulldozers. Under the APA, federal agencies had to expand the range of viewpoints they considered and then subject many of their key decisions to judicial review. By operating FWCA's environmental mandates within APA's procedural machinery, postwar lawyers and clients energized two key postwar environmental lawmaking arenas: public hearings and courtrooms. Citizens quietly passed along state agency critiques of federal dam proposals to news media. Others brandished adverse studies in public meetings, like Schuyler Bland's Merchant Marine hearing, which gave reporters vivid copy. "Say Federal Dams Will Kill Salmon!" blared one headline from a postwar newspaper in the Columbia Basin. State agencies, believing federal power jeopardized their own legal prerogatives, often quietly promoted activists' court challenges. No matter how they used the Coordination Act's critical potential, conservationists started whittling down the aura of command that federal agencies had used to remodel nature almost by fiat. Local resistance in watersheds targeted for big new federal dams began eroding older judicial precedents that had shielded federal agency action from citizen criticism. Deep, almost tectonic, changes in administrative law during the postwar years helped forge a new body of rules, ultimately to be christened "environmental law."[6]

The administrative state had grown as much from necessity as by design, a product of Americans' practical efforts to use governmental power to cope with economic collapse and global conflict. After conservatives seized control of Congress in 1938, their distaste for New Deal agencies' discretionary power prompted the first serious legislative discussions about systematizing administrative law. War shifted legislative priorities but scholarly debate and research continued to probe agencies' lawmaking potential. Both practicing attorneys and concerned legislators thought that Congress should enact new statutes to control administrative discretion. As World War II ended, administrative critics settled on two key goals: better opportunities for regulated citizens to influence rule-writing by imposing more open procedures on agencies; and the judicial review of agency actions to better guarantee constitutional rights to liberty, property, due process, and equal protection. When Congress again addressed administrative discretion by fashioning a variety of reports and bills into the 1946 APA, its sponsors intended simultaneously to achieve several purposes.[7]

Regulated business managers believed that nonfederal parties needed a fairer opportunity to participate in administrative lawmaking. As the House Judiciary Committee explained, "the bill is an outline of the essential minimum rights and procedures . . . [that] affords private parties a means of knowing what their rights are and how they may protect them." The APA itself did not require agency hearings, but section 5(b) mandated that agencies "afford all interested parties" an opportunity to participate if other federal statutes governing their work required hearings. As nearly all existing federal statutes directed natural resource agencies to conduct rulemaking hearings, the APA's broad new participatory requirement soon affected environmental lawmaking. And even though APA section 2(b) limited the definition of "party" to one that formally participated in an agency adjudication, section 6(a) expressed a strong congressional preference for widening the range of views that were entitled to shape administrative decisions. "So far as the orderly conduct of public business permits, any interested person may appear before any agency . . . for the presentation . . . or determination of any issue . . . in any proceeding . . . or in connection with an agency function."[8]

Congress's decade-long concern with controlling agency discretion focused new attention on judicial review in what became the APA's important section 10. In 1940, the House Judiciary Committee had endorsed an earlier version of the APA, vetoed by President Roosevelt, with this exasperated observation: "The law must provide that the governors shall be governed and the regulators shall be regulated, if our present form of government is to endure." The 1946 Judiciary Committee report that accompanied the APA's final passage described section 10 as "set[ting] forth a simplified statement of judicial review designed to afford a remedy for every legal wrong." Section 10 provided a seemingly expansive right of review, granting "any person suffering legal wrong because of any agency action, or adversely affected or aggrieved by such action within the meaning of any relevant statute" the right to review. While section 10 seemed to extend Congress's preference for broadening participation in administrative lawmaking at every stage, its exceptions recognized that agencies still had to exercise some discretion in carrying out their statutory duties. As the House Report noted, "the judicial-review provisions are not operative where statutes otherwise preclude judicial review or where agency action is by law committed to agency discretion."[9]

Sponsors of the APA, as well as academic commentators and private attorneys, differed on how these new mandates would reform a typical agency's administrative management of the natural world. The Portland Merchant Marine hearing, for example, raised the question about whether the FWCA, in combination with the APA, would make the Federal Power Commission (FPC), which licensed private dams on interstate rivers, more ecologically sensitive. The Federal Power Act (FPA) already directed the agency to conduct "all hearings, investigations and proceedings . . . by rules of practice and procedure." The FPA likewise encouraged the FPC to solicit views widely: "any interested State, State commission, municipality, or any representative of interested consumers or security holders, or any competitor of a party to such proceeding, or any other person whose participation may be in the public interest" could petition under FPC rules for party-intervenor status. Kenneth Culp Davis, a leading administrative law scholar, praised these provisions in 1949. They offered "broader indications of legislative policy concerning the interests to be protected" by judicial review than did the APA's "confusing" attempt to widen the scope of interests in section 10.[10]

Bernard Schwartz, the American Bar Association's Administrative Law Section editor, had played an important role in advising counsel for regulated businesses how to shape the APA during congressional negotiations. His 1953 law review article deemed Congress's passage of the APA "the most significant administrative law development during the past decade." Agency action, spurred by depression and war, had penetrated every sphere of national economic and social life. War's demands on the national state had merely been "an accentuation" of "the constant expansion of administrative authority accompanied by a correlative restriction of judicial power." The Supreme Court, dominated for fifteen years by Justice Felix Frankfurter's jurisprudence of administrative discretion and judicial deference, had supported federal agencies' vigorous deployment of broad statutory powers over the natural world.[11]

Passage of the APA offered "clear evidence of a legislative desire to call a halt to the process of administrative expansion," Schwartz thought. Early judicial decisions construing the Act led him to believe that "courts have given every indication that such laws will be interpreted in such a way as to give full effect to their remedial intent." He found it particularly hopeful that a brace of 1950 Supreme Court opinions directed the Immigration and Naturalization Service to apply the APA's judicial review mandate even in the highly politicized area of internal security deportations. By interpreting the APA aggressively in order to secure wider judicial review and to broaden the range of interests included in agency action, the "Court has indicated it still has a vital role to play," Schwartz concluded. *Wong Yang Sung v. McGrath* and *Joint Anti-Fascist Committee v. McGrath* "indicate a judicial concurrence in the widely expressed desire to put an end to the growth of administrative authority and to reestablish judicial review as a true balance of our governmental system."[12]

Two days of acerbic debate and conflicting testimony about "dams vs. fish" in Schuyler Bland's Portland hearings previewed novel ways in which motivated citizens, acting in concert with jealous state officials and dissident federal employees, were learning to make environmental law within the administrative state. Inspired by the federal Wildlife Coordination Act, conservationists generated new ecological science, forged potentially powerful political alliances, and drew unexpected media attention. Guided by the Administrative Procedure Act, citizens, state agencies, and their legal counsel pioneered innovative tactics. Familiar legal forms and procedures long used to manage postwar environmental quality spawned new legal rules and objectives. Each new statute and rule that deemed the environment a "problem" requiring legal resolution in "the public interest" fertilized the emergence of environmental law. Even those postwar laws that time and experience would prove inadequate stimulated environmental lawmaking within the administrative state.

Shortly after Chairman Bland gaveled the Merchant Marine subcommittee into session on 14 August, word reached the hearing room in Portland's downtown federal building that President Truman had just signed Willis Robertson's bill to establish the FWCA. Three days before, the president had approved the APA. While big-city law firms and Ivy League academics cared more about the APA, far-Western sports anglers and salmon packers—earnest men in flannel shirts and string ties—focused on inventing ways to use the new FWCA to reshape the legal structure that governed dam-building and fish conservation. The FWCA directed federal agency experts to solicit the views of their state colleagues about ecological impacts of dam-building and water pollution. Members of Congress and many citizen activists trusted the judgment of administrative professionals, believing them best qualified to design new federal water projects so as not to impair aquatic environments or menace fish and wildlife populations. Yet the Portland hearings opened a postwar divide that began separating agency expertise from citizen confidence.

The "credibility gap" that first appeared in August 1946 would keep widening along the Columbia River. First one platoon of experts and then another strove to open or close it. Pushing slide rules and shoving flow charts at each other, the experts' battle stimulated environmental lawmaking for the next quarter of a century. As lawmakers empowered administrators to manage the environment, regulating either Northwestern water and fish or Los Angeles cars and air, new power accreted to the administrative state. But when dissident citizens or resentful business managers resisted that new state power by resorting to remedies established by the APA, the legal system had to resolve the dilemma between public expertise and private demands. Each new environmental lawmaking responsibility reposed in an administrative agency promised future debates about its wisdom in deploying its new powers.[13]

Chairman Bland began his hearing by extolling the FWCA's promise to "coordinate" dam-building. He felt confident that more expertise could preserve Northwestern salmon and steelhead trout even as new federal dams spun more cheap hydropower throughout the region. In concert with "the state fishery agencies of Oregon, Washington, and Idaho," Bland pledged, "the Fish and Wildlife Service of the Department of Interior can coordinate their work." He advised worried sports anglers and commercial fishers that, "instead of quarreling with the engineers, . . . go to them, present the facts and work out plans showing them these conditions, and you will get good results."

Henry Jackson's opening statement honed the sophisticated political instincts that, coupled with burning ambition, were already propelling him toward the U.S. Senate. Determined to make himself both a respected ally and feared foe of conservationists and public power advocates, "Scoop" Jackson reassured State Senator Merle Chessman, the Astoria fish-packer who chaired the Oregon Legislature's Joint Fisheries Committee, that "[FWCA] is a good bill and will be beneficial to this area, which I may say is one of the first areas in the country that has adopted such a program and will bring about direct participation and coordination of all federal agencies with you." Homer Angell assured fellow Oregonians that the FWCA "will definitely tend to correlate the work of the state agencies in these Northwestern states of Oregon, Idaho, and Washington to the end that the resource—one of our great resources, the fish productivity of these states, may be preserved." He expected experts could rationally adapt fish to turbines. Bland sought to allay the skepticism many conservationists in his audience voiced about dambuilders. "The general policy of the Congress," he assured the crowd, "is now to secure coordination and cooperation between the Fish and Wildlife Service and the United States Army engineers and the Bureau of Reclamation in the drafting of any plans for any future dams in order to see that everything is properly done to preserve fish life."[14]

Oregon's Paul Needham cautiously endorsed Congress's new conservation directive. The biologist who managed his state agency's effort to raise steelhead in hatcheries below Grand Coulee Dam hoped that the FWCA "should do a great deal toward attaining the coordination and eliminating the lack of foresight in connection with planning for the preservation of these resources." Still, Needham warned, even preliminary research about Bonneville and Coulee Dams' decade-long environmental impacts was demonstrating "the dam builders have considered the salvage of fish as an afterthought."

Needham knew how high stakes had become in the Northwest. For three months preceding the House hearing, federal and state biologists had been debating over coffee and cigarettes the implications of studies that indicated cheap hydropower posed grave environmental implications for the Columbia-Snake Basin. J. T. Barnaby, U.S. Fish and Wildlife Service chief regional fisheries expert in Seattle, informed his agency's director in April 1946 that "Bonneville Dam and any other main stream structure is a definite impediment to the upstream migration of anadromous fishes." High dams, even with fishways, also killed young fish drifting downstream toward open ocean. Barnaby listed the probabilities: it was "barely possible" just one big new federal dam on the Columbia "may eventually result in the virtual extermination of all the salmon runs that now pass the site of the proposed dam," but it was "probable . . . that the results would not be so drastic but that there would be a moderate, though not excessive, mortality of both adult and fingerling salmon migrants." Should Congress, however, follow one new mainstem dam by approving a series of new Columbia and Snake River dams, Barnaby believed that "everyone interested in the maintenance of the Columbia River salmon runs should not . . . overlook the consideration of the ultimate effect: the losses incurred during the passage of fish upstream and downstream over the dams, plus the reduction of spawning and rearing areas and a general change in environmental conditions would be so serious as to make continued propagation in the headwater tributaries virtually impossible."[15]

Barnaby's Seattle and Portland FWS colleagues quietly alerted their agency counterparts in Olympia and Salem that spring who, in turn, briefed the Washington and Oregon conservation agencies' leaders. During the Great Depression, these state conservation managers had been compelled by federal law to surrender their historic constitutional powers to safeguard migratory fish. As postwar dam-building intensified, staff biologists in both state and federal conservation agencies pressed their superiors to politicize the dismal science churning out of the great dams' fish-killing turbines. Washington Fisheries Department director Milo C. Moore fired off protests to his senior senator and congressman, alerting them to his scientists' gathering fears that more dams meant no more fish. Senator Warren Magnuson and Representative Hugh DeLacy, pinned on cheap hydroelectricity's ecological/economic dilemma, in turn demanded that the Interior Department either endorse or disavow Barnaby's urgent warning.

A month before Schuyler Bland convened his hearing in Portland, Interior Undersecretary Oscar Chapman tried to reassure both Northwestern congressmen and state agency managers that his department understood "this series of dams constitutes a threat to the fisheries." Chapman vowed "a thorough study of the problem" and promised that "all the possible remedial actions should be taken before the run is spoiled." The dissidents' alliance between federal and state agency scientists mobilized enough political pressure to extract the Department of Interior's open-ended commitment to fashion "a satisfactory solution for navigation, fish, and power interests in the Northwest." From such maneuverings within the postwar administrative state grew early environmental law.[16]

Citizen activists were also learning how to use science to press their own claims for legal parity between fish and power. Warned privately by state and federal scientists about the grim studies, local people used Bland's Portland hearing to pledge constant criticism of federal expertise. Their testimony indicated how, just days after the FWCA and APA became effective, Interior's hopeful promise to devise "a satisfactory solution" to the salmon/dams crisis was stimulating new pressure on the legal system. Mert Folts led both the Oregon Wildlife Federation and his state's Izaak Walton League. New scientific warnings and optimistic rhetoric about legal duties to cooperate raised "one point in my mind about which I would like to be assured; and that is whether or not in the future projects we are to have the careful eye of the fishery protection people?" He urged the House subcommittee to consider dissident views. He hoped the new FWCA would encourage politicians to solicit alternative expertise delivered "by the people assembled here today to complain against inadequate planning." Today, he conceded, "we are forced to speak largely on the negative side. Give us the right to speak for the provisions we want on the Willamette and Columbia [river dams], then weigh the testimony of our experts. . . . Then with your help we can bring order out of confusion and progress out of chaos. Fishery asks no favors, fishery asks only for justice."[17]

Portland's IWL director Edgar A. Averill, invigorated by the Ikes' successful campaign to pass the FWCA, wryly admitted, "We are considered as rebels." Passionate and vivid, Averill's August 1946 testimony sketched the lawmaking potential that the FWCA was already unleashing. "We are in favor of research," Averill declared, "but we can research from now to kingdom come and if you do not stop this work on the dams until the research is completed, it will be too late." Science was better than guesswork, but new laws were best of all. Older laws gave dam-builders money and required them to dam rivers. Averill contended they would do so until some new law changed their mission. "We have asked and we do ask one thing," he told Bland's subcommittee, "and that is, that so far as fish control is concerned, that such control be taken away from the U.S. engineers and put in the hands of the U.S. Fish and Wildlife Service, which has an understanding of fish problems. It should not be left in the hands of those who know nothing but dams and construction, and are interested in nothing else."

With Congress about to authorize building McNary, a massive new mainstem Columbia dam near Umatilla, Oregon, and up to five new smaller upstream dams on the Snake River, Averill pleaded, "The only thing we are asking now is that no more dams be started until there has been a thorough investigation" of their fish-killing effects. When Representative Jackson primly observed "much of this information has come too late," the Portland Ike thundered, "Yes; too, too late and too little to do much good. I think that no more dams should be started until someone has been permitted to make a thorough investigation and until it has been demonstrated fully that dams will do more good than they will do harm." When chairman Bland tried to placate Averill, suggesting that "the Army engineers are the best friends that you have," the acerbic angler retorted, "Did you ever hear of the United States Army Engineers including any fishways in their plans for the construction of dams?" Describing fruitless negotiations about dams projected for Oregon's Mackenzie and Willamette Rivers, Averill characterized federal engineers' position as: "'We will do the thing we are charged with if it takes every muskrat and fish in the river. We are going to do this thing. We are charged with building the dams, and we are not charged with the protection of fish.'"[18]

Citizen activists like Mert Folts and Edgar Averill as well as official experts like Paul Needham and Milo Moore sensed, without yet fully understanding, that government power insufficiently restrained by law threatened even well-meaning legal promises to coordinate and study. Their caution proved prescient in the Northwest. Barnaby, the Seattle federal fish scientist, was muzzled after the Bland subcommittee left Portland. Interior Department superiors forbade him to share any more data with colleagues in Oregon's and Washington's conservation agencies, citizen activists, or reporters. Interior Secretary Julius Krug, on orders from President Truman, then swaddled scientific expertise in bureaucratic jargon. Krug ordered his department's contentious Northwestern agencies—Fish and Wildlife, Bureau of Reclamation, Bonneville Power Administration, Bureau of Indian Affairs—to negotiate a politically acceptable way to "coordinate" the dam-builders' duty to follow the FWCA.

By spring 1947, Interior's intra-agency "Pacific Northwest Coordination Committee" decided to ignore the department's own scientists and obscure their dire warnings that more dams threatened fish survival. Instead, Interior's Coordination Committee blandly informed the people of the Columbia-Snake Basin that "the Columbia River fisheries should not be allowed indefinitely to block the full development of the other resources of the river." Despite the Coordination Act's mandate that Interior consider ecology before damming rivers, regional politics and economics still trumped science. Of course, "the decision must be made by the Congress, with thoughtful attention to the sentiment of the people of the region," but Interior in June 1947 "concluded that the over-all benefits to the Pacific Northwest from a thorough-going development of the Snake and Columbia are such that the present salmon run must, if necessary, be sacrificed.[19]

Like Northwestern fish activists, Midwestern conservationists soon saw that each small step toward making new rules to solve one problem required further efforts to keep climbing environmental law's rising ladder. Federal dam-building agencies and their hydroelectric allies used political power and economic pressure to outflank their new Coordination Act duties. Administrative resistance to one new legal duty incited citizens to pressure legislators to enact additional rules. As federal judges interpreted the APA's section 10 to ensure wider judicial review of agency actions, both conservationist and industrial clients began consulting counsel about going to the courts to seek a better outcome when administrative interpretations of new environmental statutes confounded their sponsors' intentions.

Five months after the Department of Interior sacrificed Northwestern salmon to cheap kilowatts, Midwestern conservationists peppered department officials with criticism about agency indifference and hostility. O. L. Kaupanger of the Minnesota Conservation Committee told a panel of assistant secretaries at a special conference in Washington, D.C., in December 1947, "I think this business of talking about 'coordination' between the various agencies on water development is not even a hope. There is no such animal. . . . I think the most immovable thing on earth is an Army Engineer."

Earth was already flying in the upper Missouri Basin as the Reclamation Bureau and Army Corps of Engineers started building the Pick-Sloan Project's half-dozen giant dams and irrigation projects to remodel the watershed. "As I see the Missouri program," Kaupanger lamented, "the procedure is exactly as it has been on the Mississippi, and I presume on the Columbia; namely, this: the Army Engineers build a dam first, and then start wondering about the other things." Despite Reclamation's and the Corps' placatory talk about "enhanced recreation," the Minnesotan expressed profound doubts. "They tell us they will have wonderful fishing in the reservoirs. We are to exchange all of the waterfowl for a few lousy boat docks. . . . I would like to see the dam that will supply the needs of navigation, irrigation, water, power, and recreation. There is no such animal."[20]

Kenneth Reid, long-time director of the Izaak Walton League, dismissed administrators' polite assurances and fine language as wallpaper covering federal dam-builders' contempt for ecology and longtime alliances with local economic boosters. From his Chicago headquarters, he had spearheaded the IWL's successful lobbying campaign for the FWCA. In December 1947, he exploded when Reclamation Commissioner Michael Straus defended his agency's practice of cooperating with boosters in devising new water construction projects. "You see what a disadvantage that puts the conservation organizations at," Reid shouted, "when they are interested in these things, and when things are advanced to a point where we have to come in as objectors to something that has already been done." Straus's assistant tried to suggest that the practice could be informally improved, but Reid retorted, "I don't believe that is quite cricket [when] the other people have their nose in the door and their foot in the door before the information was available to us." Like Northwesterners who doubted federal agencies meant to give ecology equal legal status, the League director dismissed "the concept of cooperation [as] a little bit faulty." Cooperation in implementing biological surveys "has to be a two-way proposition . . . in order to satisfy the conservationists and to be fair to all the people of the United States and not just one special interest."

Reid warned that conservation activists had not exhausted their lawmaking potential by securing the FWCA. "A few general principles here actually are not criticisms of the [Reclamation] Bureau in particular, but I think are matters that we are going to have to take to Congress eventually." He told Interior's leadership that conservationists would seek new statutes to prohibit water construction projects in the National Park System, to block construction of all new federal dams that lacked completed biological surveys, to forbid trans-basin water diversions on the scale projected for Colorado's Front Range, and to designate a permanent national system of free-flowing rivers. "There has been a failure to recognize certain paramount public values on the part of the Bureau," Reid maintained, "and the Engineer Corps is equally guilty. That has caused most of our conflict."[21]

Environmental lawmaking within the administrative state accelerated after World War II when state and federal governments began enacting water pollution statutes. The IWL, which had sought new water quality laws for two decades, learned to criticize administrators for moving too slowly to enforce myriad new clean water rules. In 1948, as water quality lawmaking intensified, the IWL outlined "essential principles that should be adopted in any legislation": no degradation of clean waters during cleanup of polluted ones, ultimate federal legal authority to backstop state law-enforcement, and no cleanup delays based on funding shortages. "We are not concerned with details of [any particular] bill, but only with the basic things that we believe are essential to the attainment of the end objective."[22]

Outdoor America, the Ikes' official monthly journal, echoed Sydney Stephens' 1946 Wildlife Management Institute jeremiad, announcing in April 1949 that the group's "important questions now are: Where are we today and what will tomorrow bring?" For a quarter-century, the IWL had campaigned for tough local, state, and national clean water laws. Its leadership vowed "to encourage local, state and federal corrective action under the [new federal] pollution control law of 1948 to bring about as much as possible in the way of filth eradication, and to speed up an accurate judgment of whether the law will work or needs to be made stronger." *Outdoor America* assured its members that "the League is alert and aggressive in its hopes and plans for the future. It is thinking big, has always done so and always will." Enactment of new laws simply shifted the struggle. Conservationists would now have to monitor agency enforcement, encourage new scientific research, and "spread the word far and wide as processes are discovered for reducing or eliminating industrial pollution." Even as key states and the federal government began to use law to recalibrate the relationship between human demands and natural processes, Ikes had to get "factual statements of accomplishments [and] a forecast of expected results" so they would "be ready to go to work when the time for improving [laws] arrives."[23]

Congressional statute-writing and agency administration revealed law-makers' growing sophistication in addressing environmental problems. Administrative execution of the new laws generated more regulations. Inevitable disputes about the rules required resolution by judicial review. Each new federal environmental statute interlaced with prior precedents. A lawmaking lattice rose atop the foundation laid down by the APA and Coordination Act. Parallel postwar legal developments in nearly all the states wove dozens of new strands into the gathering tapestry of environmental law.[24]

"Present-day legislation is trending toward establishment of a separate agency—within the health department—which is given powers along with its responsibilities to abate stream pollution," *Engineering News-Record* concluded in September 1949. Since the end of World War II, "there has been a rash of such legislation." Twenty-seven states had enacted or amended water pollution laws, many of which were the "voluminous, '49-model stream sanitation code" favored by the engineers' trade journal. As soon as any postwar government, at whatever level, tackled an environmental problem such as water quality, its actions made environmental law more than possible. It became necessary—indeed, inevitable.

Vast environmental, economic, and political differences from state to state, and even watershed to watershed, ensured the sort of legal variety that encouraged legal growth. "A satisfactory sanitary code," *Engineering News-Record* opined, requires "an on-the-spot study of local needs [as] no two states, no two rivers—indeed, no two given lengths of the same river have identical conditions and needs." Leading academic water quality specialist Don E. Bloodgood of Indiana's Purdue University urged states to "authorize a board of control having broad powers so that the board can establish the necessary rules and regulations, which must change with the development of the times." His own state's new water quality statute left adoption of "the degree of waste treatment required" to "scientific investigation," which needed further "legislation providing for the necessary studies." In Oregon and California, state administrators were generating new environmental law as they tried to enforce new state statutes by revoking permits and convening conferences of municipal and industrial polluters.[25]

Early experiences with environmental lawmaking in Ohio showed how each postwar effort to tackle pollution inevitably invited further lawmaking. The 1951 Deddens Act inaugurated what the state attorney general's office deemed Ohio's "first attempt to establish a comprehensive state program of pollution control." Central to the effort was the Water Pollution Control Board (WPCB), chaired by the director of health, a gubernatorial appointee. The board's vast lawmaking potential enabled it to impose orders that polluters halt or reduce discharges, install control technology, and obtain permits specifying "the volume or strength of the permissible discharges." The board could enforce its orders by suing polluters in state court, and the attorney general was directed to pursue criminal penalties against violators.

Ambitious as the legislature's goals were, Ohio's blend of statute-passing and rule-writing ensured perennial lawmaking. The WPCB had to conduct public hearings before it issued orders and permits, and all of its work had to comply with the state's own APA, which required multiple hearings, opportunity to cross-examine agency staff, and judicial review of board decisions. Moreover, three limits on pollution control administrative action demonstrated the legislature's belief that political, economic, and scientific disputes had to shape future lawmaking in an ambitious program dedicated to preserving "public health, animal life, industrial or agricultural usage, or recreation." First, the Deddens Act did not take effect for one year. Second, the statute prohibited any regulation of "industrial wastes or acid mine drainage" until the board had assembled evidence, through contested public hearings, establishing that "there is a practical method for removing the polluting properties from the wastes or drainage." And finally, any order or permit depended on the board deciding that "the benefits to the people of the state of Ohio" outweighed "the conditions resulting from compliance." The assistant attorney general who advised the WPCB predicted "many problems will undoubtedly arise in the application of the Act" because it was "wholly untested, and Ohio's experience in this field is quite limited."[26]

Pennsylvania's example confirmed that Ohio's experience would be far from unique as one form of environmental lawmaking invariably begat others. Attorney General James H. Duff, an "ardent conservationist" and ambitious politician, had his eye fixed on winning the governorship in 1946. Sensing Pennsylvanians' demand for cleaner water, he bullied the legislature into enacting the "Clean Streams Act" in 1945. Duff reaped his electoral reward the next year, then discovered that statutory law required creation of administrative law, which generated political disputes, prompting further lawmaking in the legislature that spawned lawsuits challenging implementation of the act. Even as the Sanitary Water Board conducted ten public hearings throughout the Keystone State to devise watershed-specific priorities for controlling pollution, industries persuaded Duff and the 1947 legislative session to modify the Clean Streams Act to grant more time to study the difficult problem posed by acid mine drainage.

After hearing from "the average citizen" as well as "municipal officials, industrialists, stream conservationists, engineers, and chemists," the Sanitary Water Board adopted administrative rules classifying all waters into three categories: "those unpolluted from artificial sources, those polluted by sewage and industrial wastes, and those which were acid, particularly resulting from the mining and processing of coal." The board also exercised its broad powers under the Clean Streams Act to publish rules that required polluters to prepare plans for pollution control. Nearly 1500 cities and industrial dischargers promptly challenged the board's orders both administratively and by filing lawsuits. The coal industry won a key concession, when the 1948 legislature permitted mines to avoid installing acid control systems along pristine water bodies by merely channeling pollution downstream into "streams already contaminated." And the dairy, steel, and tanning industries persuaded the board, after extensive conferences with representatives from business and government, to delay establishing industry-wide treatment standards until further scientific research determined "the ability of waterways to support certain forms of biological life . . . under varying degrees of pollution." Commentators watching Pittsburgh's 1.5 million citizens struggle to apply the law noted "this entire abatement program must be conducted on a step by step basis." Given economic realities and technological change, "we can look forward to a more stringent enforcement of the state's avowed policy . . . to prevent any further pollution and secondly . . . to clean up present 'dirty streams.'"[27]

By early 1949, lawmakers throughout Philadelphia, Pittsburgh, and Harrisburg were coming to see that "Clean Streams" cost real money that required hard lawmaking. Faced with raising $82 million to build new sewage facilities in metropolitan Pittsburgh and $30 million just to build new plants on one of Philadelphia's major rivers, lawmakers guaranteed raucous debate about laws to apportion pollution costs among different beneficiaries. Even the first $35 million appropriated to construct water treatment plants statewide appeared to be only a down payment. Governor Duff had promised to defend "the right of the people to have clean water to protect public health, and to permit recreational uses." To secure their rights, though, the people had to make more laws. By administrative rulemaking, judicial review, and statutory enactments, Pennsylvanians were now making environmental law for generations to come.[28]

Six years into this surge of postwar environmental lawmaking, the articles editor of the *University of Pennsylvania Law Review* surveyed "programs undertaken at state, interstate, and national levels coordinating legal abatement procedures with comprehensive plans of reclamation to remedy the evil of polluted water with minimum financial burdens." Seymour C. Wagner concluded that "public and official apathy . . . and largely unfounded fears of hindering the great industrial and urban development" during the previous half-century had given way to "a relatively recent development"—"the creation of a state administrative agency with the power to make rules and regulations and enforce them by court action." Other states had embraced Pennsylvania's model by empowering their administrative agencies "with wide discretion to establish exact treatment standards." Charged with regulating both municipal and industrial discharges and pollution control systems, "it is the task of this agency more than any other single group to carry out a program designed to bring an end to pollution of Pennsylvania's polluted streams."

By 1951, the environmental lawmaking potential of a system mixing statutes, rules, and judicial review had become obvious. "To a greater or lesser extent," forty-seven of the fifty states had passed statutes delegating further lawmaking to administrative agencies that regulated water pollution. "The essential factor in all cases," Wagner observed, would be "the enthusiasm of administrative action." Pennsylvania's Sanitary Water Board not only had to manage millions of dollars of public and private abatement and control efforts that state orders and rules had set in motion, but also enforce new interstate pollution control standards in the Delaware, Ohio, and Potomac River Basins. Interstate agreements established more precise treatment goals than did Pennsylvania's own Clean Streams Act, but again "the effectiveness of the program[s] . . . depends on the efficiency with which the administrative agency carries out the legislative policy." Prospects for water pollution control impressed the *Law Review's* Wagner in 1951. "A centralized analysis of the problems of specific rivers and watersheds aimed at eliminating existing pollution and preventing new contamination," he concluded, "presage the success of this type of enforcement."

Yet even this third-year law student foresaw how each incremental lawmaking step guaranteed more debate, legal disputes, and recourse to courts and legislatures. "Conflicting economic interests, excessive financial burdens, and unresolved engineering problems" all had to be balanced by administrative agencies across the country. "The task of the [Pennsylvania] Sanitary Water Board, or its counterpart in any state," Wagner declared, "must be to . . . determine which interests have valid claims and call for legislative and judicial aid where needed." As long as revenue-strapped cities and profit-driven business polluters had recourse to their elected representatives and hired attorneys, "pollution . . . is not an evil which can be ended overnight." Like the sports anglers and state scientists who asked the Merchant Marine subcommittee in Portland to enforce the FWCA, citizens wanting to vindicate their "right to clean water" had to be political activists. "Only continuing enthusiasm will assure an ultimate solution to the stream pollution problem," the University of Pennsylvania Law Review concluded.[29]

Increasing interactions between Congress, citizens, state administrators and politicians, federal judges, and national natural resource agencies during the first fifteen postwar years outlined the basic rules for making environmental law. High principles and low motives, as well as jealousy and aggression, motivated the many actors. Clients and their lawyers, contending constantly with nature's own imperatives, pushed each constitutional branch in every state. States and the federal government often shoved one another and their pulling and tugging shaped postwar environmental law. Each lawmaker advocated distinctive interpretations of lofty but vague statutes, and dense but ambiguous regulations. Their continuous interactions wove environmental law's enduring patterns. This fertile process, which lawyers term "judicial review of agency action," empowered a wide range of citizens to use administrative law to make some of America's most important environmental law during the Cold War era.

New federal statutes, enacted in quick succession between 1947 and 1960, expressed variations of the new environmental lawmaking process outlined by the APA and FWCA in 1946. The details of each are less important than their combined contribution, which accelerated and confirmed the new pattern of making environmental law within the federal administrative state. Evidence of environmental law's postwar origins, these statutes' substantive weaknesses matter less than their cumulative administrative lawmaking impact: the 1947 Federal Insecticide, Fungicide, and Rodenticide Act (FIFRA); 1948 Federal Water Pollution Control Act (FWPCA); 1954 Food and Drug Act Amendments ("Miller amendment"); 1955 Air Pollution Control Act; 1956 Fish and Wildlife Act; 1956 Interstate Highway Act; 1956 Water Pollution Control Act Amendments; 1956 Colorado River Storage Project Act (CRSP); 1958 Wildlife Coordination Act Amendments; 1958 Food and Drug Act Amendments ("Delaney clause"); 1960 Hazardous Substances Labeling Act; and 1960 Multiple Use/Sustained Yield Act.

Every time Congress or a state legislature passed a new environmental statute after World War II, and the president or a governor signed one, they fueled environmental law's possibilities. The lawmaking process began working like Henry Huggins's doughnut machine in Beverly Cleary's 1955 children's parable. Politics would beget legislative action, which would culminate in a statute, which in turn begat administrative regulation, which in its turn begat disputes that prompted judicial decisions, which then fertilized more electoral politicking, and so on, in a frenzied dance. Witnesses tentatively began exploring environmental lawmaking's basic steps in Representative Bland's subcommittee hearing. As they soon discovered, any lawmaker could start the process—even federal agencies—as they did in the Pacific Northwest's intensifying struggles over fish and kilowatts.

Environmental lawmaking between 1946 and 1960 reflected influences unleashed by the interplay between popular politics and administrative expertise. Federalism's creative tension stimulated the administrative state to make new laws regulating nature. Controversies started and prolonged by the American constitutional system that divided governmental power between nation and states spurred environmental lawmaking. New congressional statutes generally provoked complementary state laws. Some state legislatures dutifully fleshed out a regulatory skeleton premised on federal law. Others legislated resentfully, as interests aggrieved by federal legislation simply opened another front in their pursuit of particular objectives. State administrative agencies typically followed enactment of new statutes by adopting new rules. Following Congress's lead, legislatures then responded by enacting various versions of "little APAs." Like their federal counterpart, they were intended to help citizens manage administrative agencies.

The Merchant Marine Committee's Portland hearing exposed an unintended consequence of environmental lawmaking. In summer 1946, few grasped the creative implications when conservationists began invoking, and then critiquing, governmental expertise, such as the biological surveys required under the FWCA. Precedents developed during conservationists' contests with the water management bureaucracy throughout the postwar era established a model for using scientific controversy to fertilize future lawmaking. When Congress and state legislatures started to address the broad array of postwar environmental problems—not just species loss, but air pollution, water quality, and chemical safety—their new statutes typically directed government agencies to gather data, fund new scientific research, and solicit citizens' views. By encouraging political action and scientific research in the hope of developing "consensus" around "facts," postwar environmental laws rarely accomplished definitive resolution of old or new problems. Rather, the FWCA soon established a familiar pattern. Lawmakers' reliance on expert advice stimulated citizen activism, fanned federal and state tension, and stirred local and state competition. As the scientific debates persisted, environmental law grew and changed. So, too, did environmental lawyering, as managing these multilevel debates about science and expertise schooled legal professionals to devise new practices that, in turn, generated new substantive law.

Battles that raged after 1946 over power, water, and fish in the Pacific Northwest illuminated the APA's profound impact in making American environmental law. As federal judges grew increasingly comfortable with the APA's judicial review provisions during the 1950s, their growing skepticism about unfettered agency discretion would transform natural resources regulation. Fishermen and state fish managers would keep exploiting the invitation that the APA extended to new interests in order to make new law. Ultimately, in the mid-1960s, the United States Supreme Court would heed the Portland Ikes' plea by overturning a federal agency dam license for the first time. That decision, however, reflected the APA's destabilizing effects, which encouraged both legislators and judges to think anew about the proper relationship between politics and law. Their reconsideration, undertaken in noisy klieg-lighted press conferences as well as in quiet academic classrooms, would enmesh the United States Congress, the federal courts, clients both individual and corporate, and overworked counsel. Dependent on ecology, as well as on the law's own distinctive ecosystem, environmental lawmaking occurred whenever natural forces stimulated human responses.

4

Bob Hope, "America's funny man" during the 1950s, dismissed Los Angeles smog as "a rumor spread by tourists who have this crazy idea that they have a right to breathe." The gray-brown cloud shrouding the L.A. Basin, especially in late summer and early fall, menaced Southern California's sunny image. Angelenos and the visitors who flocked to enjoy the region's Mediterranean climate and varied entertainments were fouling the Basin's air. In ever increasing numbers they came to play and stayed to live. When World War II began, Los Angeles County numbered 1.9 million inhabitants. By 1950, 2.8 million lived in the County, joining another 1.5 million who were busy turning neighboring rural counties into suburbs. Postwar prosperity freed Angelenos from public transit's iron web. Before World War II, every private car served nearly three people. By the end of the Korean War, cars had practically overtaken drivers. In 1950, Angelenos drove nearly 3 million vehicles, triple the number using county roads on 7 December 1941. Another half-million rolled onto the highways during the first half of the 1950s.[1]

Hope's smog quip drew a resigned grimace from many Americans who, in the first decade after World War II, had trouble catching their breath. Whether they tasted polluted air in Pittsburgh or New York, or saw it in L.A., they knew America's air was getting foul. Ironically, an unusual incident in a small factory town focused national attention on everyday metropolitan air pollution. A "killer fog"—coal smoke laced with chemical pollutants—shrouded the western Pennsylvania industrial hamlet of Donora in the fall of 1948. With dozens confirmed dead amid fears that hundreds more had been hurt badly enough to die, Donora's aftermath alarmed the White House. President Truman ordered the Public Health Service to conduct an urgent inquiry into the town's plight. The PHS study, published in spring 1949, recommended more research into pollution's causes, health effects, and control techniques, but no new federal laws regulating polluters.[2]

Worried citizens demanded tougher laws as they absorbed more information about how effluents from industrial production and mass mobility were degrading their lives. Truman, unable to dodge political pressure but unwilling to seek new laws from Congress, finally directed Interior Secretary Julius Krug to convene the nation's first national technical conference on air pollution in 1950. For the next decade, Truman's temporizing characterized federal air quality lawmaking as the national government deferred the hard job of making new environmental law to states and their municipalities

Donora's tragedy highlighted the postwar air quality challenge. Truman's passivity dramatized the popular response. Unwilling to wait for their national leaders to enact federal legislation, citizens in large metropolitan areas and populous states made environmental law. They raised their voices and cast their votes. They rejected pleas to wait for more technical study. They dismissed seductive political arguments from industries that argued that liberty and property gave them legal license to pollute. Citizens' political action in states and cities opened a new environmental lawmaking phase in the late 1940s and early 1950s. Air quality law premised on private lawsuits for nuisance withered. In place of the common law, new municipal ordinances and state statutes expressed ambitious public efforts to clean, or at least clean up, America's skies.

New rules empowered local and state governments to regulate private behaviors to protect public health. By 1951, the American Public Health Association (APHA) found half of the nation's ten biggest cities—Los Angeles, Cleveland, St. Louis, Pittsburgh, and New York—had adopted tough new municipal air quality ordinances. New Jersey and Maryland, planning new state legislation, authorized major air quality studies. By the time Congress enacted the first comprehensive federal air quality statute in 1963, states and localities had already earned fifteen years' environmental lawmaking experience by tackling industrial and automotive air pollution. Regulatory systems adopted after vigorous public campaigns in larger states and metropolitan areas previewed nearly every scientific, administrative, and statutory technique Congress applied to clean the country's air after the middle 1960s.[3]

California's pioneering 1947 Air Pollution Control Act (Cal APCA) delivered the dynamite Bob Hope detonated to draw laughs about smog. Cal APCA's first section declared, "the people of the state have a primary interest in atmospheric purity." The Golden State's efforts to define, defend, and extend the people's "right to breathe" invited every kind of American environmental lawmaker to the table: citizens worried about health, businesses monitoring balance sheets, scientists and engineers studying atmospheric chemistry and control technology, legislators pleasing constituents without alienating contributors, administrators struggling to enforce novel rules, and lawyers filling yellow legal pads with advice and arguments to persuade regulators and judges. During the "long decade" between 1947 and 1960—an era that historians have conventionally dismissed as environmentally indifferent—Californians' air quality lawmaking generated a sophisticated regulatory system. Their lawyers, administrators, and judges refined its basic legal principles. California's pioneering efforts inspired other Americans to devise their own state and local air quality laws. Debates among California's elected officials and interest groups both previewed and shaped the ultimate nationalization of air pollution law. But until that happened in 1970, federalism's variety encouraged productive environmental lawmaking.

Difficult legal questions about power and precedent, delegation and enforcement, rights and review, prompted more than California clients and counsel to make environmental law in the fifties. State law disputes over air and water quality paralleled federal law arguments roiling the United States Supreme Court, which was trying to square two postwar congressional innovations with the Constitution's language and tradition. On the one hand, new statutes, such as the 1946 Fish and Wildlife Coordination Act and 1947 Federal Insecticide, Fungicide, and Rodenticide Act, granted broad environmental protection lawmaking power to federal administrative agencies. At the same time, enactment of the 1946 Administrative Procedure Act directed the federal judiciary to guarantee citizens' constitutional rights to due process, equal protection, liberty, and property. Federal judges, using judicial review to reconcile agency expertise with constitutional rights, illuminated administrative law's unexpected new capacity to make environmental law.

Clients, counsel, and judges, by framing practical legal disputes about rules and statutes, stimulated citizens to use the legal system even more. The

APA restated judges' constitutional duty to guarantee citizens their procedural rights. Judges scrutinizing agency action in turn encouraged citizens to invent new ways to use administrative law to defend and define their rights. By securing their rights to be heard and to enjoy equal protection and due process, citizens were also sketching out new claims: the rights to breathe healthy air, drink clean water, and recreate in reasonably stable natural places. The APA's sponsors had not anticipated how arcane jurisprudential arguments about discretion, deference, and delegation would help American environmental law grow between the late 1940s and middle 1960s.

Across the continent from the harried California commuters crawling through a smog-choked San Fernando Valley, quiet fury disturbed the Supreme Court's cool marble halls during the fifties. Two towering postwar legal minds battled, publicly and privately, to answer a question that the Constitution's framers had not asked: had citizens intended to grant their elected officials authority to empower unelected administrators to improve environmental quality? William O. Douglas's and Felix Frankfurter's administrative law duel, as personally tawdry as it was philosophically rarefied, unleashed environmental law's creativity and adaptability. Even as the great justices hacked away at each other to control the Court's administrative law docket, state and local environmental lawmaking accelerated. Each new effort to protect the public's newly discovered "right to breathe" by applying states' traditional policing power remodeled older legal doctrines of liberty and property. Challenge and response ricocheted through the legal system. Though not a lawyer, Bob Hope was no dummy, either. Ordinary Americans were making environmental law by practically applying "this crazy idea about their right to breathe."

Public health specialists acclaimed California's 1947 air quality statute as "the most important and influential air pollution legislation in the country." The legislature enacted Cal APCA, the first comprehensive statewide air pollution statute, principally at the instigation of Southern Californians. Local officials first applied its sophisticated regulatory mechanisms in Los Angeles. California's and Los Angeles's efforts to control both mobile and stationary-source emissions pioneered legal techniques other states and the federal government copied. Enforcement challenges under Cal APCA stimulated perennial legislative tinkering in Sacramento. As regulated industries tried to modify new rules, their resistance familiarized both advocates and judges with the evolving doctrine of judicial review. Dirty air fertilized environmental lawyering. Precedents generated by Californians who were making air quality laws established important guideposts for regulating other environmental contaminants in the postwar era.[4]

The L.A. Basin's economy more than doubled between 1945 and 1954, causing "moderate to heavy" smog to choke lungs and obscure dramatic mountain ranges forty times per year. The chemical industry's trade journal characterized "smog" as "a nebulous term at best." Even so, in 1948 *Chemical Engineering* saluted Southern California residents who "rightly demanded prompt corrective measures" as "pioneers." Optimistic about the prospect of using corporate scientific and management expertise to serve public purposes, the journal commended activists whose political pressure "may help other areas to reach the goal of scientific community betterment."[5]

Air pollution galvanized political action. Worried citizens dealing with dirty air ignited a volatile mixture of politics and legal action. Rhetoric and resistance transformed the L.A. Basin into an environmental lawmaking hothouse in the late 1940s and early 1950s. The Pasadena Citizens' Anti-Smog Action Committee allied anxious parents of preschoolers with savvy technical professionals. Local environmental activists began recruiting new members and lobbying elected officials as soon as Los Angeles County exercised powers conferred by Cal APCA to create the state's first Air Pollution Control District in 1948. By 1954, co-chair Francis Packard reported that 31,000 citizens, businesses, community groups, and politicians received the Anti-Smog Action Committee's regular mailings. He announced affiliations with thirty-four other civic groups that were scattered across the Basin and already using state and local laws to clean SoCal's air and defend the public's health.[6]

Like Pacific Northwesterners exploiting the Wildlife Coordination Act after 1946, Californians quickly learned to tap air pollution law's creative potential. A recurring lawmaking cycle ensued. Each new postwar environmental statute—to conserve fish, clean air, or purify water—invariably prompted executive branch agencies to promulgate an initial wave of administrative rules. Practical enforcement experience, encountering nature's own unruly sovereignty, then sent rule-writers back to their legal pads to try different methods. Their next administrative iteration again justified new rules and statutory amendments. Human social counterparts mimicked nature's complex and intricate ecological cycles. Politics and law, science and economy, culture and art all intertwined to create sinuous chains of legal cause and effect. Even as the Golden State innovated air quality regulation, Californians were also inventing new legal techniques to curb water pollution. Attorneys and clients steadily built new laws atop older precedents. Lawmakers invariably applied experiences learned in one medium—both natural and political—to solve problems that arose in the other.

The same 1947 assembly session that enacted Cal APCA directed its Interim Fact-Finding Committee on Water Pollution to study the problem and to report recommendations. The committee's report painted a septic scene for legislators returning to Sacramento in 1949. Urban or rural, California's waters were sickening people and damaging nonhuman biota. Burgeoning wartime industrial and residential growth had overwhelmed Los Angeles County's brand new Pasadena sewage plant almost as soon as its valves opened. Hailed at its 1939 dedication as the nation's finest, in 1949 it was abandoned. Unable to absorb even treated waste from Pasadena, the county's intermittent streams became emergency drainage channels that carried raw sewage directly into Long Beach Harbor. Rural Central Valley rivers serving Modesto, Stockton, and Tracy had become industrial sinks as food processors simply ignored old public health statutes and dumped harvest effluents into waters running at late summer lows.

Alarmed by "this relentless flow of waste," the 1949 assembly promptly passed the Dickey Water Act. After Governor Earl Warren signed the bill, administrative regulation began supplanting "inadequate remedies offered by the common law" of nuisance. *Stanford Law Review's* editors commended California's new method of making environmental law. Regulating pollution enabled lawmakers and polluters to act prospectively. Instead of awaiting actual damage or guessing the outcome of a court case, administrators and industries could rationally use technology, science, and capital to adapt pollution control to different climate and drainage factors.[7]

California Water Code sections 13000 to 13064 created a complex legislative, administrative, and judicial system to attain the Dickey Act's ambitious goals. Section 13005 empowered a new State Water Pollution Control Board to coordinate nine new regional boards tasked with restoring state waters' cleanliness and purity. Section 13001 broadly defined "pollution" as "impairment of the quality of the waters of the State . . . to a degree . . . which does adversely and unreasonably affect such waters for domestic, industrial, agricultural, navigational, recreational, or other beneficial use." In each major drainage, the Dickey Act empowered regional boards to write and enforce rules establishing each water body's appropriate quality. After adopting rules that set the desired quality level, the boards enjoyed the authority to compel new polluters to obtain discharge permits that in turn specified the quantity of added effluents necessary to safeguard the specified quality goals.[8]

Complex as was the job of prospective regulation, the new water quality act also directed regional boards to apply the new permitting process to existing polluters. "The duty is placed on the regional boards," observed *Stanford Law Review*, "to seek out existing sources of pollution and issue requirements governing them." Water quality boards could order other state and local government agencies to conduct inspections and to write analyses to justify the new powers. California's century-old water quality laws had depended on individual nuisance suits filed by private plaintiffs or bold public prosecutors. In sharp contrast, the *Law Review* concluded, the new Dickey Act "vested the regional boards with enormous power."

The assembly correctly anticipated that such vast new regulatory power would prompt resistance, or at least spark disputes. The Dickey Act therefore established a complex review system. Potentially, a polluter aggrieved by a board order to get or observe a permit enjoyed rights to multiple administrative and judicial hearings. Disputes were bound to occur and the Dickey Act even encouraged them. Much of the new water pollution system required regulators to use emerging scientific and engineering expertise and to construe novel statutory language. Lawmaking opportunities therefore abounded. Stanford Law School editors anticipated how postwar administrative lawmaking would help germinate environmental law. They surmised that judges who reviewed permittees' complaints about administrative action would "likely . . . decide on a case-by-case basis, giving considerable weight to the findings of the regional boards." This approach made judges constructive lawmaking partners, rather than functioning either as "merely a rubber stamp of approval on . . . the boards" or "substituting the inexperienced decision of a court for the more experienced judgment of an administrative tribunal."[9]

Politics and economics, as well as expertise and precedent, influenced California's experimental water quality lawmaking. Water, like air, exposed tensions locked within consumer capitalism. Air pollution regulation alarmed drivers and car manufacturers. Water quality law energized water users. California's powerful agri-businesses had already persuaded the assembly to exempt agriculture from the Dickey Act's new regulatory system.

Discharge permits and rules had to ignore planting, fertilizing, cultivation, and harvesting of crops. The act also forbade regional boards from defining irrigation's effects on soil and water as "pollution." Vested legal rights to divert water for irrigation avoided water quality permitting. Regulators thus had to ignore field runoff that was polluted with chemicals and silt, a toxic mixture that irrigators called "tailwater." Discharge permits could not restore ponds contaminated with toxic salts that constant irrigation leached from the soil. At least two, and often three, members of each five-member regional board had to represent irrigated farmers and their processor customers. Their economic influence ensured that unrelenting political and legal pressure would continuously reshape California's new rule-writing and order enforcement system.

A bustling state like California posed infinite ways to harm water quality. For example, a new suburban housing development might reshape stream topography and require a thousand new sewer hookups. Oil and gas drilling might snake pipelines through wetlands and punch wells through riparian zones. Proposed factory settling ponds might require new water appropriation rights. The Dickey Act preserved older state law water regulations enforced by the Public Health Department, Fish and Game Commission, Public Works Department, Agriculture Department, Investment Department, Industrial Relations Department, and Natural Resources Department. A myriad of local sewer, sanitary, and garbage districts also still enjoyed broad authority to manage water use. Although the new State Water Pollution Control Board possessed vague authority to "formulate a state-wide policy for control of water pollution," policymaking had to give "due regard for the authority of the regional boards." And the assembly not only specifically acknowledged existing regulatory systems but preserved individuals' common-law rights to sue with regard to water pollution nuisances. "Conflicts in administration may arise," predicted the Stanford Law School editors with monumental understatement. "However, in actual practice, adroit management at the regional level may smooth over any possible deficiency inherent" in the new water pollution legal system.[10]

While regulators struggled to understand and enforce California's new water quality system, Harold W. Kennedy and Andrew O. Porter were adroitly using politics to manage the state's other new environmental regulatory system. The Los Angeles County Air Pollution Control District's two chief attorneys advised the nation's second-busiest air quality agency in

1955. Only New York City, with three times L.A.'s population, had to govern more pollution sources. Both native Californians, Kennedy and Porter were in the middle of their legal careers. Kennedy had graduated from Boalt Hall in Berkeley, the Golden State's top law school, and Porter had earned his J.D. from Harvard Law School. Their government client not only had to make new rules to cope with numerous stationary and mobile sources that emitted exotic pollutants into uncooperative geographic and climatic features, but the L.A. air quality district and its lawyers had to work within a political system that divided lawmaking power between the state capital in Sacramento and their own community.

Their first attempt at environmental lawyering convinced Kennedy and Porter that Cal APCA was working for Los Angeles, would work statewide, and should inspire nationwide emulation. At the practical level, Cal APCA's fusion of ambitious statutory goals with broad administrative discretion was successfully using law to combat unhealthy air. As a matter of law, its impeccable constitutional lineage derived from the state's expansive "police power" to protect its citizens from an array of public health and safety threats. Some version of the statute could be replicated in other states, since all enjoyed some measure of their colonial predecessors' common-law police power heritage. Air quality counsel Kennedy and Porter entertained no constitutional doubts that the states enjoyed vast potential to make environmental law to safeguard their citizens' public health. "The only limitations upon the full police power of the several states to control completely the air pollution nuisance," they wrote in 1955, "are the provisions of the United States Constitution." And despite its guarantees of due process, equal protection, and property ownership, a half-century of police-power jurisprudence convinced Kennedy and Porter that "no constitutional limitations . . . would prevent a satisfactory solution." So powerful was the state's interest in defending public health that it could "destroy an established business, regulate the manner of doing business and the use of property or prohibit it altogether, or require large expenditures for equipment" as long as state lawmakers reasonably intended to serve the public welfare.[11]

The Los Angeles air quality district had been deploying its lawyers to make a vast quantity of new environmental law since 1948. Cal APCA empowered district staff to not only write law in the form of administrative rules, but to enforce it. The district adopted the rules, interpreted them in cases of dispute, and revised them in light of new science and practice. District personnel even enjoyed law enforcement authority: they wore badges, compelled production of business records, entered factories for inspections, and stopped and inspected vehicles. "The most useful provisions of the act," Kennedy and Porter noted, "are the rule-making power and those relating to the permit system." Initially, the district had established rules that restricted emissions from stationary sources. All new pollution sources—factories, refineries, dry cleaners, incinerators—had to obtain permits. To secure the required permit, applicants had to furnish detailed technical proof that controls would keep emissions within permitted limits. And although Cal APCA "grandfathered" polluters already in operation in 1948, automatically permitting them to discharge pollutants, district rules that specified the types and quantities of legal emissions empowered revocation even of "grandfathered" permits.

Over seven years, L.A.'s air quality district had required industries to obtain over 13,000 new discharge permits. Legal duties imposed by their permits committed regulated businesses to spend $180 million installing emission control technology. Retrofitting existing stationary pollution sources had already required polluters to spend nearly $30 million. Court challenges brought by industry had argued that the district's rules exceeded Cal APCA's intent. Permittees also contended that the act abridged the California Constitution, but Porter and Kennedy overcame all their litigious resistance. The California Court of Appeals thoroughly dismissed industry's objections in 1955 and the U.S. Supreme Court peremptorily rejected industry's federal constitutional arguments a year later. State air quality lawmaking had become so established and popular by the mid-1950s that local elected officials were actually jostling with the governor to claim leadership in strengthening Cal APCA.

Kennedy and Porter, fresh from winning their first appellate victory, told a national legal audience in 1955 they were now advising their air quality client to think bigger. They were drafting new rules to use stationary source regulation as a springboard to tackle the ubiquitous internal combustion engine. "There is a serious air pollution menace . . . from invisible gasoline vapors" spewed from more than a million cars and trucks into SoCal's periodic temperature inversions, they warned. As "apparently nothing can be done about the temperature inversion," they were advising the district how to make new mobile source rules under existing statutory authority. Legislative politics were beyond the scope of their duties, but Kennedy and Porter disclosed that their agency was headed up to Sacramento again. Local air quality regulators as well as Los Angeles' top elected officials intended to seek new powers from the California Assembly to "eliminate the emission into the atmosphere of gasoline vapors (hydrocarbons) from industrial sources, control automobile exhausts, the largest source of hydrocarbons, . . . and reduce all other industrial pollution through more stringent standards governing permissible emissions."[12]

First generation environmental lawyers such as Kennedy and Porter doubted neither the necessity nor justice of their mission. "Given strict enforcement, a will to do the job and the latest scientific aids, there is ample legal authority to abate all known sources of air contaminants." With pardonable pride, they cheered Los Angeles for "leading the nation in the emphasis placed upon an air pollution abatement program." Though Cal APCA was novel and rudimentary, the statute "together with the more than one hundred rules adopted by the district which have the force and effect of law, is adequate or can be made adequate to deal with the difficult and involved problem." Both veteran environmental regulators and bright law students concurred that environmental regulating inevitably required intensive political action. Stanford Law School editors believed the new regional water quality boards needed "public support . . . and public co-operation" to make the Dickey Act succeed. Kennedy and Porter, though irritated at times by citizen accusations of administrative timidity or favoritism, thought "even the severest critics of the district have not claimed [Cal APCA], together with the rules, has failed to furnish sufficient legal tools with which to work."

Californians made environmental law on many fronts in the 1950s. Even as they launched the state's water quality law, ongoing disputes about enforcing the new air quality rules and fine-tuning Cal APCA kept environmental lawmaking momentum in high gear. Los Angeles County's most powerful elected official, Supervisor Kenneth Hahn, called a December 1954 press conference to announce that he intended to seek further improvements in the 1947 APCA. For the most part, Hahn reported, the L.A. Air Quality District was making good progress in permitting and monitoring stationary source emissions. But even the infant science of smog demonstrated that Angelenos' cars produced far more pollution than their factories, incinerators, and refineries. Hahn directed district legal staff to propose amendments to the county's six-year-old air quality ordinance to regulate auto exhaust. Not to be outdone, Los Angeles mayor Richard Paulson boldly announced he was flying to Sacramento when the legislature convened in January 1955 to demand new state laws to require that new cars sold in the state meet emission standards.

Hahn and Paulson enjoyed a powerful ally in Sacramento. The new governor, Goodwin Knight, had convened California's first air pollution conference shortly after taking office in 1953. His predecessor, Earl Warren, who had just become President Eisenhower's first Chief Justice of the United States, had himself lobbied the Assembly to enact Cal APCA in 1947. Warren's sterling environmental record as governor, coupled with the Golden State's progressive reputation for tackling hard environmental problems, had already paid national dividends. Warren won the 1948 vice presidential nomination to run nationally with another Republican governor, New York's Thomas Dewey. The GOP's presidential nominee's pollution fighting reputation in Albany matched his earlier crime fighting record in New York City. Unlucky in the national elections, Warren came home to Sacramento, where he soon approved an expansion of Cal APCA in 1949 to empower multi-county Air Pollution Control Districts. Republicans all, Hahn and Paulson in the Southland along with Warren and Knight in Sacramento intended to keep their party marching in the vanguard of postwar pollution lawmaking. Governor Knight marked his first anniversary in office by quickly adopting the state air quality conference's recommendation to appoint a cabinet level pollution advisory committee in 1954.[13]

Watching California's car-dependent popular culture closely from its Detroit redoubt, "the auto industry prepared to do battle anew with a ghostly enemy, the acrid smog that persistently invades and imperils Los Angeles." The *New York Times* reported in late 1954 that this titanic battle between the country's preeminent industry and fastest growing big state carried national implications. Auto manufacturers sent a task force of engineering vice presidents to explain to Golden State lawmakers the daunting technical challenges that confronted their industry. Chrysler's Paul Ackerman warned that taxpayers would revolt if Los Angeles County or the state tried to require emissions control technology on private cars. Ford's Victor Raviolo calculated that even the simplest type of catalytic converter would cost Angelenos an extra $400 million to equip their cars. "Mayor Paulson would have quite a time," noted the steel industry's national trade journal, "trying to force the owner of a ten-year-old relic worth $100 to install a $150 catalytic converter."[14]

Bob Hope's mock jibe—blaming outside rumormongers who didn't appreciate L.A. air's unique qualities—hit an Angeleno nerve. Even if "tourists" were the real whiners, and not, say, Pasadena parents, complaints about smog revealed local business leaders' deepening concern about air quality's economic impacts. Southern California depended on immigration from other areas of the country to fuel its growth. If word got out that the area's air was unsightly, and maybe even dangerous to breathe, Americans might stay away. They might relocate from Des Moines to Denver or, even worse, to San Diego. SoCal corporate, political, and educational leaders worried that air pollution might threaten to burst their phenomenal postwar economic boom. "City and county officials are talking seriously," an engineering journal reported in October 1955, "about the possibility of having to restrict building of new industrial plants and expansion of old."

UCLA medical school dean Stafford Warren advised Los Angeles County leaders that smog indeed posed a serious public health threat. County air quality regulators in the early 1950s commissioned the dean to devise a public warning system. As implemented by a bevy of new administrative rules, the warning system echoed contemporary civil defense practices. When any of four designated pollutants reached specified concentrations as determined by Air Quality District monitors, the county declared "Smog Red Day." In the direst conditions, local governments could exercise their inherent police powers to curtail vehicle traffic and industrial operations. The Los Angeles Basin's leading media, spearheaded usually by the *Los Angeles Times*, bannered articles about white-coated scientists teaming with grease-spattered engineers to find solutions to pollution. The Air Pollution Foundation, headquartered in L.A. by 1955 and generously funded by corporate contributions, joined nationally prominent research facilities, such as Battelle Labs outside Columbus, Ohio, and the Southwest Research Institute in Pasadena, to study air pollution's health effects. Cal Tech atmospheric scientist A. J. Haagen-Smit, under contract with Los Angeles' air quality agency, had published some of the earliest explanations of the photochemical reactions that produced smog.[15]

Pioneer environmental lawmakers had, well before the postwar lawmaking surge, understood the judicial branch's inherent limits. Courts could only decide discrete disputes between adversaries. Lawsuits against polluters based on old common-law principles of property, contract, and tort had utterly failed to prevent widespread environmental degradation. Isolated judgments for trespass or nuisance that awarded monetary damages or enjoined only the most flagrant forms of industrial pollution, proved too costly for individual litigants. Paying a few plaintiffs here and there amounted to little more than the cost of doing business, business managers and their counsel concluded. Prevailing theories about pollution litigation seemed to require that judges balance the economic benefits of production against the monetary costs suffered by a handful of unlucky, agitated plaintiff property owners. Given that method of "balancing the equities," antipollution lawsuits might remain a regulators' weapon of last resort but nuisance theory would steadily become a minor legal curiosity. "Air pollution has become such a serious problem in many places that reliance on a common-law nuisance action is no longer satisfactory," Kennedy and Porter advised lawyers in 1955. Expressing the modern view, the Stanford Law School editors thought "experience has shown the pollution problem in California cannot be safely left to private initiative."[16]

Federal and state statutes after World War II that empowered administrative agencies to make environmental laws unintentionally transformed the judicial branch. Judges began learning how their two principal duties—to resolve disputes by interpreting laws and to constrain state power within constitutional boundaries—actually made them important lawmaking partners. By guarding constitutional rights—due process and equal protection foremost—and patrolling constitutional boundaries, judges became unexpectedly important environmental lawmakers. The Marshall Court's heyday in the first quarter of the nineteenth century had plainly established the United States Supreme Court in particular, and the federal judiciary in general, as the nation's authoritative constitutional referee. Judges wielded unique authority to determine whether legislators had delegated administrators appropriate rule-writing power; whether congressional statutes had proper textual authority in constitutions; and whether the balance of power among the legislative and executive branches needed adjustment. The 1946 Administrative Procedure Act, and its state counterparts, reemphasized another fundamental judicial duty: that of protecting citizens against the government by affording them an impartial venue in which to challenge administrative acts beyond the government's delegated powers. Congress's penchant for solving environmental problems by enacting new statutes, such as the 1946 Coordination Act, as well as citizens' invocation of new environmental rights premised on older laws, regularly posed hard problems about the amount of lawmaking power the Constitution allowed Congress to delegate to the President's agencies. The postwar judiciary had to continually resolve these problems, making more environmental law all the while.

Foremost among the judges who unlocked the APA's capacity for postwar environmental lawmaking were Supreme Court Justices William O. Douglas and Felix Frankfurter. Both had joined the Court when President Franklin Roosevelt and Congress, desperately fighting the Great Depression, were transforming the relationship between the national state and American nature. One of the New Deal's most durable legacies was federal power's projection into every facet of the American environment. In 1939, the year of Frankfurter's and Douglas's appointments, the Army Corps of Engineers was starting to perfect its hydroelectric management of the Columbia River at Bonneville Dam. The Interior Department's Bureau of Reclamation had nearly completed an even vaster impoundment behind Grand Coulee Dam, 200 miles upstream, and Tennessee Valley Authority dams were inundating hundreds of thousands of southern acres beneath massive reservoirs dedicated to power production and flood control.[17]

Douglas's emerging environmental convictions eventually caused him to renounce his New Deal preference for public power expansion. Deciding cases that challenged federal agencies' dam licensing and construction during the fifties changed his views about water and power. Instead of heralding dams as social dynamism in action, Douglas increasingly characterized them as problematic human interventions into natural processes that possessed their own sovereignty and deserved a measure of legal dignity. Frankfurter, by contrast, consistently respected administrators throughout the postwar years. When teaching law in the 1920s, he expounded the theory that the Constitution justified Congress's use of administrative agencies to regulate, and even to provide, electricity. Even as postwar dam-building accelerated, Frankfurter's Supreme Court opinions continued to portray river management as simply another form of social welfare policy. By transforming river basins into hydroelectric plantations, the national state was strategically deploying social power into fields of action that demanded expert management. On a postwar Supreme Court badly riven by legal and personal rivalries, Douglas's and Frankfurter's clash about administrative management helped change American law's relationship with the natural world during the second half of the twentieth century.

Their first decade of service on the Supreme Court spurred Douglas and Frankfurter to develop clashing theories about the proper relationship be-

tween federal courts and executive branch agencies. Douglas, sensitive to
changing public opinion, championed activist, almost democratic judging.
Frankfurter, ever the dedicated New Dealer, deemed the judiciary ill-suited to
manage the complex American economy and polity. Ten years' jurisprudential rivalry only deepened their personal enmity. After 1950, Douglas's and
Frankfurter's repeated clashes over judicial review of agency action transformed the Administrative Procedure Act. By requiring judges, lawyers, and
clients to reconsider the relationship between citizens and the state, the APA
stimulated creative thinking about law's relationship to nature.

On a personal level, Douglas and Frankfurter loathed one another. They
waged their struggle to dominate the Supreme Court's APA jurisprudence by
means both Olympian and petty. Their battle for the soul of administrative
law soured the Court's working atmosphere. Their bitter rivalry hastened the
deaths of two chief justices who unsuccessfully tried to maintain judicial
comity. Their clash complicated the task of both private citizens and public
agencies trying to predict the federal government's future course in natural
resource regulation. Unseemly and irrational though it was, their mutual
disdain, spanning two decades under three chief justices and four presidents, inspired Douglas and Frankfurter to refine administrative law jurisprudence. Douglas accelerated environmental law's emergence from
administrative law's postwar crisis by challenging his rival for control of the
Court's duty to review agency action.[18]

In April 1949, his tenth anniversary of joining the Supreme Court, Justice
Douglas addressed the New York City Bar Association. The former Columbia
and Yale Law School professor carefully cultivated his rough-hewn public
image. Powerful political friends and a curious media publicized the justice's regular hiking trips in his native Washington state and rambles
through the world's wildest places. Yet Douglas still cared a great deal about
the approbation of New York's legal community. He had ridden the rails to
the city in his early twenties to attend Columbia Law School. There, he began
his meteoric rise, first as a legal scholar and then as a New Deal administrator. Douglas counted many friends among the city's elite attorneys and
judges. His 1949 Cardozo Lecture thus sought to burnish his reputation as
the Court's most dynamic member. He also intended it to cement the New
Deal Court's claim to serve as the nation's ultimate guarantor of constitutional democracy.[19]

Many of Douglas's listeners hoped that the postwar Court would stabilize the trajectory of its administrative jurisprudence. Although the Cold War was deepening, Truman's 1948 reelection triumph had rearmed liberalism with a fresh four-year mandate for government intervention into the economy. The New York City Bar Association included many attorneys who made a lot of money representing powerful corporations that had challenged New Deal regulation of business activity. Douglas knew the Court's sharp departures in the later 1930s from its pro-enterprise precedents had fueled fierce corporate political criticism. Roosevelt's appointment of five justices between 1937 and 1941 led many commentators (not all of them hostile) to portray them as FDR's judicial water boys. Conservative attorneys and their clients weren't the only critics who disapproved of too much economic regulation on its merits. Many contended that frequent reversals of precedent devalued the judiciary's principal function of defending predictability in a turbulent world.[20]

Douglas thought the New York Bar's plea for judicial passivity craved mere "static security." Laudable in itself, "security can only be achieved through constant change, through the wise discarding of old ideas that have outlived their usefulness, and through the adapting of others to current facts." Precedents constructed the Constitution's "architectural scheme," but 150 years of Supreme Court litigation had bequeathed justices literally thousands of precedents. Only by deciding new cases in light of their own experiences and contemporary conditions could appellate judges solve the chief problem of constitutional adjudication, that of "keep[ing] the power of government unrestrained by social or economic theories that one set of judges may entertain." To "master the sudden storms of an era," Douglas concluded, "it is better that we make our own history than be governed by the dead. We too must be dynamic components of history if our institutions are to be vital, directive forces in the life of our age."[21]

Douglas's frank advocacy of politically sensitive judging collided head-on with the jurisprudence articulated by Supreme Court colleague Felix Frankfurter. Two years earlier, Frankfurter had delivered the Cardozo Lecture to the same audience on another mild spring evening. Judges, he told the New York Bar in 1947, risked political oblivion by courting the public too freely. Deciding cases differed fundamentally from passing laws. Frankfurter warned the "only sure safeguard against crossing the line between adjudication and legislation is an alert recognition of the necessity not to cross it and an instinctive, as well as trained, reluctance to do so." Frankfurter admired, even worshipped, Oliver Wendell Holmes, Jr.'s forthright acceptance of the judge's political function in a democracy. Nevertheless, he preached a purer doctrine of judicial restraint. Frankfurter's first biographer, Joseph P. Lash, summarized his philosophy as mixing functional segregation and judicial deference: "By a policy of judicial restraint and by rising above their private views," Frankfurter hoped that "the Justices would avoid usurping the powers of the Executive and Congress and becoming, as Brandeis had cautioned, a 'super-legislature.'"[22]

Frankfurter, the cool critic of lawmaking judges, idolized lawmaking administrators. A leading scholar suggested in 1950 that "The Administrative World of Mr. Justice Frankfurter" orbited around the twin suns of administrative expertise and judicial deference. One of the brightest stars on the Harvard Law School faculty for twenty-five years before his Court appointment, Frankfurter used his Byrne Professorship of Administrative Law to expound his beliefs. In lectures, articles, and books he argued novel social problems created when private capital clashed with public necessity compelled the "recognition of the place of administrative processes in modern government." The new men who staffed these new governmental forms— men Frankfurter shamelessly cultivated during exclusive private Law School seminars for those he deemed worthy—impressed him with their ability, energy, and patriotism. Early in the New Deal, he wrote his former mentor, Henry Stimson, "Above all, we can no longer afford to do without highly trained, disinterested government personnel."[23]

Once on the Court, Frankfurter's numerous opinions that reviewed agency actions strove to instill confidence in the decisions. He knew these newly powerful administrators; he had steered a vanguard of Harvard Law School graduates into the burgeoning New Deal agencies. "The attraction of such posts," he informed Fortune's readers in 1936, "is not money but the opportunity for men of genuine ability to do really useful work and to try their mettle on problems worthy of the best powers." As early as 1930, Frankfurter had insisted that "administrative agencies must be made adequate instruments for expressing the social policies which they were set up to further." So pronounced was his jurisprudence of administrative deference, "his acceptance of the place of administrative expertise and his insistence upon limitations of judicial control," that "Justice Frankfurter tends to lose sight of the need for making sure someone can review agency action," law professor Bernard Schwartz warned. "As Justice Frankfurter sees it," he concluded, "courts have nothing to do with the wisdom of challenged administrative action."

In an important 1943 decision about federal agencies' licensing powers, NBC v. United States, Frankfurter characteristically elevated executive capacity and deprecated judicial review: "Our duty is at an end when we find that the action of the Commission was based upon findings supported by evidence, and was made pursuant to authority granted by Congress." Courts had neither the capacity nor constitutional mandate to govern America, he wrote in a 1940 opinion. They "are not charged with a general guardianship against all potential mischief in the complicated tasks of government." Administrative agencies, by implication, should enjoy such a trust.[24]

Both Douglas and Frankfurter zealously endorsed FDR's New Deal Democracy. Both claimed, disingenuously, that Roosevelt's call to the Court came out of the blue. Melvin I. Urofsky, Douglas's biographer, deemed their "quick minds, loyalty to the New Deal, and personal friendship of the President of the United States" great assets to the nation. Each authored numerous Court opinions that approved unprecedented expansions of administrative power over the economy and society. But their shared commitment to New Deal principles of executive leadership and vigorous public sector intervention could not prevent their growing disdain for each other from hardening into contempt expressed as openly as the Supreme Court's cloistered atmosphere allowed.[25]

Joint service on behalf of FDR, their shared hero, quickly exposed the two justices' incompatible styles, straining their relationship from the outset. Neither had yet joined the Court when FDR's abortive 1937–1938 "court-packing" effort gave both an opportunity to demonstrate their political loyalty. Frankfurter advised Roosevelt privately to vet prospective judicial nominees to ensure fidelity to their patron's constitutional views. Publicly, he authored newspaper columns implying majorities had the right to create appellate courts to match their philosophy. Loyalty in this losing fight won Frankfurter his coveted nomination to the Supreme Court in January 1939. Douglas, then chairing the Securities and Exchange Commission, joined FDR confidantes Harry Hopkins and Missy LeHand for drinks in Harold Ickes' Interior Department office to toast the new justice, whom he hailed as a fellow "symbol . . . of the liberal cause."[26]

Douglas's own appointment three months later quickly revised his estimate of his new colleague. He discovered the "liberal" Supreme Court aspirant had strangely metamorphosed into "judicial independence" Frankfurter. More annoying still, Frankfurter was quietly continuing his after-hours advising of New Dealers from FDR on down. Douglas, ever the activist on and off the bench, thought Frankfurter's public pose of disinterested rectitude "duplicitous," in light of his almost pathetic private need to be consulted and flattered by powerful men. Frankfurter's biographers have speculated that his robust defense of judicial deference camouflaged this penchant for *ex parte* policy advocacy: keeping the Court out of controversy helped keep journalistic and political light from uncovering his private role as New Deal counselor. Reflecting forty years later, Douglas believed Frankfurter's camouflage concealed his contempt for colleagues and for the judiciary's constitutional function. With Chief Justice Charles Evans Hughes, Douglas soon fretted about Frankfurter's habit of behaving as if he were still tutoring Roosevelt and his New Dealer pupils at Harvard. When Frankfurter scathingly dismissed "Bushy Hughes" as an elderly makeweight one too many times privately, Douglas "finally chose a different path."[27]

Frankfurter returned the criticism both publicly and privately. He found Douglas's concern for public opinion disgraceful and proclaimed impartiality as his judicial credo: "I have no rigid social philosophy; I have been too intent on concrete problems of practical justice." Douglas's recurring fascination with elective politics repelled Frankfurter. To his diary in 1943, he confided deep concerns about his colleague's ambitions: "I am shocked to have this Court made a jumping-off place for politics. . . . This Court has no excuse for being unless it's a monastery. . . . We know all of the instances [of judicial politicking] and the experience is unedifying and disastrous." As Douglas continued to figure in press speculation about the 1944 presidential campaign, Frankfurter spilled bile across his diary. "Not long after Douglas came on the Court it was plain as a pikestaff to me that he was not consecrated to the work of this Court but his thoughts and ambitions were outside it. And for me such ambition in a man corrupts his whole nature." When Douglas's name popped into early articles handicapping the 1948 Democratic nomination race, Frankfurter's public and private damnations "bec[a]me almost an obsessive concern," his biographer sadly observed.[28]

On a postwar Court deeply divided by personal rivalries, Frankfurter's disdain for Hugo Black further darkened his views of Douglas, Black's good friend as well as Court ally. He denounced their "political" method of judging as little more than cloakroom lawmaking: "How malignant men like Black and Douglas not only can be, but are," he penned to his diary. Justices who counted votes hardly deserved to be considered judges at all, Frankfurter exploded one day in 1948 to Arthur Schlesinger, Jr., who was writing a long magazine article about the Supreme Court's troubles. "At the core of such an attitude," Schlesinger recorded Frankfurter as saying, "was of course the assumption of [sic] belief that there is no such thing as law and that law and opinions are just ways of clothing themselves in legal jargon. . . . Such an attitude was of course just as wicked as it was dishonest."[29]

Frankfurter's prejudices had at least a nominal basis in fact. Douglas did enjoy politics, delighted in Washington gossip, and considered himself presidential timber. In his memoirs, he confessed enough interest to welcome entreaties from FDR's White House about running as vice president in 1944 and again from Truman in 1948. Despite his retrospective claim—"I never had Potomac Fever"—his willingness to consider two offers of the vice presidency bespoke at least a mild interest. To critics both on and off the bench, who scorned his interest in public opinion, Douglas responded that all appellate judges of any intellect had opinions and that the task of the judge was to use honest intellectual effort to conform ideology to the Constitution's neutrality. He thought his friend and Columbia Law mentor, Chief Justice Hughes, penetrated Frankfurter's self-deceptive pose of disinterested scholar. Recalling Hughes's aphorism that "a judge's decisions were based 90% on emotion," Douglas observed Frankfurter's "skein of life was woven with a design that was duplicitous, for no one poured his emotions more completely into his decisions, while professing just the opposite." To make a Court majority, his rival would become rude and relentless, a dishonest intellectual bully, the worst kind of academic showman wearing the garb of judicial salesman. In later years, Douglas diagnosed Frankfurter's problem as "short man syndrome." His taunting of opponents on the Court and in "the Establishment" concealed his deep need "to be accepted by them and honored and admired by them."[30]

Frankfurter's passive judicial review jurisprudence maddened Douglas. His rival's "so-called hands-off policy" of judicial abstention and deference to agencies simply stripped federal courts of their chief duty to defend citizens from unwarranted government interference. He welcomed "activist" judges, such as Black and Earl Warren, who tried to construe constitutional provisions and congressional statutes "in the spirit as well as the letter in which they were written." Frankfurter and "the Harvard cabal," by contrast, invented complicated policies that allowed government to go unchecked. Not only did judicial deference have to imagine a "fantasy" world of politically aware citizens, it encouraged judges to evade the judiciary's highest duty, "vindicat[ing] the rights of the oppressed." At his life's end in the mid-1970s, writing in Richard Nixon's Watergate shadow, Douglas saw Frankfurterism recur in plainer form: "That is the real reason why the Supreme Court is said to be overworked and should let others do the work. Big business [and] power politics . . . could not possibly have it otherwise."[31]

Truman's first Court appointee, Harold Burton, detected the icy distance that separated two of the Court's brightest stars and biggest egos as soon as he took the oath in the fall of 1945. The conscientious, popular Ohio senator noted the Douglas-Frankfurter rivalry split the Court into a "civil liberties" faction, in which Frank Murphy and Wiley Rutledge fell into line behind Black and Douglas, and the "judicial restraint" alliance of Frankfurter, Robert Jackson, Stanley Reed, and Owen Roberts. Burton himself, more sympathetic to governmental power in all fields and less sure of the judiciary's constitutional competence to handle "political questions," initially sided with Frankfurter. Burton's modest legal scholarship elicited professorial tutorials thinly disguised as collegial discussions in which Frankfurter sedulously cultivated the rookie justice. By 1946, Burton had become an uneasy "swing man." He thought Frankfurter excessively eager to uphold administrative action and preclude judicial review of personal liberty claims. But lacking both Douglas's deep passion for the natural world and his prickly inclination to pick fights, the Ohioan gradually fell into line behind Frankfurter. Burton's *First Iowa Hydro-Electric* opinion for the Court in 1946 sustained the Federal Power Commission's discretion to ignore state law in licensing an Iowa River dam. *First Iowa* thus evidenced Frankfurter's powerful current still pulled colleagues in his wake.[32]

Postwar water policy dramatized Douglas's and Frankfurter's escalating battle. The struggle to control a North Carolina river's hydropower pitted three of the South's biggest utility companies against Virginia farmers and their Truman Administration allies in the early 1950s. The Roanoke Rapids case exposed how environmental lawmaking within the administrative process was dividing Douglas and Frankfurter. The Federal Power Commission had sided with the private power companies by licensing their proposed Roanoke Rapids dam in 1950. Public power forces earned Supreme Court review of the FPC decision by arguing that Congress had indicated a strong preference for nationalizing the river's hydroelectricity. Frankfurter's 1953 opinion in *Chapman v. FPC* refused to revoke the private dam license. He rationalized the decision by relying on both the 1930 Federal Power Act's broad grant of discretion to the agency and the 1946 *First Iowa* decision that sustained its administrative expertise. Congress, Frankfurter wrote, properly made a "general grant of continuing authority to the FPC to act as the responsible agent in exercising the licensing power" that the Constitution conferred on the federal government. Given the "breadth of authority granted to the Commission [as] the permanent disinterested expert agency of Congress," the disappointed license opponents were simply asking the Court "to intimate a preference between private or public construction at this site." The Constitution had wisely placed this policymaking decision beyond judges' prerogative.[33]

Douglas's vigorous dissent, joined by Black and Chief Justice Fred Vinson, charged that Frankfurter's casual deference to agency discretion missed both Roanoke Rapids' constitutional and environmental significance. For Douglas, the case turned not upon administrative expertise but the public's interest in the water. "Roanoke Rapids is a part of the *public domain*," he wrote. The Court's deferral to agency discretion "inferred that Congress . . . was utterly reckless with the *public domain*." Along navigable rivers, which the Constitution placed squarely within Congress's control, the public's rights resisted "this raid on the *public domain*." Even FPC expertise could not sanction "such an unconscionable appropriation of the *public domain* by private interests," Douglas concluded.[34]

Dying fish marooned in slack water pools behind power dams made their own contribution to environmental law. Natural dynamics began shifting the judicial review battlefield. The Cold War intensified demands for cheap hydropower, moving Frankfurter's duel with Douglas over administrative discretion and judicial deference from the Southern Piedmont to the Pacific Northwest. A trio of desperate legal fights over dams proposed for Washington, Oregon, and Idaho rivers illuminated administrative law's capacity to create environmental law. In the nation's hydroelectric homeland, the FPC was busy licensing municipal and private power dams in watersheds crucial to survival of salmon and steelhead trout. Both Oregon and Washington, working in concert with emboldened citizen activists, tried interposing state fish conservation laws to block new dams in the early 1950s. The FPC rejected both challenges by licensing new dams to block Oregon's Deschutes and Washington's Cowlitz Rivers. On the Snake River, which formed their common boundary in Hells Canyon, Oregon and Idaho managed to persuade the FPC to trade permanent closure of the river for modest fish conservation measures. Douglas disagreed vigorously with all three agency decisions, but Frankfurter secured enough of his Court colleagues' votes to win tactical victories through 1957. The two judicial giants' public posturing did, however, help conservationists win strategic advances in Congress that enabled Douglas's vigorous judicial review philosophy to finally prevail in the 1960s.

Citizens and state conservation agencies scored a surprising preliminary victory over agency authority in 1954 by swaying opinions on the Ninth Circuit Court of Appeals. The Far West's federal appellate court had ruled against dam opponents on the Cowlitz River in 1953. Chapman tied the circuit judges' hands, as well as those of Washington State. "The Federal Government has the jurisdiction over navigable rivers," concluded the Ninth Circuit, "and it is within the power of the Congress and the Executive to prescribe the policy in relation thereto." Even "if the dams will destroy the fish industry of the river, we are powerless to prevent it," the three judges observed with a mix of sadness and wonder. Douglas wanted the Supreme Court to review the FPC's Cowlitz decision, but could not persuade three colleagues to join him.

Untrammeled administrative discretion's ecological implications, upheld by Frankfurter's limitless logic of judicial deference, dismayed the same three Western appellate judges who had sustained the Cowlitz license. They rebelled in 1954 against the FPC along the Deschutes River. State of Oregon v. FPC maintained that the power agency had improperly ignored Oregon's traditional constitutional duties to manage its non-navigable waters and safeguard its migratory fish. When the FPC asked the Supreme Court to reaffirm Chapman by reversing the Ninth Circuit's Deschutes decision, Douglas still could not best his rival. Over his bitter dissent, the Supreme Court reinstated the FPC license in 1955. The decision found that assessment of the Deschutes dam's potential to damage fish "is within the exclusive jurisdiction of the Federal Power Commission [which] . . . acts on behalf of the people of Oregon, as well as all others, in seeing to it that the interests of all concerned are adequately protected."[35]

Frankfurter's impregnable Chapman barrier apparently blocked judicial review in the Far West. Opponents of the FPC's Hells Canyon dam license therefore tried another courthouse in 1956. They calculated a different, more self confident appellate court would find a way around *First Iowa*, *Chapman*, and Frankfurter. They wanted judges to reach some of the knotty economic and conservation issues buried in the agency's thousand-page administrative record justifying its Hells Canyon license. The District of Columbia Circuit Court of Appeals courthouse, just down Capitol Hill from the Supreme Court, heard the vast majority of judicial review lawsuits that arose out of federal agency actions. More familiar with the Administrative Procedure Act and more self confident about their judicial prerogatives, D.C. Circuit judges seemed more inclined to reconsider the constitutional and ecological implications of unreviewable administrative discretion. Yet as soon as Judge Wilbur K. Miller defined the key issue in Hells Canyon as "agency judgment," Frankfurter's impress dictated the decision. "Our review of the Commission's orders . . . is quite limited in scope," the D.C. Circuit began. "When we have determined whether the agency violated constitutional or statutory provisions, and whether its decision had a substantial basis in the evidence considered in its entirety, we are done." Frankfurter had written his *Chapman* opinion so tightly to preclude what he scorned as judicial second-guessing. A law school commentator guessed that the D.C. Circuit stopped thinking as soon as it characterized the Hells Canyon case as one "emphasizing the broad discretion allowed the FPC in factual determinations by the [Federal Power] Act." Douglas alone among his Court colleagues wanted to reconsider the appellate court's decision.[36]

Superficially labeling the 1950s as a decade dazed with prosperity and comforted by consensus unfairly pigeonholes an entire era. World War II's triumph, which quickly turned into the Cold War confrontation with Communism, Alan Brinkley has argued, "increased popular sensitivity to America's image [and] helped create support for some of the ambitious liberal reform efforts of the postwar era," such as civil rights, antipoverty campaigns, and environmental protection. Americans' conceit about their "exceptional mission" bequeathed "an appealing sense of hope and commitment . . . reflecting a confidence in the character and commitment" of their society. Reformist impulses encouraged clients, lawyers, and judges to experiment with legal tools that moderated administrative power's impact on ecology. Justice William O. Douglas's challenge to judicial deference was unmooring an administrative law jurisprudence that privileged administrative convenience above science and popular opinion. Congress and many states were making new environmental law to express citizens' growing uneasiness about the price that prosperity extracted from natural systems. By the end of the fifties, new statutes and judicial decisions were destabilizing older interpretations of "the public interest," equipping law that protected air, water, and their nonhuman inhabitants with new critical bite.[37]

Virginia Democrat A. Willis Robertson chaired the influential House Select Conservation Committee from the New Deal into the postwar era. The nation's most prominent midcentury environmental lawmaker, he sponsored the 1946 Fish and Wildlife Coordination Act, inciting new legal critiques of federal water projects. Courtesy U.S. Fish and Wildlife Service.

Justice William O. Douglas fought to invigorate judges' power to hear environmental-law claims. Contemptuous of judicial deference, he clashed repeatedly with Justice Felix Frankfurter about the effect of the 1946 Administrative Procedure Act on environmental disputes. Courtesy Yakima Valley Historical Museum.

The Anderson Ranch Dam in southern Idaho, like many postwar federal dams, spurred conservationists to develop new legal tactics. Conflicts over water, fish, and recreation fueled environmental lawmaking throughout the postwar years. Courtesy Idaho State Historical Society.

The 1948 federal water quality act challenged both activists and politicians to make environmental law. Local struggles to update primitive municipal sewage systems, like this one near Boise, Idaho, spurred important lawmaking well before the landmark 1972 Clean Water Act. Courtesy Idaho State Historical Society.

Citizens from Los Angeles to Cleveland promoted key air-quality laws after World War II. Before the federalization of clean-air law in the 1960s, factories like this zinc smelter in northern Idaho faced a welter of state and local legal controls. Courtesy Idaho State Historical Society.

Postwar economic expansion stimulated environmental lawmaking, but affluence restrained critics and limited the legal restraints on consumption. Dredge mining that scarred mountain country, like this Idaho meadow, proved politically difficult to control with state or federal laws. Courtesy Idaho State Historical Society.

Americans flooding outdoors after World War II gave recreationists new arguments to safeguard natural resources. Crucial environmental lawmaking alliances linked field-sports enthusiasts with new fun-seekers, like these river rafters near Boise, Idaho. Courtesy Idaho State Historical Society.

Bruce Bowler, pioneer environmental lawyer, testifying on behalf of his long-time conservation client, the Idaho Wildlife Federation. From his Boise office, this solo practitioner helped innovate key environmental law tactics and principles well before 1970. Courtesy of the Bowler family.

Bruce Bowler's environmental law practice centered in the small capital city of Boise, Idaho, where just blocks separated key lawmaking forums —courts, the Statehouse, and government agencies. Courtesy Idaho State Historical Society.

Bruce Bowler's second-floor solo law office in Boise's modest Sonna Building was the nerve center of postwar environmental lawmaking in the state. Conservation clients got his services for free or at steep discounts. Courtesy Idaho State Historical Society.

In settings such as this congressional field hearing in northern Idaho in the late 1950s, citizens, administrators, and politicians were forging environmental law before the "environmental decade" of the 1970s. Courtesy Idaho State Historical Society.

5

"Publication of Rachel Carson's *Silent Spring* in 1962 can be described as the start of the modern environmental movement," according to John Opie's *Nature's Nation: An Environmental History of the United States.* Carson's graceful indictment of unrestrained chemical use on crops, trees, and even humans spotlighted the unknown risks of DDT, the one-time postwar wonder chemical. Her velvet thunderclap reverberated like *Uncle Tom's Cabin,* Harriet Beecher Stowe's antebellum antislavery novel. When CBS TV broadcast a 1963 prime-time Sunday night documentary that restated Carson's arguments, most Americans got their first glimpse of the one-time government scientific writer. They liked what they saw. Carson's calm strength made her a formidable adversary for the chemical industry and its political friends. "Environmental protection became part of the national agenda" that night, Opie maintained. "Environmentalism, with ecology as its science, moved into the American mainstream and began to steer the national agenda in government, science, and industry."[1]

Some historians and legal academics have contended that environmental law only emerged after *Silent Spring* catalyzed a mass environmental movement in the mid-1960s. In their estimate, without Rachel Carson, environmental law would have taken shape later, more slowly, or perhaps not at all. Environmental lawmaking's fifteen-year backdrop, however, brings *Silent Spring* into sharper focus. Carson's critique expressed and affected beliefs millions of Americans shared broadly, but did not itself create those beliefs. Although public opinion demanded more laws after 1963 to protect people from environmental harm, *Silent Spring* did not create that demand, though Carson's quiet passion shaped some of its objectives. Americans' shared personal and civic experiences—what they had done, seen, and thought before 1963—laid a cultural powder trail that *Silent Spring's* bright flame ignited.[2]

Some dozen years before *Silent Spring* appeared, Aldo Leopold's *A Sand County Almanac*, a posthumous collection of conservation and ecological essays was published. Scarcely a handful of wildlife managers, biological scientists, and conservation activists noted its publication in 1949. Leopold's valedictory commanded far more attention when republished, four years after *Silent Spring*, in a cheap paperback edition. During the Cold War chill, *Sand County* scarcely rippled the surface of American public life. Leopold anticipated Carson's plea for a new ethic of environmental restraint, rooted in ecological wisdom and philosophical humility. Though environmental lawmaking after World War II had started readjusting basic legal principles that privileged private property above public safety and elevated individual liberty over community security, few legislators responded to Leopold as their successors did to Carson.[3]

Carson's book intensified a new phase of environmental lawmaking after 1962, while Leopold's went largely unnoticed in 1949. Most Americans quickly hailed Carson as a heroine, while few noted—and fewer long remembered—Leopold's work or testament. The fifteen years that separated Leopold's quiet passage from Carson's celebrity map a cultural divide. The divide's dimensions suggest why *Silent Spring* accelerated lawmaking and *Sand County Almanac* did not. One side of the divide dips back before 1949, when general popular indifference acquiesced to environmental degradation. The other side of the divide rises toward 1963, when public concern mounted about the earth's future and humanity's survival.

Between 1949 and 1962, three simultaneous cultural shifts challenged, then destabilized, traditional popular values that Americans used to subordinate nature to society. Outdoor recreation boomed. Suburbs flourished. And widespread prosperity gushed across the landscape, floating millions toward a level of material security previously known only to a relative handful of the wealthy. Cultural ferment fertilized legal change. Citizens made more law at all governmental levels to restructure important aspects of their relationship with nature. They empowered the national government to make and enforce many of the most powerful environmental laws. Cultural transformation during the fifties, however, still preserved Americans' customary definitions of freedom and prosperity. Even new laws that regulated uses of the natural world reflected optimism that well-drafted rules would ameliorate difficult problems. Hardly any of the environmental laws enacted during the sixties required many people to reconsider consumption, prosperity, and success. And though some new environmental laws after 1960 restrained personal behavior, most citizens still defined America's characteristic creed as private freedom to pursue mass prosperity. They resisted imposing public sanctions that aimed to elevate the long-term common good above everyday private comfort.

AMERICANS AFIELD

A first important postwar cultural transformation sent unprecedented numbers of ordinary people afield. Ever-diminishing numbers still worked in nature as of old, transforming natural resources into products for human consumption. Against this dwindling minority, millions more left their homes to explore, hike, boat, and kill animals and fish as hunters and anglers. Recreating taught them new skills, which inculcated new values. During their billions of hours afield together in the fifties, millions of Americans learned new lessons through recreation that helped trigger and then sustain environmentalism in the 1960s.[4]

Outdoor recreation's new postwar popularity challenged America's most visible conservationist action group, the Izaak Walton League, as it struggled through a wrenching leadership transition. Kenneth Reid's October 1948 heart attack had hit him in his Chicago office, not along a trail. For more than a decade, he had directed the nation's preeminent conservation activist organization. Indefatigable in advocating Ikes' priorities—healthy land, clean water, and the creatures they nourished—the acerbic Reid drove himself and his tiny staff hard. He relished playing conservation gadfly. His job description might have read, "Make yourself a nuisance to administrators, elected officials, and industrial managers whose factories pollute water and foul air." IWL worked most fiercely and effectively on its home turf, the Upper Midwest and Ohio Valley. Two promotions sparked by Reid's deteriorating health in 1949 left lasting effects not only on the group's staff, but on environmental lawmaking. William Voigt from IWL's Western field office in

Denver replaced Reid as executive director. And a crew-cut, globe-trotting Yale dropout of early middle years, Joseph W. Penfold, succeeded Voigt in Denver. Rocky Mountain experiences just after World War II convinced Penfold that Americans' enthusiastic pursuit of outdoor leisure promised fundamental changes in their legal relationship with the natural world. Penfold pushed the IWL in the 1950s to endorse a national recreation policy, and in 1959, Congress agreed by creating the Outdoor Recreation Resources Review Commission. Penfold drafted the early proposal that inspired the ORRRC.[5]

Joe Penfold, a minister's son from central Wisconsin, grew up fishing, canoeing, and camping in the lands left behind when the nation's logging industry moved west, away from the North Woods around the Great Lakes. New Haven, Connecticut's varied charms proved uncongenial to the flannel-shirted fisherman. He loved to read and write but chafed under Ivy League academic rules and social hierarchies. Before graduating, Penfold left Yale to crew on merchant ships plying international waters in the late 1920s, eventually earning his seamen's union card. During the 1930s, he left off seafaring, then gradually stopped wandering the country, until, captivated by the New Deal's promise to empower citizens who traditionally had been relegated to the margins of society, he joined the federal workforce full-time. World War II's mobilization then tapped Penfold's interest in economic policy. He moved from supervising work relief to the agencies that coalesced into the wartime Office of Price Administration.

Emergency detail to the OPA's Mountain West region brought him back to the Rockies' Front Range, which he had toured by foot and car during the early 1930s. He admitted later that he fell in love with the Western outdoor lifestyle as a middle-aged federal bureaucrat. Still single when the war ended, Penfold went abroad again as a United Nations refugee field assistant in China. After being "shot at by both sides, at the same time" in the Chinese Civil War between Communists and Nationalists, he returned to Denver. By now married and a father, he began socializing and hiking with a group of conservationists gathered around charismatic National Park Service regional manager Arthur Carhart. On Carhart's recommendation to Voigt, the Izaak Walton League hired Penfold in 1949 as Western Field Representative.[6]

From his Denver office, he began mobilizing conservationists throughout the Mountain and Far West to critique postwar federal dam-building and water diversion projects. The postwar recreation boom was cresting in the early 1950s. Millions of ordinary Americans were enjoying time off outdoors. Penfold nevertheless later recalled the "contempt" with which both government water managers and their agribusiness allies viewed nonconsumptive values and pursuits. "They had no concern for any of our concerns: esthetic, outdoor recreation, and related uses of water and land," he mused a quarter-century later. "They really thought that we were a little screwball."[7]

Between the late 1940s and early 1960s, increased numbers of outdoor recreationists steadily forced one-time skeptics to revise their caricatures. Hunters and anglers led the way afield, their numbers soaring in the fifties. Between 1948 and 1958, reported the U.S. Fish and Wildlife Service, fishing license sales rose 43 percent and hunting license sales 30 percent, while national population increased just 19 percent. If those growth rates persisted into the sixties—and FWS saw no reason not to plan accordingly—states, cities, and the federal government would have to add 46 percent more public fishing waters and 57 percent more public shooting areas just to keep pace with the Eisenhower Era recreation boom.[8]

Recreation on all types of public lands skyrocketed. Land managers accustomed to serving loggers, miners, and ranchers—constituents organized around economic production from natural resources—faced a values revolution when recreational shock troops went afield. During the ten years after 1945, total annual visits to national forests boomed 250 percent, from 16 to 40 million. One-quarter of all the new visitors who went to Smokey Bear's domain did so to hunt or fish. Proximity proved decisive: three-quarters of the national forests lay west of the Continental Divide, but fully one-third of the Forest Service's annual visitor days were registered in the heavily populated Northeast, Southeast, and Midwest. Throughout the vast reservoir system created during the New Deal by the Tennessee Valley Authority—from the lowlands of western Tennessee to the foothill flanks of the Carolina Appalachians—recreational boater and angler use quadrupled between 1947 and 1956.[9]

Outdoor magazines reaped what prosperity sowed, their pages cheerfully encouraging even larger crops of new recreation enthusiasts. Glossy cover art, "how-to" articles crammed with detail, and advertisements that promoted gear to lighten the load, shorten the trail, or nail that wily buck abounded in the publications. Hunters and anglers for over half a century had been nurturing a rich magazine tradition. Field and Stream, Outdoor Life, and Sports Afield dominated the postwar era. Millions of readers subscribed at home or leafed through copies at gas stations and barber shops. All had been publishing since the 1890s and all occupied vital commercial junctions centered in New York City's web of advertising, publishing, and retailing. Their readers were overwhelmingly male, but the postwar rush afield swept along nearly as many women as men. By the early 1960s, outdoor magazines were portraying recreation as a truly national outdoors awakening. Readers of both sexes often started and continued their journeys of discovery in the magazines' pages, filled with first-person accounts of going afield and bright with the colors of nature and commerce.[10]

President Harry Truman shared few of the new recreationists' aims. His brand of Fair Deal liberalism recruited postwar federal water policy to serve national security. In early 1950, he formed a presidential commission that stumped the country to jump-start massive new federal dams in the West and South. The Cooke Commission was ostensibly gathering information to help the president reform executive branch water agencies. Its members understood that the president really intended to rally political supporters to push Congress to authorize more water projects. In mid-summer 1950, commission field hearings were canvassing the West. Joe Penfold's Denver testimony about Westerners' new passion for recreation put the Izaak Walton League into a distinct minority. Immediately preceding him at the lectern, Colorado's Water Resources Board director had sketched a bright picture of the state's economic future if federal commissioners ignored "a handful of conservationists who don't need to have any attention paid to them."[11]

Western water lawyers and project managers dismissed Penfold as a harmless crackpot, but his testimony intrigued Morris Cooke, the old Progressive public power academician who chaired Truman's commission. A quiet chat in Cooke's hotel room that night surprised Penfold. The commission wanted to hire him as a recreation consultant in Washington, D.C., writing up its final reports. Nothing Penfold did that summer appreciably affected the commission's work, since Cooke gratified Truman by calling for more big dams, public power projects, and comprehensive planned development of the nation's river basins. Penfold's capital sojourn, though, convinced him of two indisputable facts: Americans' rush afield showed no sign of abating, even as the Korean War exploded; and federal agencies had absolutely no idea how to respond to the unprecedented surge.[12]

Almost as soon as the Cooke Commission endorsed dams in Echo Park as key components of the Colorado River Storage Project (CRSP), conservation activists began battling the massed forces of Western water developers and federal water managers. New recreationists provoked this first big postwar environmental collision. Cultural change fanning political controversy could, Penfold came to see, create legal change.

The Echo Park controversy finally subsided after Congress and the Eisenhower Administration capitulated to conservationists in 1956 by eliminating new dams in Dinosaur National Monument in Utah and Colorado. Echo Park illuminated the recreation revolution's legal potential. Its purely political outcome made no new environmental law immediately. As Mark Harvey's *Symbol of Wilderness: Echo Park and the American Conservation Movement* summarized, "Opponents of the dam had no legal weapons to block or delay the project. . . . [They] had little choice but to operate solely in the political arena." Nevertheless, the conservation coalition that bested two presidents and their Reclamation Bureaus, congressional majorities of both parties, and powerful Western constituencies favoring more dams, promised legal change.[13]

Echo Park's most tangible legal product became the 1964 Wilderness Act. Congressional sponsors introduced the first wilderness bills in 1956, even before the controversy had subsided. When the Wilderness Act became law, Harvey concluded, it overhauled the federal land management legal system. A distinctive new category of protected area, designated by Congress and the President, dedicated public lands to both ecological preservation and nonmotorized human recreation. "In the broadest sense," Harvey thought Echo Park spotlighted "a generational clash in American conservation and environmental history." After the mid-1950s, "a new generation of preservationists, represented by such groups as the Wilderness Society and the Sierra Club, . . . advocated greater protection of national parks and wilderness areas and sought to take advantage of changing economic and social trends including a rise in educational levels, greater geographic mobility, and steady growth in the numbers of people moving out of cities and into suburbs and expressing a fondness for natural beauty." Harvey, like cultural historians Roderick Nash and Samuel Hays, believed that "these societal changes after [World War II] created new demands for 'amenities' like wildlife protection and access to parks and wilderness areas, and established the foundation for what later came to be termed the environmental movement."[14]

Joe Penfold helped harness the movement to environmental lawmaking, encouraging recreationists to exercise their sovereignty by using law to secure their objectives. He thought the Echo Park controversy's political eruption marked a big cultural shift in American values. "Protection of a national monument against the intrusion of men-built developments such as Echo Park Dam . . . [was] part of the overall context of protecting and preserving outdoor recreation opportunities." The intense political struggle over Echo Park continued for six years at the national level, and required that traditional conservationists seek support from the new postwar recreationists going afield. Penfold deemed "the Dinosaur fight . . . germane to the particular course of events . . . because it served as a catalyst which brought together for the first time perhaps in the history of the country all of the conservation organizations and societies." Unlikely at the outset, national political pressure finally defeated the dams in Congress. Like the Ikes' 1945–1946 push for the FWCA, Echo Park boosted members' morale. This "long and hard fight demonstrated again, perhaps for the first time, that there was a real strength in the conservation movement."[15]

Field and Stream celebrated its sixtieth anniversary as the Echo Park controversy peaked in 1955. A million monthly issues fanned across the country from its New York offices, read by perhaps another 3 million hunters, anglers, campers, and hikers. Billing itself as "America's Number One Sportsman's Magazine," *Field and Stream* covered not only Echo Park but disputes about land, water, and wildlife management throughout North America. Conservation Editor Harold Titus reminded readers of Echo Park's historic context. His magazine had long advocated laws to restrain public property's conversion into private profit and his numerous columns defending wild rivers in Dinosaur National Monument offered "attempt[s] to preserve satisfactory segments of the old America that was." He believed *Field and Stream's* conservation mission remained timeless even as it proved timely: "This task of conserving something of our old heritage is not anything less than an endless struggle . . . to keep our natural resources alive and functioning. It means rushing through the meeting of one emergency only to face another. It is no longer necessary to fight for one thing, another will need all our efforts—and right now. It has been thus from the beginning, and perhaps will be for all time. At least it will be until man is so reconstructed that all selfishness and greed and short-sightedness are eliminated from his nature."[16]

Struggle, cooperation, humility, responsibility, and restraint composed

Field and Stream's conservation canon in the mid-1950s. Millions of recreationists who encountered the natural world began subscribing to its tenets. Their individual jaunts afield forged a powerful realm of shared experience. Postwar outdoor magazines' articles and editorials guided them along a trail toward the sixties' environmental movement. Many recreationists packed new values for their changing journey: more flexible than domineering, more democratic than deferential, more esthetic than economic, and more skeptical than enthusiastic about traditional institutions' claims to exercise power over the natural world.

Although Harold Titus certainly contributed less than Rachel Carson to Americans' postwar environmental awakening, he sketched many of the same themes that she eloquently expressed. *Silent Spring* appeared as Titus ended his thirty-year career writing *Field and Stream's* monthly "Conservation" column. He wrote to "supply ammunition [to] the individual, like the one reading this sentence, who is up there on the firing line and either battles to glory or goes down to wretched defeat." Titus stressed citizens' duties to learn, cooperate, and oppose power if need be. He counseled conservationists to infuse political vigilance with ecological wisdom. "Conservation" columns in *Field and Stream* anticipated Carson's 1962 plea for mindful activism: "The earth's vegetation is part of a web of life in which there are intimate and essential relations between plants and the earth, between plants and other plants, between plants and animals. Sometimes we have no choice but to disturb these relationships, but we should do so thoughtfully, with full awareness that what we do may have consequences remote in time and place."[17]

Titus prepared his audience to enlist in the movement for environmental quality that stimulated so much sixties' lawmaking. Going afield during the Eisenhower years, millions of Americans acquired new knowledge about nature, and about their own relationships with natural systems. Citizens had learned enough about their place in nature after 1949 to make Carson's 1962 critique of unregulated chemical spraying fit concrete situations they themselves understood. The outdoor recreation boom opened the way for the transformation in values and behavior that Carson's book prompted. A significant constituency of Americans afield— hunters, anglers, male and female outdoors enthusiasts who neither shot nor fished—embraced Carson's reformulation of Leopold's basic question: How can we live comfortably within nature while respecting natural processes?

Harold Titus had endured enough twentieth-century wars to remind *Field and Stream* readers that the Korean armistice opened the conservation movement's third postwar period. "Praying this one sticks," he hopefully observed, "Each time there has been a tremendous upsurge of interest in working with our natural resources—forests, fish and game." The Traverse City, Michigan, native had, like Penfold, grown up amid the logged-over North Woods. A veteran, like Leopold, of service on a state game management agency, Titus proudly confessed he peppered his *Field and Stream* "Conservation" column with Leopold's ideas in the 1930s and 1940s. Leopold, Titus claimed, used him "as a tool . . . to hasten public acceptance of the technical approach to wildlife problems." From the mid-1930s to the early 1960s, he wrote "Conservation" to serve three purposes. He sought to motivate outdoor recreationists to act politically. He encouraged traditional field sportsmen to expand the conservation movement to welcome the new waves of recreationists. And he scrutinized government and business proposals that menaced healthy natural systems and public rights.[18]

Between 1951 and 1960, cartoons and short epigraphs—from Izaak Walton, Aldo Leopold, even Voltaire—bannered "Conservation" in each month's *Field and Stream*. Longtime managing editor Van Campen Heilner and art director Hermann Kessler assigned staff cartoonist Walter Dower to enliven Titus's text with sketches that signposted evolving attitudes about humans in nature. Pithy and wry, Dower's editorial cartoons summarized Titus's ongoing meditation about how outdoor recreation could safeguard the health of natural systems on which that recreation depended. Titus and Dower counseled skepticism about accumulation of material wealth, criticized established political structures, and preached respect for natural systems. They wrote and drew passionately to promote common democratic action in defense of cherished places and traditional practices. Their monthly "Conservation" column in *Field and Stream* helped nurture postwar recreation into an environmental lawmaking force. Taken together, Titus's hard-boiled prose and Dower's pungent penwork politicized complex cultural issues, carrying conservation to the brink of the environmental movement that Carson inspired.

The Echo Park controversy intensified Titus's criticism of federal dams for neglecting recreational and ecological values. The October 1951 "Conservation" column featured Dower's cartoon that depicted recreationists clad in flannel shirts and billed caps, toting fishing rods and shotguns, flocking to-

Figure 5.1

ward the Capitol, purposeful but leaderless (Fig. 5.1). Organized proxies for
citizens at large, they challenged the experts who touted expensive engineering works. The following summer, Titus decided Army Engineer and Reclamation Bureau dams and canals were not only ignoring citizens' pleas but
flouting the 1946 Wildlife Coordination Act by failing to consider biological
impacts. Dower's June 1952 cartoon portrayed the columnist's favored solution: a powerful new body of government employees and citizen experts to
weigh what would, twenty years later, be termed "environmental impacts of
major federal actions" (Fig. 5.2). *Field and Stream* never advocated replacing
expertise with passion to make environmental decisions, but Titus's proposed "Natural Resources Council of America" accorded equal weight to nature's needs and recreationists' values. He thought natural systems and
outdoor pursuits deserved as much legal weight as big dams and suburban
houses.[19]

"Conservation" critically diagnosed the political economy of resource exploitation. In 1953, Titus and Dower inveighed against outmoded political
structures that enthroned miners, loggers, and land developers. They be-

Figure 5.2

Figure 5.3

lieved that unrestrained capitalism conferred political advantages on a minority who disregarded ordinary people's equally legitimate aspirations for environmental quality (Fig. 5.3). Even as the Cold War constrained social criticism, Titus argued that corporate resource users often rigged politics to pursue goals inimical to the national good. His brand of dissent, mild by the standards of the earlier labor movement or later environmental crusade, refused to celebrate traditional power relationships. Businessmen who damaged natural systems were neither heroes of the struggle against Communism nor wizards of capitalism. Instead, as Titus's September 1956 column and Dower's illustration argued, the public good outweighed private profit. "Ordinary citizens" enjoyed legal rights to recreate that deserved as much

Figure 5.4

Figure 5.5

protection as suburban developers' rights to restrict access (Fig. 5.4). Private property's social dimension overcame libertarian notions in which ownership connoted exclusivity. Titus considered the nation's suburban land rush "an alarming situation to contemplate." Through text and cartoons, *Field and Stream*'s "Conservation" cautiously explored alternatives to prevailing postwar consumption and land use assumptions.[20]

Titus and Dower valued individual action as well as conservation activism's community component. Their May 1954 "Conservation" column contended that conservationists should forthrightly avow their beliefs. Dower's cartoon sat a sword-wielding, slouch-hatted, plaid-shirted outdoorsman astride a rearing steed (Fig. 5.5). Titus's alarming report about Lake Erie pollution ladled praise on citizens who organized to pressure state regulators to take stricter action. Activists, in Titus's estimate, had to practice a higher form of citizenship based on individual virtue and courage, community self restraint, and visionary strategy. Echo Park inspired conservationists to believe they could use politics to change laws. The controversy made David Brower, Ira Gabrielson, and Howard Zahniser national figures. Their blended gifts of zeal, tactical sense, and persistence infused Echo Park Dam's opponents with the passion of outnumbered, righteous heroes. Conservation advocacy began resonating with that certain tone adversaries found intolerable and, when expressed too loudly or for too long, irritated even neutral observers.[21]

Figure 5.6

"Conservation's" May 1958 column clearly demonstrated Titus's and Dower's political sympathies. A dark image depicted their warning about businesses manipulating poor rural people to endorse shortsighted projects that benefited wealthy investors. Shadowy, corpulent, cigar-smoking puppet masters, crouched in the shadows behind stage, dangled marionettes dressed as "conservationists" (Fig. 5.6). Keenly attuned to advertisers' needs and subscribers' desires, *Field and Stream's* management still gave Titus and Dower a loose rein. Their work bestowed "attaboys" on activists who opposed the consensus that heralded prosperity. The column's words and pictures often fiercely criticized aspects of American government that elevated projects favored by the powerful few over the public's real good.[22]

Titus and Dower encouraged recreationists to think critically and act politically. Along with other outspoken activists in the later fifties, they appealed to a nation still timid about criticizing leaders who regularly warned them about pulling together to defend their "way of life" against evil, alien influences. For example, in 1958, few concepts appeared more patriotic than personal freedom expressed through technical innovation and automobiles. Scientific forestry, supervised by some of the nation's leading silvicultural experts, seemed proof of America's superiority. Elected officials were encouraging their appointed agency experts to acquiesce to new pressures, West and East, for unrestrained motor vehicle access to public lands and "selective logging" in the Adirondack Forest Preserve of New York State.[23]

Titus confronted both conservation problems in January and May 1958. Since the early 1950s, he had been warning about adventurous outdoorsmen who used military surplus jeeps to reach country previously beyond the most audacious hiker or well-heeled horse-packer. February 1952's column cited Leopold's cautionary note about building more new visions "in unlovely minds" than new roads across lovely lands. Most "venturesome" jeep jockeys doubtless were fine people, Titus conceded, but "easy access to . . .

wilderness areas attracts the thoughtless and heedless as well." By fall 1957, Titus concluded democratized recreation, though promising the conservation movement new allies, conferred no democratic right to drive, fly, or motorboat into every acre of the public's lands and waters. When a handful of congressmen followed Echo Park's resolution by introducing the first wilderness system bills, "Conservation" hailed their "pioneering effort." Their campaign, Titus hopefully noted, "will gain wider attention and stronger support as time goes on. It had better, if we expect to preserve any section in its natural state!"[24]

Titus grew alarmed enough about motorized vandalism to head the January 1958 "Conservation" with Dower's blunt cartoon that pictured a jeep full of yahoos carving deep ruts across a high alpine meadow (Fig. 5.7). He saluted Montana's conservation agency for making rules to restrict four-wheel-drive vehicles to existing roads and trails. "Those taking the long view and with a true love of the wilderness in their hearts" should urge their own state and federal land managers to zone vehicles out of vulnerable public lands. Titus tied Western off-roading to Eastern logging in July, urging New Yorkers to resist plans to "open up" the Adirondack and Catskill backcountry. Dower's cartoon, entitled "Last Wilderness," poised a watchful deer before old-growth woods, its only fallen tree an elderly giant toppled in a windstorm (Fig. 5.8). Dower illustrated Titus's contention that trees should

Figure 5.7

Figure 5.8

fall in a designated wilderness when natural forces decided the time and place. "Conservation" continued to praise the nation's largest legally protected roadless wilderness and boost federal wilderness. By 1961, Titus inspired *Field and Stream* to formally endorse a congressional wilderness bill three years before its enactment.[25]

Titus's audience included many of Joe Penfold's constituents. The Izaak Walton League's Western Field Director sensed that the millions going afield from their suburban homes could spur big changes in natural resources policy. In late summer 1956, as he prepared to move from Denver to Washington to become the League's National Conservation Director, Penfold reflected on recreational trends. While driving through a big national forest in southwestern Colorado a couple weeks earlier, he told the National Conference on State Parks in a speech at Jackson Lake, Wyoming, "I found 85 cars crowded into a campground designed for 16." A week later, as he motored toward Denver through the Roosevelt National Forest, "there was a car parked every place where there was room to pull off the road, and a lot of places where there wasn't." Eager to sample a bit of their public lands' allure, "there was a family picknicking [sic] just about every place along the creek where there was a spot big enough to spread a picnic lunch." No surprise, there, Penfold reported: one southwestern Colorado national forest's visitorship boomed 700 percent in the first decade after World War II. Penfold's adopted state, home to only 1.5 million residents, hosted more than twice that many every summer, "most of those folks coming West specifically to take advantage of the recreation resources we speak of." People went outdoors for lots of reasons, he told the parks conference. Unintentionally perhaps, Penfold offered a recreation rationale that also accounted for the parallel rush from city to suburb. Postwar people with the time and means to do so were searchers. A citizen afield, like a new homeowner, sought "space and the opportunity to recreate himself, away from the noises, smells, and glare of modern society."[26]

SUBURBIA, SWEET SUBURBIA

Americans celebrated peace after 1945 by procreating. Amorous activities unleashed a second cultural transformation: construction of millions of new homes across unsettled lands to house booming numbers of young children. Young families simply overwhelmed a housing stock dormant since the mid-1920s. Of course, after World War II, many people still resided in great cities and small towns and many Americans remained unmarried. But the skyrocketing birthrate that propelled the suburban rush after World War II upended the nation's definitions of "home" and "hearth." America's population growth rate nearly matched India's in the fifties. As many people moved each year between 1947 and 1962 into suburbs as had arrived annually during the immigration peak before 1910. New suburbanites inhabiting new homes in green fields soon perceived new environmental threats that menaced their families and they explored novel ways to defend their hearths and progeny.[27]

Penfold's suburban seekers included Tom and Betsy Rath, a fictional couple inhabiting a small tract house in southern Connecticut. Tom caught the train every weekday into New York City, where he labored as a copywriter at an advertising firm. A World War II paratrooper, Tom had written to Betsy, his "girl back home," that "the important thing is to find a kind of work you really like, and something that is useful. The money doesn't matter." But as 1954 approached 1955, Tom, now the father of three small children, felt driven to seek another job, at a new television network broadcasting programs he detested. "The sole reason he wanted to work for United Broadcasting Corporation," author Sloan Wilson wrote of Tom Rath's motives, "was that he thought he might be able to make a lot of money there fast." When offered the job, Rath returns to break the news to his current supervisor, who asks plaintively, "But why are you leaving now?" Rath's answer simplifies the complex suburban and baby-boom pressures reshaping American middle-class life in the fifties: "Money. I have three children and I need more money than I think I can make here in the immediate future." As soon as Tom tells Betsy he may land the UBC job, she has their little house appraised, contacts a realtor, and begins to shop for a new suburban house twice as expensive.[28]

Sloan Wilson's fictional suburban protagonists in his best-selling 1955 novel, *Man in the Gray Flannel Suit*, resembled the mythical couple who puzzled John Keats. His 1956 satire, *The Crack in the Picture Window*, asked, "How did John and Mary Drone come to inhabit a box of their own in one of the fresh-air slums . . . spreading like gangrene" across "rural tracts that might better have remained in hay?" Keats wondered if middle-class suburban living was undermining not only natural integrity but social values. Visiting a new subdivision sprouting in the northern Virginia suburbs across the Potomac from Washington, he observed bulldozers "battering down pines, leveling knolls, churning the area into a level red-clay sea." Built on "bulldozed slime," the new houses reminded him of the worst robber baron excesses a half-century earlier: they were "a waste of natural resources and a menace to the public's emotional health."[29]

Crack in the Picture Window reads quaintly today and its wry criticism accomplished little. The suburbanization rate in the first decade of the twenty-first century exceeds even the most hectic house-building days of the baby boom. Yet by linking suburbanization and cultural transformation, Keats's book glimpsed the environmental dystopia crouching within a thousand peaceful Levittowns. "Today's housing developments," Keats charged, "are conceived in error, nurtured by greed, and corrode everything they touch." To house the Drones, the Raths, and millions of actual white middle-class aspirants on whom Keats and Wilson modeled their fictional characters, builders created "neither city nor country, but a combination of the disadvantages of both," *Picture Window* observed. "Illusory" images sold the new houses. "Illusory" estimates of net worth sold their buyers on mortgages exceeding their capacity to pay. Suburban anomie, epitomized by the lonely young wife staring out of the cracked picture window at strangers rolling by in station wagons, seemed like the buyers' just desserts, Keats thought. By "confusing things for experiences," the suburbanites "built only a lot of houses," not a community's "balanced society of men, women, and children wherein work and pleasure are found and the needs of all of society's members are served."[30]

Three years after he embedded a catchphrase in Americans' lexicon, *The Organization Man's* William H. Whyte, Jr., returned to the suburbs. For *Life* magazine in 1959, he drove around the edges of America's sprawling metropolitan complexes. Their environmental transformation worried him as much as the cultural shifts he pilloried in his best-selling account of middle-class white-collar culture. "Take a last look," Whyte wrote of "The Vanishing U.S. Countryside." Its meadows, woods, and creeks should be "fixed in your memory," he advised *Life's* readers. "If the American standard of living goes up another notch, this is about the last chance you will have."[31]

Adam Rome used Whyte's lament to explore suburbanization's paradoxical effect on suburbanites' environmental values. His important 2001 study of suburbanites' engagement with environmentalism, *Bulldozer in the Countryside*, extended an insight first suggested in 1987 by Samuel Hays in *Beauty, Health, and Permanence*: in the very process of re-creating themselves as suburbanites, a decisive core of ordinary Americans "played an important role in the emergence of environmentalism." Even as they scalped the land to subdivide it into lots, suburban migrants told themselves they were moving from center cities to seek something greener, more healthful, more "natural." Rome and Hays suggested that rising postwar prosperity was replacing the imperative to produce and conserve with the opportunity to pursue amenities. Americans' search for the "good life" was steadily supplanting their long "struggle to survive." This epochal shift in values that had defined nature's purposes for Americans before 1945 promised political change.[32]

The soaring American birthrate swelled family size between 1946 and 1960. Americans built more suburban homes because they needed more space to handle their growing families. Elaine Tyler May has found that they also devoted far more time and money to child rearing than their parents or grandparents had. Young suburban parents cared deeply about their children's future. Children, nurtured and privileged as they had not been before, symbolized America's postwar promise, according to William Chafe.[33]

The health and safety of all these young families began influencing lawmakers' priorities. Toward the end of the fifties, millions of parents identified nuclear fallout as a perilous global concern. Closer to home, the food on their family tables seemed newly vulnerable to chemical poisoning. Environmental lawmaking expressed postwar suburbanites' dedication to protect both families and homes. They put new emphasis on guarding personal safety from technological and environmental threats, causing lawmakers to instill a measure of caution by adjusting rules that had favored production. Even before *Silent Spring* appeared in 1962, families' fears about chemicals and health illustrated suburbanites' potential to remodel law to protect their safety. Their cautious lawmaking, however, revealed the limits that still restrained environmental law.[34]

The 1947 Federal Insecticide, Fungicide, and Rodenticide Act (FIFRA) replaced the 1910 Insecticide Act and established at postwar's outset an important environmental law principle: uniform national standards should regulate manufacture and sale of chemicals that could sicken people and pollute natural systems. Congress also invoked its Commerce Clause power to begin limiting the ways buyers could use chemicals such as agricultural poisons. FIFRA federally regulated agricultural chemical safety, largely preempting inconsistent state laws that had created a patchwork of legislation. Critics—from free-market libertarians to community environmental activists—have identified numerous shortcomings in FIFRA's administrative system. However, numerous changes to the law, made by both Congress and executive branch agencies, have retained its primary regulatory tools: mandatory pre-sale registration and safety-centered labeling. Sixty-year-old legal methods still structure one of the most important federal laws intended to safeguard human health and ecological integrity.[35]

FIFRA's primary legal innovation required manufacturers to register a wide range of what the statute primly termed "economic poisons" with the U.S. Department of Agriculture (USDA) before they could be sold. To register products for sale, section 3 directed the manufacturer to attach to each container a prominent label bearing pre-approved text. The label warned that the contents were toxic to humans and a wide variety of life forms. It disclosed the primary active and inert ingredients and had to offer concise instructions for safe application. Section 6 delegated wide administrative discretion to USDA to make rules defining proper labels. For example, FIFRA empowered the agency to adopt registration rules specifying what "instructions for use . . . are necessary and adequate for protection of the public." Section 6 also authorized USDA's rules to define exactly what language would provide "an adequate warning or caution statement." Violations of FIFRA's registration or labeling provisions exposed a manufacturer to both administrative fines by the government and civil liability to injured users, who included those whose plants, fish, birds, and animals had been wrongfully poisoned.

Section 4 authorized USDA, at its discretion, to cancel a poison's registration "in order to protect the public," thereby making further sale illegal. Even proper registration lasted only five years. FIFRA thus required manufacturers to register economic poisons regularly, each time supplying both the federal government and the public a wide range of information about the product's purposes, composition, and toxicity. Section 6 authorized USDA to revise its registration thresholds as science and practice warranted. To assist in rulemaking and enforcement, the agency could hold hearings and compel manufacturers to submit evidence "to determine [if] economic poisons, and quantities of substances contained in [them], . . . are highly toxic to man."

Failure to comply with FIFRA's registration rules, or failure to label the products in accordance with the rules, exposed agricultural chemical manufacturers to criminal liability under federal law for the first time. The House of Representatives Agriculture Committee, which wrote most of the statute, noted with satisfaction that nearly all interested parties—chemical manufacturers, farm lobbies, and state agriculture agencies—endorsed FIFRA. Even though the act imposed new criminal penalties for violating new duties, the agribusiness industry still sought "highly desirable" uniform laws "for the protection of the public, so that manufacturers may have Nation-wide distribution with a minimum of conflict between the labeling requirements of the various [state] laws."[36]

William H. Rodgers, Jr., a young environmental law professor at the University of Washington in 1970, deemed FIFRA's first quarter-century a record writ large with failure. USDA's Pesticides Registration Division (PRD) had never failed to register a chemical if the manufacturer challenged the agency's tentative registration rejection. A 1964 interagency agreement enabled the Departments of Interior and Health, Education, and Welfare to comment on proposed registrations, but PRD had never used another agency's environmental or public health protest to refuse registration or to cancel a registration already made. Congressional hearings in the mid-1960s established, to Rodgers's satisfaction, FIFRA's obsolescence. "It is time to rewrite the basic pesticides legislation," he argued. USDA's cozy relationships with the chemical industry and agribusiness prevented adequate public oversight. Though FIFRA's intent was laudable, its clumsy administrative system permitted lawful applications of legal poisons to cause environmental damage. After *Silent Spring* aroused readers, various congressional investigations "inflamed the public" about the many dangers posed by DDT and other persistent agricultural chemicals. "The climate for wholesale reform of the registration process," Rodgers estimated, "will never be better." In 1970 as in 1947, "opportunism . . . is the key to legal reform."[37]

Rodgers's scathing critique of FIFRA nevertheless revealed an important postwar "back story": public concerns about food safety and chemical pollution had twice persuaded Congress to legislate new limits on agricultural poisons. First in 1954, and then more decisively in 1958, public agitation led legislators to scrutinize and strengthen the regulatory system. Both times, Congress resorted to an older system of administrative control established by the 1905 Food and Drug Act. Though postwar reforms appeared too tentative, Rodgers believed they showed how modernized federal laws could keep food safe and protect natural environments. Seen as environmental law experiments, food safety amendments in the fifties help recover environmental law's historic perspective. As baby boom parents and their children adopted new values about nature and technology, becoming more environmentally literate and passionate, postwar precedents showed them how to do more environmental lawmaking.

Since 1938, the Food and Drug Act had empowered the Food and Drug Administration to establish "tolerances," rules limiting the amount of pesticides that food could contain before being deemed "adulterated" and unsafe for consumption. FDA tolerances, based on data supplied by USDA and information gathered from the public at hearings, made it illegal to sell adulterated food. Extensive public hearings in 1950, as the chemical-agricultural era dawned, led FDA to promulgate DDT tolerances in 1955. FDA, however, had not used its rulemaking power to set general tolerances across the whole spectrum of agricultural chemicals. Food industry concerns about FIFRA's uncertain effect on older food safety law prompted Congress's first postwar adjustment to chemical regulation, the 1954 Miller Amendment to the Food and Drug Act.[38]

The Eisenhower administration brokered a deal that tried to calibrate FIFRA's chemical regulations to the Food and Drug Act's tolerance setting machinery. Chemical manufacturers, national farm groups, food processors, and the grocery industry endorsed the compromise that became the Miller Amendment, which eliminated public hearings but kept FDA's prerogative under the Food and Drug Act to make tolerance rules. Chemical manufacturers could initiate rulemaking by submitting toxicity and application data, which had to be kept confidential by the agency. FDA could convene advisory committees, which could include the public, to help fashion rulemaking responses to industry petitions. The agency could also simply publish tolerances on its own motion, with no real opportunity for public comment or scrutiny of the manufacturer's data. Tolerances had to incorporate the FDA's documented findings about "the ways in which the consumer may be affected by the . . . pesticide chemical or by other related substances that are poisonous or deleterious." (21 U.S.C. § 346a(b)) The Miller Amendment's most important legal innovation empowered FDA to establish a "zero tolerance," forbidding the sale of any food product that contained any measurable trace of a particular chemical. Yet the agency could, based on its scientific evidence and administrative discretion, also exempt chemicals from the tolerance system entirely.[39]

Relentless expansion of chemical agriculture soon provoked the first postwar food chemical environmental crisis. Coming four years after the Miller Amendment, the late 1950s "cranberry scare" illustrated how quickly public concern could boil into popular hysteria. Citizen passion, informed by the developing science of ecology, mobilized quick environmental lawmaking. Members of Congress would not be accused of standing idly by as families keeled over at their holiday tables. The furor erupted over Thanksgiving cranberries. Media enthusiasm pushed reluctant administrators into the limelight and a cabinet secretary literally had to feed his family allegedly tainted berries under news photographers' flash bulbs to reassure both consumers and food sellers. Little red berries also revealed big tensions between USDA's application of FIFRA's generous pesticide registration regime and FDA's interpretation of its long-standing mandate to ensure the safety of the nation's food.

The media coverage, and lawmakers' response inside agencies and the Capitol, indicated how energetic environmental lawmaking was becoming even as the law's structure remained rudimentary and fluid. Three times, in less than a decade since DDT's release to the public, scientific and popular concerns had motivated legal change. Though partial and hesitant adaptations to technological change, FIFRA, the Miller Amendment, and the Delaney Clause nonetheless revealed environmental law's systematic expansion. In its growth mode, the field was responding to new scientific information, cultural values, and political pressures.

The "cranberry-chemical cocktail crisis" fanned public pressure on environmental lawmaking. The Eisenhower administration preferred legal change through industry initiative instead of public pressure as a matter of principle. A lifelong staff man, the president trusted agencies' expertise and deplored crisis management under media spotlights. Eisenhower had long resisted worldwide public clamor to stop atmospheric nuclear testing. He dismissed splashy campaigns that claimed to show that nuclear fallout poisoned babies' milk, believing them factually unsound and politically suspect. By regulating cranberry-growing chemicals at the same time it soft-pedaled weapons bans, however, the administration could show appropriate sensitivity to Americans' concerns about food safety. Tentative as the remedy for cranberry cocktail hangover proved to be, enactment of the 1958 Delaney Clause to the Food and Drug Act gave the public more leverage with elected officials. Growing public concern about environmental toxicity, whether from atmospheric nuclear radiation or chemicals sprayed on food, was remodeling older public health rules into basic environmental protection law.[40]

Cranberry growers and their chemical suppliers during the mid- to late 1950s developed a new herbicide, aminotriazole, which promised effective weed control followed by rapid dissipation without apparent damage to wetlands in which berries grew. The PRD registered aminotriazole under FIFRA in January 1958 for use on that year's crop. PRD accepted industry data showing the compound left "no residue" if properly applied. The next spring, cranberry growers joined orchardists and the pesticide's maker to petition FDA to use its Miller Act authority to set an aminotriazole tolerance that would enable more widespread use. In the meantime, however, Congress added the 1958 Delaney Clause to the Food and Drug Act, provoking a clash between competing priorities: cheaper food and safer eaters.[41]

At least for cranberries, safer eaters won. The Delaney Clause directed FDA to bar the sale of any food containing any additive "found to induce cancer when ingested by man or animal." Even if the data were unclear, FDA was to err on the side of precaution. Congress also forbade the sale of any food containing any additive "found, after tests which are appropriate for the evaluation of the safety of food additives, to induce cancer in man or animal." Aminotriazole's tolerance rulemaking offered a test case for the Delaney Clause. After agency scientists convinced the administrator of the herbicide's carcinogenic potential in May 1959, FDA refused to promulgate a tolerance, making cranberries that bore any trace of aminotriazole "adulterated" under the Food and Drug Act and hence illegal for sale. Further testing in the autumn revealed, contrary to industry claims, that the herbicide was not dissipating after application in New Jersey's cranberry bogs. FDA then seized nearly a half-million tons of sprayed cranberries, just as the holiday marketing season was hitting high gear. Health, Education, and Welfare Secretary Arthur Fleming justified the dramatic action by revealing internal agency findings about the chemical's carcinogenicity.

Growers, grocers, and the chemical industry squealed. Consumers blanched. The Eisenhower administration fashioned a shaky compromise: bulldozers buried seized cranberries under TV cameras' watchful eyes; unsprayed cranberries were certified safe for consumption; angry growers got nearly $9 million in compensation; and the secretary's wife had to invite the nation to her family's holiday table, via mass media, to witness the secretary and Mrs. Fleming serving unsprayed "safe" cranberries.

Despite agribusiness rage, Congress refused to repeal the Delaney Clause. Consumers' new worries about agricultural chemicals did not, however, move USDA, which simply registered aminotriazole under tighter FIFRA restrictions. The PRD persisted in maintaining generous registration rules for DDT. To complete the compromise, and to demonstrate that public fears of cancer-causing foods were not entirely groundless, Congress broadened the Delaney Clause to cover color additives the next year. Now, foods both "natural," like fruit, and "artificial," like baked goods containing fruit, were proclaimed "cancer-free." USDA's leisurely FIFRA fact-finding about DDT's health effects would meander along until 1963, when the storm unleashed by *Silent Spring* pushed congressional committees and presidential commissions into new action.[42]

AFFLICTING THE COMFORTABLE

A third postwar cultural transformation made the first two—outdoor recreation and suburbanization—possible. Ordinary Americans rediscovered a paradox most had not confronted for a quarter-century: prosperity's cunning, ambiguous allure. Most Americans gloried in postwar material security after twenty-five years of war and want. While new experiences recreating, procreating, and homemaking encouraged many citizens who reveled in economic growth's blessings to start counting its environmental costs, few perfected their new accounting skills. Comfort dulled their intellectual appetites. Inertia restrained most from pursuing the subject to its cautionary conclusions. Americans, for the most part, remained unwilling to acknowledge consumption's environmental toll. Few questioned the political economy that exhorted production, consumption, and wealth.[43]

John Keats, satirically investigating "the real effect of automobiles on our landscape and on the nature of our society," pleaded for "an honest product, honestly priced." The Insolent Chariots paid homage to social theorist Lewis Mumford's 1957 address about Americans' obsession with automobiles. Keats's best-selling 1958 book skewered Americans' penchant for buying big, option-packed cars on credit. Not only did debt financing enrich lenders and car dealers without benefiting consumers, but customers' use of credit to "buy more car than [they] want or need"—what Keats dubbed "the Cadillac syndrome"—distorted automobility's functional promise for ordinary Americans after World War II. The car culture fouled air. Highways destroyed precious farmland and open space. Unsafe cars maimed and killed unfortunate drivers. And elephantine sedans and station wagons wasted scarce fuel and diverted social capital into unproductive investments. "Pursuit of happiness seemed the nation's single-minded intent" after the war ended, Keats lamented. "Irresponsible consumers" during "a decade of noisy, glittering drift" chased images and avoided reality. When credit buyers ended up paying interest charges that effectively doubled a vehicle's list price, the entire system teetered on the brink of amorality, or threatened to plunge into immorality's abyss. "Where is the morality," Keats wondered, "of selling a car to a man obviously incapable of paying for it unless he is willing to deprive his family of many necessities?"[44]

Keats contrasted Henry and Edsel Ford: the grandfather had promised to equip every American family with a practical personal vehicle, as long as it was black. His grandson's eponymous 1957 model, wasteful of resources and dangerous to boot, epitomized the auto industry's "indifference to real people's needs." For Keats, the ideal American car fused "the Roman virtue of practicality and the Scottish virtue of thrift." He appealed to buyers to carefully assess their real transportation needs by asking, "Why do I live where I live? . . . Why and when do I really need to drive? . . . Is this what I really either need, or want?" If they honestly answered these hard questions, Americans of all economic levels should then seek to buy "a cheap, safe, practical, simple, sturdy and economical automobile." Something along the lines of the then-novel Volkswagen that was slowly beginning to appear on new car lots in the late fifties fit the bill: "sensible cars . . . rationally marketed and honestly priced," the little imports' "virtues [are] the virtues of all efficient machines." Keats's wry humor thinly concealed *Insolent Chariots'* moral core: thrift, restraint, and order should characterize the optimum relationship between Americans and their cars. For him, these "producer virtues" offered a pungent reminder, not only of a better past, but of consumption's social and environmental costs.[45]

Lary May, writing in 1989 about postwar culture and politics, contrasted Keats's "producer" values with shiny rivals for the nation's allegiance: personal fulfillment and material consumption. Little about the postwar economy indicated Scottish thrift was winning the beauty contest. Between 1945 and 1960, American GNP soared 250 percent. Per capita income in 1960 was a third higher than in 1945, despite a population that had grown by 40 million. "The astonishing growth of the American economy represented the single most impressive development of the postwar years," William Chafe has contended.[46]

Criticism of American society and its prosperous polity emerged in spite of, or perhaps because of, unparalleled economic comfort. The cohort of critics that Richard Pells has dubbed "liberal minds in a conservative age" wrote passionately about, and for, Americans as consumers. Keats, along with Vance Packard, William Whyte, and Sloan Wilson, infused their critiques with paeans to what Daniel Horowitz has termed "producer values." Both their fiction and journalism sketched an alternative vision to fifties' prosperity, "a virtuous life based on civic responsibility, honest callings, unalienated work, widespread property ownership, and personal independence." By finding a mass market for their writings and eschewing intellectual trappings, postwar social critics interrogated topics integral to environmental law's emergence: suburban housing developments, cars and families, corporations and advertising. Precisely because their works won a mass audience of what Horowitz dubbed "middlebrow readers," the postwar social critics enable better appreciation of environmental lawmaking's limits in a prosperous majoritarian democracy.[47]

Critical—often passionately so—about consumerism, middlebrow writers surveyed a postwar society that felt qualitatively different to Americans who had endured the Great Depression and won World War II. As early as 1954, cultural historian David Potter discerned new values forged by those whom he fashioned "the people of plenty." Coming of age at a time when employed white Americans could reasonably expect to enjoy material security and realistically imagine their children inhabiting an even more comfortable future, inhabitants of what social historian Dale Carter has termed "the Ike Age" forged new values that distanced them from their Depression and wartime heritage. They displayed apparent concern about society's state and worried about its prospects, but stopped short of making radical adjustments to ingrained structures of property and authority. As citizens, they exercised political power to make laws ameliorating, but not halting, environmental damage caused by the increasing consumption of goods produced by the accelerating transformation of natural systems to satisfy human wants.[48]

Between 1955 and 1960, the market for social criticism absorbed popular books by John Keats, Vance Packard, William Whyte, Jr., and Sloan Wilson. Packard's wildly successful trio—*Hidden Persuaders* (1957), *Status Seekers* (1959), and the frankly conservationist manifesto, *Waste Makers* (1960)—scrutinized advertising techniques, class structures, and product obsolescence. In 1956, Whyte's *Organization Man* mixed magazine journalism—he was a rising senior correspondent for *Fortune*—with social science to explore the new worlds of work and family that middle-income white Americans were constructing within businesses and governments staffed by suburbanites. Although former ad-man Wilson wrote fiction to deliver his criticism, his targets were Whyte's, too: suburban Americans who, through their purchases and careers, were carpeting former farmlands with subdivisions and peopling city office towers with beleaguered strivers. *The Man in the Gray Flannel Suit*, the fifth-best-selling fictional title of 1955, represented Wilson's bid to recast the still fluid values of corporate suburbanites before they hardened into what he feared were destructive social molds.

Legal historians pick their way cautiously across cultural landscapes. An organic link does join rules to the ruled, but many filters can cause legal change to lag behind social developments. Even when cultural fluidity seems pervasive, legal historians recall that law exists, in large part, to brake the process of transformation. Law differs from television and computer gaming, for example, because rules operate to preserve that which has long endured from the corrosive effects of that which is in motion. Despite this caution, an environmental history of environmental law should consider how Americans explained the consequences of postwar prosperity.

Popular reading habits offer clues to the contradictory ways that prosperity pushed environmental lawmaking. Keats's *Insolent Chariots* and his genial alarm about suburbanization, *Crack in the Picture Window*, promised enough sales to justify his publisher hiring one of the period's most popular cartoonists, John Osborn, to illustrate them. And both justified the optimism, going into paperback the year after they appeared. Yet neither critique cracked the Top Ten nonfiction best-seller charts. *Crack in the Picture Window*, for example, sold far fewer copies than titles about home improvement, cooking, and etiquette. *Chariots'* implicit critique of suburban living (and driving) appealed to far fewer readers than Jean Kerr's wildly popular comedy of suburban manners, *Please Don't Eat the Daisies*.[49]

Americans' postwar environmental law system arose atop inherited assumptions, buttressed by unquestioned premises. Despite cultural ferment, most Americans remained loyal to deeply rooted values that inherently limited the new laws' capacity to safeguard the world they sought to protect. Durable dual prejudices favored superficial behavioral adjustments over deep ethical change and private liberty instead of public direction. Retained together, traditional beliefs generated an incomplete, unstable legal field. American environmental law proved increasingly irrelevant to manage the primary forces of consumption, ambition, and individualism that still disorder the natural world to serve humans' self interest. When the pace of lawmaking slowed after the 1970s, the beliefs and behaviors that produced environmental damage persisted.

Environmental law's creation during postwar economic prosperity crippled its capacity to restrain and reform the very actions that produced the imperatives for its invention. Americans were willing only to adjust their private behaviors at the margins. They continually subjected even those legal restraints to traditional political pressures. Unchecked, their voracious appetites created a system of environmental law unable to forestall crisis by the twenty-first century.

New knowledge learned from living in nature taught incomplete lessons about the consequences of life at the world's economic apex. Lacking the collective discipline to tailor their enduring economic structures and political values to ecology's education, postwar Americans' new environmental law system compelled no real reckoning with the postwar economic boom. Even the most ambitious environmental lawmakers expected technical adjustments to ingrained American values would enable the earth infinitely to support mass prosperity. Environmental lawmaking in the postwar era blunted legal change to protect material prosperity. Its creators used legal rules to reduce the risk of collective failure instead of using law to redefine national success.

6

Minnesota Democrat John Blatnik hammered the House of
Representatives Public Works Committee's third straight executive session into order on Thursday morning, 13 April 1961.
Three hours later, most members began shuffling papers and
glancing at their watches. They soon had to scurry across Independence Avenue, or through the tunnel beneath it, to be
recorded "present" when the House convened at 1:00 P.M. The
chairman began thanking members for their constructive contributions to "mark-up," the crucial brushwork done privately
as a congressional committee sifts staff analyses, agency comments, and members' own amendments to fine-tune a complex bill. Their tedious, technical debate satisfied Blatnik, the
committee's legal staff, and emissaries from the new Kennedy
administration that Public Works had completed writing a federal water-quality bill that most members would endorse. Securing a "do pass" recommendation, sending H.R. 4036 on to
the House, and adopting a lengthy report explaining the legislation would take just a few minutes at the final committee session. Blatnik's House Democratic leaders and their Senate
counterparts could then move this "must-pass" bill to enactment before the 87th Congress adjourned for the summer.

H.R. 4036, the 1961 Water Pollution Control Act Amendments, followed a precedent set in 1948, when the Federal Water Pollution Control Act (FWPCA) originally declared the
United States' legal primacy to protect interstate water quality.
In 1956, the Eisenhower administration joined bipartisan majorities on Capitol Hill to extend and strengthen FWPCA. For

five years before Public Works took up H.R. 4036, Public Health Service and Justice Department regulators had been enforcing rules to limit pollution's degradation of the interstate waters along which most Americans lived. Measured strictly by page count, most clean water law in 1961 still came from states and municipalities. Yet subnational governments now made environmental law on this important, visible subject under federal discretion and direction. Enactment of the 1948 and 1956 laws established the national government's constitutional authority to write more "clean water acts" whenever citizens decided water pollution problems required federal law solutions.[1]

Environmental lawyers, like all of their professional colleagues, have borrowed inveterately. Lawmakers constantly reached across doctrinal borders and ecological systems searching for legal tools to meet urgent needs. When Congress legislated national rules for clean water in the 1960s, it was also setting precedents for the simultaneous nationalization of air quality law. "A . . . dominant influence in the genealogy of the Clean Air Amendments of 1970," William H. Rodgers argued in his 1977 *Environmental Law* handbook, came from "the federal regulatory experience in the field of water pollution." "Intermittent legislative activity gradually strengthened the federal presence in both fields . . . [as] terms, concepts, [and] procedures borrowed from one field [were] applied to the other."[2]

Cross-fertilization between water and air regulation tapped the same constitutional grant of legislative power, Article I's Interstate Commerce Clause. Pollutants fouling the Missouri River eluded the capacity of either Missouri or Kansas state laws to protect their common boundary water. Hydrocarbons belched from truck engines carrying steel made in Gary, Indiana, shrouded air in Chicago, Illinois. In each instance, pioneering state and local lawmaking revealed the need for national rules equally valid on both sides of political boundaries. Local people came to realize the value of air and water law enforced by the strongest agent, the United States government, whose authority to do so was conferred by Article VI's Supremacy Clause.

An environmental history of New Frontier lawmaking clarifies environmental law's postwar heritage and gradual emergence. Fifteen turbulent, prosperous, frightening years of Cold War peace energized what Richard Andrews termed "a diverse range of constituencies representing previously separate aspects of environmental protection . . . into a broad movement demanding changes in both the substance and the process of environmental policy." Citizens sought "stronger federal policies to protect the environment from the impacts of urban and industrial growth." Federal laws about water and air pollution reflected crucial lawmaking activity from the 1950s, Andrews's *History of American Environmental Policy* acknowledged. Clean water statutes enacted in the early 1960s "began a gradual nationalization of the authority to set and enforce water quality standards." He also observed "a similar evolution . . . in air pollution policy," as new federal statutes "beginning in 1963 . . . shifted federal policy from modest support of state and local initiatives to a fully nationalized framework for air pollution regulation."[3]

ACROSS THE WATER QUALITY RUBICON

Chairman Blatnik warned House Public Works members to get ready for another busy session at what he intended to be their next, and last, meeting. Not only did they have to finish marking up the 1961 clean water bill, but they still faced their usual heavy pork barrel workload, in which they had to weigh colleagues' pleas for new dams, highways, and sewer plants. Just as the chairman prepared to gavel the committee into adjournment, Florida Republican William C. Cramer unveiled another new sheaf of amendments to H.R. 4036. Blatnik exploded. "We have waited for two or three weeks to get through our subcommittee reports. . . . We are in a terrific jam or bind. My God, I am not trying to close off debate, but give us a little help. We are working under a very severe and burdensome limitation of time under the load we have." Cramer retorted, "The proposed amendments would be constructive [or] I wouldn't have wasted three or four days, as I did on it [sic]." Blatnik sputtered back, "We have discussed this amendment over and over again. . . . Our position is clear and we will listen as far as time will permit us, but I hope the gentleman will understand the circumstances."[4]

Throughout H.R. 4036's markup in Public Works, Cramer had spoken as a "states-rights man," the principal advocate for a brand of federalism that tried to maintain states' water quality prerogatives under FWPCA. He knew governments would have to make more law to abate pollution and protect public health. Constituents were demanding cleaner water. Most appeared ready to follow more and stricter rules limiting pollution discharges. But

Cramer wanted legislatures, governors, and state administrators to keep designing water pollution control's emerging structure. A fiscal conservative, he tried to limit the FWPCA's appropriations to build municipal sewage treatment plants. The one-time county attorney for fast-growing Tampa–St. Petersburg, Cramer objected to Blatnik's preferred funding formulas, which directed more federal money to smaller cities, like those in the chairman's Iron Range district. A local political dealmaker before coming to Washington in 1957, Cramer criticized the new authority that federal administrators wanted so they could reshuffle construction priorities already announced by state agencies. He suspected the New Frontier agency lawyers arrayed before the committee's tiered seats wanted to aggrandize their own lawmaking role and he thought they wanted to boost their power by limiting not just states and cities, but Congress as well. Cramer's amendments reopened the touchy constitutional issue of just how much legal authority the nation should deploy by using federal agencies and courts to regulate pollution within state boundaries.

Blatnik's and Cramer's genteel acrimony signaled congressional disagreement about priorities and pork, not principles and precedents. The Floridian was not challenging Congress's constitutional right to legislate for clean water. Instead, he and Blatnik were fencing over procedures, details, and budgets. Both conceded the federal government's constitutional power to make laws safeguarding interstate waters' purity under Article I's Interstate Commerce Clause. The most famous postwar conservative, Ohio senator Robert Taft—"Mr. Republican"—tiptoed Congress into the water quality Rubicon when he spearheaded enactment of the 1948 FWPCA. President Dwight Eisenhower, a self-described "modern Republican," carried the federal government across the river by proposing and signing the FWPCA Amendments in 1956. Some Public Works members even contended that the federal government had established its constitutional competence in the 1899 Refuse Act, which empowered the Army Corps of Engineers to clear rivers and harbors of physical pollutants in order to improve navigation.[5]

Robert E. Jones, Jr., recalled a bit of Depression-era history for his Public Works Colleagues as the Blatnik-Cramer colloquy simmered. Once the United States got into the dam-building business in a very big way during the New Deal, said the Alabama Democrat, federal management of vast river basins made national water regulation a concrete reality. Federal dams large and small, spanning rivers and creating reservoirs in nearly every member's district, attested to the potentially limitless sweep of the Interstate Commerce Clause.[6]

"Beginning in 1970," Richard N. L. Andrews has argued, "U.S. environmental policy entered a fundamentally new era." Two distinctive features defined this new era, his 1999 *History of American Environmental Policy* contended: "a greatly enlarged federal role in environmental protection," based on new laws enforced by a new government bureau—the Environmental Protection Agency (EPA); and "greatly expanded access for citizen environmental advocates both to administrative procedures and to the courts for recourse."[7]

"Environmental law emerged in the early 1970s," Richard J. Lazarus agreed in 2004. Lazarus wrote *The Making of Environmental Law* to tell "a fascinating and revealing story" about "how environmental law first emerged . . . in the manner and form that it did in the 1970s." "The 1970s were an extraordinary decade for environmental law," Lazarus argued, "the formative decade" in which Congress enacted and three presidents signed "dramatic, sweeping, and uncompromising" federal statutes. And even after presidential enthusiasm waned, "environmental law found its institutional supporters elsewhere . . . the most significant [being] in Congress and the federal judiciary and in the rising environmental law public interest community."[8]

Andrews and Lazarus downplayed environmental lawmaking before 1970. Neither considered state and local laws important or substantial. Environmental law's currency appreciated in proportion to its proximity to the Capitol. Having made only "a smattering of emerging . . . environmental laws" by 1970, Lazarus contended, states and municipalities surrendered sovereignty to Washington, D.C. Thus diminished, they docilely discharged only their new function of "implementation, albeit subject to federal oversight." Nationalization of environmental law after 1970 simply overwhelmed federalism. "Despite some resistance," Lazarus concluded, "most states had begun to develop their own environmental programs and agencies by the end of the 1970s."[9]

Both Andrews and Lazarus assigned huge significance to one feature of environmental law: its nationalization. President Richard Nixon's televised signing of the new National Environmental Policy Act on 1 January 1970 marked a historical watershed. By investing nationalization after 1970 with epochal significance, Andrews and Lazarus discount much of the legal evidence they painstakingly assembled to write *A History of American Environmental Policy* and *The Making of Environmental Law*.

Federal environmental lawmaking did surge in the 1970s. Congress and executive branch agencies made volumes of new laws. Yet the most important laws—especially such keystones as the 1972 "Clean Water Act" and 1970 "Clean Air Act"—ratified jurisdictional shifts that began at least a decade or more earlier. Lawmakers in the 1970s neither had to invent new legal tools nor define new objectives previously thought beyond environmental law's scope. Historical evidence about the enactment of federal water and air statutes clarifies how the nationalization process unfolded steadily during the decade of the 1960s.[10]

The 1961 Federal Water Pollution Control Act Amendments continued the process of nationalizing environmental law that began in 1948 and accelerated in 1956. John Blatnik's Public Works Committee was working while a legal clock ticked. FWPCA would soon expire because the outgoing Eisenhower administration had vetoed its reauthorization, citing budget concerns. The president, constantly feuding with congressional Democratic majorities during his last two years in office, adamantly intended to leave his successor a balanced federal budget. His deep concerns about the costs—ideological as well as fiscal—of expanding the federal government's size had enabled Eisenhower to translate popular disaffection with New Deal regulation into two sweeping Republican political victories in 1952 and 1956. Not surprisingly, the old general later subtitled the first volume of his memoirs *Mandate for Change*, recounting his 1952 victory and first presidential term.[11]

Ike and his Public Health Service water quality advisers accepted the constitutional principle of federally regulating pollution that fouled interstate waters. Eisenhower's administration drafted and strongly endorsed the 1956 water quality law. It gave regulators new authority to supplant local and state law with federal enforcement, if polluted water threatened public health and safety.[12]

The president prided himself on modernizing Republicanism to meet postwar complexities. No doctrinaire when it came to wielding federal power, Eisenhower got the federal government building interstate highways and public schools, vaccinating children, and regulating food additives. He saw no inconsistency between trying to restrain federal spending and regu-

latory growth while deploying federal law to help state and local governments meet demonstrated human needs. His endorsement of the 1956 clean
water extension bill, coupled with his signature on 1954 and 1958 bills that
expanded federal regulatory power to keep chemical contaminants from the
nation's food supply, complicates both contemporary criticism and later histories that claimed that Eisenhower constitutionally objected to federal lawmaking about the nation's natural environment. Instead, he vetoed the 1960
clean water bill because of budget worries, not philosophical objections to
either cleaner water or stronger national legal authority. Congress, led by
Democrats, wanted to more than triple the federal share of water treatment
costs, a price he thought too high. And liberals like Blatnik wanted to make
federal cost-sharing permanent, inaugurating another open-ended fiscal obligation that Eisenhower believed would impede efforts of state and local
initiatives to evolve their own pollution regulation codes. "By holding forth
the promise of a large-scale program of long-term Federal support, it would
tempt municipalities to delay essential water pollution abatement efforts
while they waited for Federal funds," chided the president.[13]

John Kennedy's State of the Union address, delivered in the House chamber just three months before Blatnik convened the Public Works Committee's markup sessions on H.R. 4036, dramatized the new president's
enthusiasm to spend money his predecessor tried to save. Kennedy contrasted Republican penury and state-rights purity with Democrats' eager-
ness to pay more attention to, and to spend more money on, abating water
pollution. His new Health, Education, and Welfare (HEW) secretary, former
Connecticut congressman Abraham Ribicoff, backed Kennedy's bold words
and generous promise by recommending clean-water statutory language
that followed New Deal precedents.[14]

By using the 1961 Federal Water Pollution Control Act Amendments to in-
vest the federal government heavily in the sewage treatment construction
business, Ribicoff and Kennedy, as well as Blatnik, intended to follow
Franklin Roosevelt's and Harry Truman's examples. Like the New and Fair
Dealers who used water project appropriations to promote public provision
of electricity and irrigation water, the New Frontiersmen sought to spend
money to shape policy. H.R. 4036 would literally cement federal responsibility for policing interstate water quality into permanent law. Not only did the
Kennedy administration's bill reorganize the federal effort by giving the
president direct management of HEW's pollution-control efforts, it obli-

gated the national government to write ever-bigger grant checks to help cities and states pay for the new sewage treatment plants that had been going up across the country since the late 1940s.[15]

Blatnik and his staff, along with HEW's legal counsel, jousted with Cramer over his amendments when Public Works convened for one more executive session markup on 18 April 1961. Both sides understood they were not lawmaking in a vacuum. Fifteen years' worth of environmental law—most sketched by the states, some scribbled by the cities, a little outlined by Congress—covered their desks. Looking back on their work, environmental law scholar William H. Rodgers, Jr., understood that John Blatnik's committee did not invent modern American water pollution law. Public Works members and staff certainly conducted intense legal arguments about amending a statute as important as the FWPCA, but all understood that they served as custodians, as well as architects, of water quality law.

Georgetown Law School's Rodgers authored one of the first systematic explications of environmental law in 1977. His *Environmental Law* handbook nevertheless reminded practitioners, scholars, and students that contemporary legislating emphasized both the field's organic character and its national pedigree. Even though "water pollution law begins with an intimidating 90-page Act of Congress," the 1972 "Clean Water Act," the newest federal water quality statute "is but a predictable convergence of several historical forces." Often overlooked in the seventies and even today, the 1972 act *amended* a quarter-century's worth of existing federal laws. "In many ways a novel and remarkable legislative effort," Rodgers noted that the 1972 Act "still is rooted deeply in the past, expressing principles well accepted for generations." By the same token, Blatnik and Cramer, despite their political differences, understood in 1961 that they were arguing about *amending* the Water Pollution Control Act of 1956, Congress's second use of federal constitutional authority over interstate water and commerce to assist municipal and state governments in controlling pollution. Rodgers's *Environmental Law* stressed how history shaped water quality lawmaking, noting that "after its initial appearance in 1948, the Federal Water Pollution Control Act was amended five times prior to the major revisions of 1972."[16]

When Public Works' last markup session started considering Cramer's amendments to H.R. 4036, Blatnik and his Florida adversary knew that other lawmakers, past and present, there and elsewhere, sat at their elbows. These seasoned members of Congress, advised by talented legal counsel, explicitly acknowledged local mayors and state administrators were making water quality law even as the committee met. Both Blatnik and Cramer grasped the legal significance and political implications of decisions already made and precedents established since 1948. Chief counsel Jerry Sonosky reminded the committee that even the Eisenhower administration had admitted that important jurisdictional questions had already been settled. Despite the president's veto of the 1960 extension bill, his aides assumed the federal government could, if it chose, regulate pollution that crossed state lines; could, if it chose, preempt local control over pollution that fouled coastal waters, such as New York's or San Francisco's great bays; and could, if it chose, legally intervene to force recalcitrant states to control intrastate pollution sources that dirtied interstate waters, such as the Great Lakes.[17]

Cramer, though a budget hawk and local government champion, endorsed Eisenhower's views. He was not trying to turn back the lawmaking clock, he assured Public Works. He was not wasting their time or spending his political capital on a futile philosophical gesture. Instead, Cramer argued, Congress in 1961 was debating policy, not settled principle: not *whether* to use federal law to assist states and municipalities, but *how* to spend federal money, file federal lawsuits, and write federal agency rules and orders.

"As a matter of policy there is a difference of opinion *as to the extent to which* the Federal Government should enter into water pollution situations and enforcement situations," Cramer observed to committee colleagues as he presented his first "clarifying" amendment. Not a matter of constitutional right, but a debate about prudential degree, preoccupied the committee the rest of the morning. State agencies and even interstate agencies along the Ohio and Potomac Rivers, and around the tri-state New York harbor were already making and enforcing law to curb pollution. Cramer simply wanted to "giv[e] more teeth to the existing State agencies" by focusing federal intervention on demonstrated pollution problems along navigable interstate waters that states and cities had been unable to solve using their own law. Absent "some definition limiting the Federal responsibility, . . . then the Federal Government will take over the entire enforcement." He wanted to preserve and even strengthen what he termed "a proper partnership . . . in the enforcement section [and] partnership on spending the money."[18]

Like Eisenhower and other Republicans, Cramer divided the basic issue of managing the nation's waters into "partnership" versus "dictation." Pollution's partisan rhetoric borrowed from hydropower debates during the postwar years. Eisenhower had talked a lot about "partnership" during the fifties' sharp debates over public power and irrigation. Partnership paid him personal political dividends even after his administration drastically curtailed Truman administration spending on new dams. But Eisenhower's "no new starts" order burdened Republicans who were trying to retain Western seats in the 1956 and 1958 congressional elections. In 1961, Kennedy promised that his new Interior Secretary, Arizona's Stewart Udall, would reopen the federal dam-building spigot in the same message in which he urged Congress to reauthorize the water pollution control act.[19]

Eisenhower had embraced water policy "partnership" primarily as a means to restrain Congress's spending habit without sacrificing the president's ability to articulate natural resource priorities. Cramer, however, genuinely wanted water pollution partnership to encourage nonfederal lawmakers by enlisting local people to care for their nearby waters. By limiting federal administrators' authority to intervene in water pollution cases, he hoped both to save federal money and to empower lawmakers who lived in polluted watersheds.

The Floridian conceded federal law could reach, and already was policing, major interstate waters and the nation's coastal waters. He was even willing to have the 1961 bill extend federal regulation to intermittent streams and subsurface aquifers that fed interstate waters. Cramer sympathized with conservation activists' letters and testimony. Like them, he wanted to empower federal administrators to issue federal water quality control orders, based on federal studies, and to regulate polluted streams that posed technical, scientific issues beyond the power of a single state to resolve. What he opposed, however, was excluding state governors and their administrators altogether from the fact-finding and order-writing process, as Secretary Ribicoff's HEW aides were proposing.[20]

Prodded by Blatnik and loyal to Kennedy, the Democratic majority on House Public Works turned back each of Cramer's amendments. H.R. 4036 went to the full House, where its adoption perpetuated national environmental law precedents while innovating federal environmental law administration. President Kennedy's signature on the 1961 FWPCA Amendments pumped billions more federal dollars into the construction of local sewer works. It empowered HEW to sue polluters without obtaining governors' consent. But New Frontier clean water law retained a core principle of the 1948 and 1956 federal water pollution statutes: it left real lawmaking authority with the states. Congress amended FWPCA three more times—in 1965, 1966, and 1970—before "the major revisions of 1972," Rodgers would later write. And each set of amendments, even the "comprehensive programmatic and regulatory creation" adopted in 1972, "expressly disavow[ed] a purpose to preempt state and local authorities by federally conceived effluent limitations and standards of performance." In fact, section 510 of the 1972 Clean Water Act, Rodgers emphasized, "preserv[es] maximum autonomy to other jurisdictions, even within areas of admitted federal competence."[21]

FOOTHOLD IN THE AIR: CLEAN AIR LAWMAKING

Two Los Angeles law professors wrote the first draft of air quality regulation's postwar history. James Krier and Edmund Ursin, Harvard Law graduates teaching at UCLA by 1977, wrote *Pollution and Policy: A Case Essay on California and Federal Experience with Motor Vehicle Pollution, 1940–1975*, to stress the continuities and contingencies that created state and federal laws to control air pollution. Their book's title evoked environmental law's postwar incrementalism. They wanted lawyers and policymakers to analyze legal developments in air quality control as a historic continuum between 1940 and 1975 because "at least in this instance, the past has indeed been prologue in many important respects."[22]

The Californians' explanation of postwar air quality lawmaking detected two historic patterns: states and localities made the first important strides in cleaning the air and the national government nationalized clean air law well before the seventies. "The events on which we focus are typical of most environmental problems," Krier and Ursin contended. "History," they argued, "especially the history of policy made in a many-layered federal system, does not develop in a nice linear progression of significant event followed by significant event." Rather, "the process of making pollution policy . . . has been one of least steps along the path of least resistance, [its] history far more one of reaction than initiative [as] events, not foresight, ushered in each stage of intervention." When governments intervened by making new laws, state action "tended to consist in curative rather than preventive measures . . . designed to preserve so far as possible the prevailing social patterns—whether of business practice, citizen behavior, or the distribution of authority among local, state, and federal governments." Representatives

Blatnik and Cramer in 1961 had come to the same conclusions: environmental lawmaking was not a federal preserve, nor the New Frontier of the 1960s a distinct, revolutionary moment.[23]

Krier and Ursin's air law history described a postwar lawmaking line dance that moved to federalism's rhythmic refrain. Technological innovation, cultural responses, and economic reverberations punctuated the cumulative process of legal change. To cope with worsening air pollution, big states and populous local governments initiated postwar lawmaking. As Chapter 4 showed, California led the way in 1947. Water quality law emerged in much the same way after World War II, originating in Harrisburg, Sacramento, Albany, and Columbus before Capitol Hill or 1600 Pennsylvania Avenue took much notice. State leadership then prompted federal financial assistance, which invariably generated political pressures for federal intervention when the environmental problems proved intractable. This long process of legal change helps explains why the same Congress that extended federal water pollution enforcement authority in 1956 also enacted the pioneering 1955 Air Pollution Control Act (APCA). "The years 1954–1955 were the first of real significance with regard to development of a federal interest in air pollution," Krier and Ursin found. Nature's own agency—a serious November 1953 smog incident in New York City—stimulated renewed pressure for national action from people living in larger states and municipalities.[24]

Two Republican senators, California's Thomas Kuchel and Indiana's Homer Capehart, successfully pressed the Eisenhower administration in 1954 to convene an interagency task force to assess current federal air pollution remedies. Kuchel hoped that Eastern concerns like the New York smog coupled with Western initiative—California's Air Pollution Control Act— would convince the president to keep their Republican Party in environmental lawmaking's vanguard. Both senators believed that executive branch interest in air quality lent vital political support to their legislating efforts. Consistent with the old general's penchant for orderly staff work prior to executive action, the Public Health Service, responsible since 1948 for federal water pollution regulation, recommended in late 1954 that Congress should meet the air quality challenge and authorize "a broad federal program of research and technical assistance."

Twice Eisenhower sent presidential messages to the 84th Congress, which took office in 1955 with new Democratic majorities, in which he recommended air quality action. Consistent with partisan sniping in other social policy fields in the mid-fifties, congressional Democrats seized the political initiative by upping the budgetary ante. Congressional action united generous liberals, imbued with the New Deal spirit of using government spending to solve public problems, with determined partisans, who were eager to gain electoral advantage as they headed into the 1956 campaign season. The Democrats controlling the 84th Congress outran Eisenhower and Kuchel. The 1955 APCA appropriated 66 percent more money for scientific research and technical assistance to nonfederal governments than the president had proposed.[25]

Kuchel persuaded his congressional colleagues that federal air quality lawmaking should lead to further, more effective action by cities and states. The national government could deploy its unmatched expertise, while "the primary responsibility for the regulatory control of air pollution rests with the States and local governments." Consequently, the new APCA empowered HEW to start both engineering and public health studies intended "to improve knowledge, provide technical assistance, and 'stimulate . . . increased attention and greater resources to the prevention and control of air pollution.'" Modest as was the new federal presence in making air quality law, four years of Public Health Service studies stimulated Eisenhower to call the first National Conference on Air Pollution in 1958. Krier and Ursin concluded that the conference's report "demonstrat[ed] the health effects of invisible, gaseous pollutants," enabling Senator Kuchel to earn the APCA's four-year extension in 1959.[26]

Committee work on the APCA extension bill converted Ohio Republican congressman Paul Schenk into another fervent advocate for more federal regulation of auto emissions. The Cincinnatian used his seat on a traffic safety subcommittee to quiz Public Health Service experts about vehicle exhaust's safety threats. What he learned spurred him to introduce bills in 1957 and 1958 that empowered HEW to ban the sale of motor vehicles that discharged enough unburned hydrocarbons to endanger human health. Unsuccessful in the 85th Congress, Schenk finally overcame both administrative reticence and industry objections in 1959. Passed in the same session that extended the APCA, the Schenk Act ordered HEW, through the surgeon general, to begin formulating air quality criteria. Administrative rules with the force of law, these first scientific efforts to relate emissions concentrations to human health established an important benchmark for future federal air-quality rulemaking. "The decade [of the 1960s]," Krier and Ursin found, "opened with Congress's first automotive pollution legislation, [which] led to increased Public Health Service emphasis on the automotive exhaust problem."[27]

Federal scientific research inspired more state and federal air quality lawmaking. The Schenk Act presumed the federal government would use criteria studies to propose additional enforcement tools. Pacesetting again, California enacted its first comprehensive statewide stationary source regulatory system in 1959, followed by its first mobile source law the next year. By the time HEW convened the second National Air Pollution Conference in 1962, both the Kennedy administration and key congressional leaders agreed that the federal government needed to keep at least abreast of state lawmaking in Sacramento. Auto emissions in urban areas, an environmental problem with broad national economic and social implications, commended a stronger federal regulatory role even to skeptics like Alabama congressman Kenneth Roberts, who chaired the chief statute writing subcommittee.

Congress temporarily extended the 1955/1959 APCA to give HEW more time to complete follow-up studies about air quality and public health. The surgeon general had already expressed the judgment, in his first official report on *Motor Vehicles, Air Pollution and Health*, that "quantitative research information [was] needed to serve as the basis for equitable and appropriate judgments as to the limitation of discharges of various pollutional [sic] substances from motor vehicles." Congress and leading states were bidding against one another to develop the most effective administrative methods. Despite intense auto industry resistance, air quality lawmaking was on the verge of nationalization.[28]

Between December 1962 and July 1965, California's pioneering example inspired unprecedented unanimity among state and local air quality lawmakers. Political, technical, and legal limits prevented local- and state-based clean air law from controlling pollutants that crossed boundaries while both commuters and industrial output crossed state lines. Pressure for nationalizing air quality law from the local and state level eventually persuaded Congress and President Lyndon Johnson to establish the first comprehensive federal regulatory system to tackle both stationary and mobile polluters. Lobbies for city mayors, county commissioners, and urban managers united in December 1962 to approve a policy statement endorsing their new view:

properly regulating air pollution, long deemed one of the "primary responsibilities and rights of the states and local government," now required federal legal leadership. The American Medical Association endorsed the push for federal preemption. By late 1962 even Eisenhower's last HEW secretary came on board, convinced that "the federal government should have abatement authority in the case of certain interstate air pollution—authority it already had with respect to water pollution."[29]

Congress enacted and Johnson signed the 1963 Clean Air Act, a substantial advance modeled on the 1961 water quality act. Directed principally at stationary air pollution sources, the Clean Air Act directed HEW to promulgate rules to establish air quality criteria. States and municipalities could either use federal criteria as baselines or devise their own more protective laws, but federal standards now built the floor below which lesser lawmakers could not descend. Congress and the president, having accepted federal responsibility to spur stationary source lawmaking, next turned to the tougher problem—cars—and an even more difficult issue, the cultural values they embodied and the vast industry they had built.[30]

Senator Edmund Muskie (D-Maine), who chaired the new Special Senate Subcommittee on Air and Water Pollution, began challenging Representative Blatnik's considerable environmental lawmaking authority on Capitol Hill. Muskie, who displayed more political ambition than his counterpart, poured tremendous energy into making pollution law his signature issue. Conservation lobbyists and the national media increasingly watched the Senate side of Capitol Hill. The man from Maine welcomed their attention. His nationwide subcommittee hearings in 1964 produced a scathing report that attributed fully half of America's dirty air to engine exhaust. The Automobile Manufacturers Association tried to fight the last war by vainly contending that state-based rulemaking best suited their industry. President Johnson still doubted the wisdom of spending political capital to battle the nation's most powerful, profitable industry. He pleaded with Muskie in February 1965 to conduct "discussions with the auto industry designed to lead to elimination of the auto exhaust problem." Muskie ignored Johnson's preference for quiet consultations and pressed ahead with his plan to complete air pollution law's nationalization.

Democrats won crushing congressional majorities in the 1964 elections. "Landslide Lyndon" became president in his own right. Vietnam had not yet fractured his party on Capitol Hill nor soured relations between congressmen and the White House. Muskie, emboldened by his soaring national reputation as a pollution fighter, quickly introduced and won congressional passage in October 1965 of the Motor Vehicle Pollution Control Act (MVPCA). According to Krier and Ursin, "the federal program of automotive pollution control was underway."[31]

By 1966, Congress and President Johnson had nationalized air quality lawmaking. President Kennedy and Congress had done the same by 1961 for clean water. William Rodgers's *Environmental Law* handbook and Krier and Ursin's *Pollution and Policy*, written with a decade's perspective, both concurred about the New Frontier's legal significance. Rodgers reminded environmental lawyers that, to advise clients effectively, they had to understand the historical roots of federal air quality law. When the Clean Air Act passed in 1963, he insisted, "federal regulation got a foothold." The 1967 federal Air Quality Act expanded that foothold to a regulatory beachhead. Even the keystone to contemporary air quality law, the 1970 "Clean Air Act," actually amended these 1960s statutes to preempt looser state stationary source regulation altogether.[32]

The landmark 1970 legislation, popularly known then and now as the "Clean Air Act," actually *amended* the 1967 law. It broke out of the New Frontier's regulatory beachhead. Yet, like federal clean water law since the early 1960s, the nationalization process still acknowledged state and local lawmaking's existence and authority. The Clean Air Act, according to Krier and Ursin, declared "the primary responsibility for air pollution control was to be left with state and local governments," where it had resided since the first federal air pollution law in 1955. Although the "1970 [Clean Air Act] amendments represented an abrupt and radical departure from the established regulatory path," Rodgers emphasized how its section 116 "disavows [Congress'] intention to preempt state and local regulation, except in limited circumstances." This "important policy pronouncement," he believed, attested to federal environmental lawmakers' decision to "build on the common law superstructure . . . the experience of hundreds of years of attempting to control air pollution by the application of nuisance and other common law doctrines."[33]

Nationalized air pollution law preserved the postwar preference for encouraging local lawmakers to experiment with methods suitable for their distinctive problems and objectives. Introducing his mobile source bill in 1965, Muskie told Senate colleagues that "the California experience should

be used as the basis for a national program of automotive pollution control."
A Golden State administrative agency had been promulgating vehicle air
quality rules since 1960. Californians bought over 10 percent of the nation's
total car output, giving its lawmakers the clout to force changes in how Detroit worked. Despite some Californians' suspicion that their state agency
deferred too much to car industry arguments, Muskie's 1965 MVPCA
adopted California's lawmaking model.[34]

The nation's first antismog law empowered HEW experts to adopt emission standards for all new vehicles, effective with the 1968 model year. The
new administrative rules mixed government compulsion with industry innovation: as long as carmakers could satisfy regulators their products complied with the new federal laws, "the means of compliance were up to the
manufacturers." By implication, the federal statute preserved California's,
and all other states', prerogative to set tougher standards than HEW pre-
scribed. When Congress revisited its 1965 handiwork two years later, it
made explicit what had previously been implied: not only could California
set stricter auto emission standards, HEW "faced the burden of showing
that the federal standards would, in fact, be adequate" to solve distinct local
problems faced by smog-choked metropolitan areas, such as the Los Angeles Basin and New York City.[35]

FEDERAL ENVIRONMENTAL LAW BEFORE EARTH DAY

Federal lawmakers during the New Frontier understood states and localities
had been regulating air and water pollution for decades before the 1960s.
They also knew the Constitution, which shaped Americans' political and legal traditions, encouraged subnational lawmaking. Both keystone federal
pollution control laws therefore tied national standard setting to state implementation plans. Section 110 of the 1970 Clean Air Act and section 303 of
the 1972 Clean Water Act both acknowledged that state administrators, processing testimony from their fellow citizens who breathed the same bad air
and drank the same dirty water, best understood how to apply new federal
rules to attain the laws' ambitious goals.[36]

Environmental law appeared steadily during a long, complicated process
of legal change. Commonly mistold, environmental law's origin story ob-
scures its past by oversimplifying its birth. "In popular perceptions the 'envi-

ronmental era' began in 1970," Richard Andrews has observed, but "in reality, American environmental policy has far older roots [and] has developed in the larger context of American history." Broadly defined, "environmental policies [are] the actions of government . . . [that] have affected the natural environment." They have assumed various legal forms, "from colonial precedents and constitutional principles to subsequent laws, regulations, and other policies . . . establishing private rights, public restrictions, and economic incentives." American environmental law, therefore, includes "not only the recent burst of legislation intended to protect the environment, but all of the policies by which Americans have used the powers of government to exploit, transform, or control their natural surroundings."[37]

Common misunderstanding of environmental law's origins has at least a grain of truth. After 1970, governments at all levels used "fundamentally new" methods to "protect public health, safety, and environmental quality." Yet "today's environmental policies are the legacy of a long history." Although "the label 'environmental policy' was coined only in the late 1960s, . . . the existence of environmental policies . . . dates back not just the thirty years since the first Earth Day, but the two hundred-plus years since the establishment of the current constitutional regime, and the nearly four hundred years since European empires colonized North America."[38]

Andrews contended that European colonizers in North America began using law—state action expressed as binding laws that cumulatively generated public policy—to regulate people's use of nature. As "they established both colonial and community policies for governing . . . use of [the] natural environment to support themselves and produce good for export trade, . . . colonists set the precedents for some modern policies, such as the regulation of wildlife and common rights to navigable waters." Even "the attitudes of the United States' founders, and the principles which they incorporated into the Constitution and early statutory policies, were not invented overnight, but were deliberate adoptions or rejections of colonial concepts and precedents." Both public and private law—rules embodied in government policy as well as those that individuals observed in arranging their own affairs—established enforceable norms "for land and natural resource use and for the protection of public health." Ancient English principles of property—"rights to use or transform the environment and its resources, responsibilities that went with those rights, and restrictions governments might impose on the exercise of them"—coexisted with "explicit government policies" that regulated "land and water use, water pollution, forest and mineral resources, fish and wildlife."[39]

An environmental history of environmental law spotlights nature's own lawmaking agency. Andrews contended that the natural world itself made legal change. Natural features and forces exercised sovereignty's prerogative from the outset by enforcing conditions that European colonizers who encountered North America had to respect or disregard at their peril. "American environmental policies were thus powerfully shaped," Andrews observed, "by the characteristics of the American environment itself"—"a land mass three thousand miles wide . . . governed by a temperate climate . . . fertile soils, sweeping grasslands, untouched concentrations of minerals, forests of giant pine, fir, redwood, and sequoia, an almost unimaginable abundance of wildlife . . . environmental conditions formed by centuries of ecological dynamics." Infinite in number, fluid in character, the ceaseless interrelationships between powerful natural and ubiquitous human influences left environmental law in their wake, Andrews understood.[40]

One of the first systematic instruction manuals for law teachers and students defined environmental law as "an amalgam of common law and statutory principles" that in turn composed a system of "planetary housekeeping . . . concerned with protecting the planet and its people from activities that upset the earth and its life-sustaining capacities." Nonhuman legal agency matters because "environmental law focuses upon people from the perspective of their external surroundings, both natural and artificial." Environmental law constantly and inevitably percolated throughout Americans' social structures. Influenced by and simultaneously reshaping cultural institutions, environmental law "does not live in isolation from other legal specialties," William Rodgers has observed. It thus "borrows heavily from tort and property law, . . . functions within constitutional limits, . . . [and] involves the interpretation of contracts, enforcement of the criminal law, an understanding of trust responsibilities, the complexities of tax law, . . . issues of antitrust, . . . [and] the intricacies of legislation."[41]

Environmental law's lengthy pedigree, stamped by natural agency and social imperatives, has made it one of the American legal system's hardy perennials, "surprisingly persistent—almost stubbornly so," wrote Georgetown Law School's Richard Lazarus in 2004. Humans have had to interact with nature simply to survive in the twenty-first no less than in the seventeenth century, he observed. Rules governing "the kind, degree, and pace of [ecological] transformations resulting from human activity" thus depended fundamentally on "the ecosystem's dynamic complexity [which] supplies the context for any regime of law that seeks to govern human activity that transforms the natural environment."[42]

Earth's own sovereignty has perpetually operated through influences that even the most sophisticated natural sciences have only slowly revealed. Even while using them to transform the natural world, humans have had to adapt their rules to natural features and forces. Americans' ceaseless capacity to reinvent their social lives has infused environmental rule making with contingency. No wonder, Lazarus reckoned, environmental lawmaking triggered vigorous debates. Its makers were always acting amid "conflicts over enormous natural resources wealth, human health, and sharply contrasting values" while the earth itself perennially recast the terms of the discussion.[43]

Lazarus, like Rodgers and Andrews, has tied modern environmental law to its ancestral parents: natural resource regulations grounded in property principles and police power regimes developed through the tort law of nuisance. Both lawmaking parents fertilized distinct constitutional justifications for environmental lawmaking. Natural resource conservation laws have depended on some form of "state property" clause, typified by the Constitution's Property Clause. Unlike the federal government, state constitutions have long granted "general police powers" to control unwanted private activity. Both lawmaking sources have encountered restraints. "Each theory of sovereign authority underlying environmental law—whether property or tort—has . . . constitutional and political limits on the extent to which government can impose ever more stringent restrictions on the exercise of private property rights that threaten environmental values." And both lawmaking sources evolved different enforcement modes over time. "The modern pollution control laws seek, in effect, to answer questions regarding allowable pollution that were once largely addressed by courts in common law nuisance litigation, but which now elude the institutional competency of the courts in the more technologically and economically complex modern society."[44]

Environmental law's history cannot be untangled from Americans' distinctive social and political history. Andrews catalogued American environmental policy's "distinctive features": the "distrust of centralized power and authority"; a "heterogeneous patchwork of statutes, purposes, instruments, agencies, and levels of government"; and a mixture of "legislative, administrative, or direct popular decision-making." Americans' combined, incremental, cumulative lawmaking fashioned a system distinct among the world's advanced states for its "overwhelming concern with domestic issues, . . . expansive deference . . . to private rights to transform the environment for economic gain, and the correspondingly weak powers . . . accord[ed] to public agencies.[45]

Environmental policymaking, even before "the unprecedented political attention [paid] to the environment since 1970," ensured an unstable outcome, Andrews has argued, because "the pervasive influence of federalism [requires] constant renegotiation of the tension among national, state, and local governments." And if settled rules do manage to survive the negotiations, they constantly erode because "the active role of an independent judicial branch" has afforded "broad rights of access and redress" not only to "business and labor organizations but . . . citizens in general to challeng[e] the environmental actions of government agencies themselves."[46]

"Let us be realistic about it," Representative William Cramer told his House Public Works colleagues as they struggled to finish writing the 1961 Water Pollution Control Act Amendments. "You and I know there are a lot of politics involved in who does what on streams, and so forth," he mused. "And the policy question is who will have the lead in it—the Federal Government or the State, and over what cases." To that fact, Alabama congressman Robert E. Jones, Jr., replied, "It just seems to me we are talking about usurping some jurisdiction. Suppose it is pollution in New Orleans contributed to by Red Wing, Minnesota, then the City of New Orleans might file some complaints against Red Wing, Minnesota, because it is in navigable waters." Read by a lawyer, as well as by a historian, their New Frontier colloquy guaranteed perennial legal change. [47]

FROM THE FILES OF BRUCE BOWLER, POSTWAR ENVIRONMENTAL LAWYER

7

"BE IT RESOLVED that the Idaho Wildlife Federation supports [the Federal Water Pollution Control Act] and requests the $45 million annual appropriation for municipal aid for sewage treatment be increased to the needed $100 million annual appropriation to properly do the job and that an undersecretary in the Department of Health, Education, and Welfare be devoted fully to water pollution problems."
—Bruce Bowler, Chair, Fish Committee, Idaho Wildlife Federation Annual Meeting (1958)

"They call us fish folks sometimes, or fishheads, or wildlifers, but nevertheless we are your neighbors, and we are the grocers and druggists and even the farmers, and all the people that make up the economy that like to get upon these [public] lands."
—Bruce Bowler, Member, National Advisory Board Council, U.S. Bureau of Land Management (1965)

The House of Representatives subcommittee hearing in Seattle's federal courthouse had barely begun. The chairman, Democrat Robert E. Jones, Jr., was still welcoming witnesses and guests in his raspy Alabama drawl, a syrupy tone rarely heard in Scandinavian-inflected Puget Sound country. Junior staff clerks—just a few, as this was only a subcommittee field hearing— shuffled papers on their laps at seats in the jury box. The senior clerk whispered instructions to the stenographer, a middle-aged woman who regularly transcribed witness testimony in the Pacific Northwest's largest federal courthouse. Chairman Jones's subcommittee colleagues were still scanning their agendas to determine what kind of face to put on for the small audience and tiny knot of press photographers. Outside, a cold fall wind rattled the windows, promising rain— nothing new for the Pacific Northwest as Thanksgiving week loomed. Work would end by mid-afternoon, it being a Friday, so members could fly back to either Washington, D.C., or their districts to mix constituent calls with some family time.

Thick folders rested on a table behind the senior clerk, who now seated himself just behind Jones's left elbow. The brown manila expandable files held testimony prefiled by witnesses unable to travel to Seattle but interested enough to submit their views for the record as the Public Works Committee's Subcommittee on Natural Resources and Power developed a new federal clean water act. Early that morning, 22 November 1963, clerks had inserted a lawyer's letter sent from Boise, Idaho, the previous day into the folders. Jones and his senior clerk never had a chance to glance at the two pages on simple letterhead, the kind of low-cost stationery favored by solo practitioners in small towns.[1]

Shortly before 9:45 A.M., a court employee slipped into the back of the courtroom and whispered to a reporter, a courthouse regular she recognized. Simultaneously, the chief judge's clerk strode through the swinging door from his boss's private chambers and whispered to the committee clerk. Startled, the clerk leaned forward, put his hand on the chairman's shoulder, and whispered into his right ear. Jones, his face suddenly, keenly alert above his ever-present cigarette, covered the microphone before him and leaned over to pass the shocking message to his senior Republican colleague. Each then pivoted in the other direction to whisper to party cohorts seated along the subcommittee's oak table. Simultaneously, from the corridors beyond, an excited hum surged to an audible buzz punctuated by shouted questions.

Nearly two thousand miles southeast, President John Kennedy lay dying in an emergency room in a Dallas hospital. Chairman Jones abruptly, but politely, adjourned the water pollution hearing. Members retired from the ornate courtroom to the spartan jury room, one group gathering around a small black-and-white television, another perched on a table next to a desk radio. A handful of senior court staff, duty-bound to remain near the chief judge, shared their consternation. Ten days later, after Congress helped lead the American people in mourning the assassinated president, staff would finally read Bruce Bowler's letter.[2]

The Idaho environmental lawyer had submitted testimony on behalf of his client, the Idaho Wildlife Federation. As IWF's outside counsel, a position which paid little enough in fees even when he was writing its briefs and testimony, Bowler had been handling legal work for the state's premier conservation organization since the early 1950s. During the decade before that, he had offered informal advice about legal matters in his capacity as an IWF board member. For a quarter-century before 1963, Bowler had belonged to the federation, as well as to the Ada County Fish and Game League, the largest of the IWF's constituent clubs around the state. Upwards of 20,000 primarily white male anglers, hunters, and hikers—and their families— were asked to contribute $25 per year to the Federation. In a typical year in the early 1960s, IWF's annual budget rarely exceeded $5,000.[3]

From the files of Bruce Bowler, until now untapped by environmental and legal historians, emerges the complicated, unexpected picture of one practicing lawyer who helped invent American environmental law. Drawn from scores of neatly organized boxes, packed with thousands of pages that document a professional life during the postwar's quarter-century, Bowler's practice reveals a new legal field taking recognizable shape. Created in the Intermountain West by Bowler and his clients before the "environmental decade" began in 1970 and beyond elite academic circles and rarified national politics, environmental law originated when ordinary people strove to use law to solve actual problems.[4]

Bowler considered his legal work on behalf of conservationists a civic duty. For every thousand dollars in fees billed to the IWF and other environmental clients, probably another ten thousand came from the ordinary sorts of clients that small-town lawyers, from Idaho to Florida, advised and represented: businesses negotiating contracts, families buying property or preparing wills, young couples adopting babies, and the occasional petty criminal representation of a white-collar family's wayward teenaged son spicing the quotidian mix. Bowler's solo practice earned enough to pay his home mortgage, law office expenses, and the costs of raising three young sons with wife Beth. Both natives of southern Idaho's "Magic Valley" had left in the mid-1930s to attend the University of Idaho, four hundred miles north in Moscow. Beth had, by the early 1960s, grown used to Bruce's annual winter drives north into the mountains above Boise to attend IWF conferences.[5]

Two months before writing testimony about water pollution, Bowler had informally celebrated the twenty-fifth anniversary of his admission to the Idaho Bar. After graduating from the University of Idaho College of Law at the relatively advanced age of 27, he opened his practice in the state's capital city. Bowler grew up in Shoshone hunting, fishing, and rambling on the irrigated high desert cradling the Snake River, some 150 miles east of Boise. Passionate, patriotic zest for Idaho's countryside, both its wilderness peaks and irrigated croplands, made him the ideal president of the Ada County Fish and Game League. Quiet and methodical, his indefatigable manner of practice had already made him a respected regional and national environmental lawyer. Standing just over five-and-a-half feet tall with thinning dark hair, Bowler valued his status as a respected professional in Boise's small legal community. In the little capital city of barely 50,000, Bowler didn't *find* time—he *made* it—to recreate. Each week, he passed along a smidgen of woodcraft and some of his joy at being outdoors to the Boy Scout troop he led. With pine-fringed, sagebrush hills north of town and canal-laced dairy pastures barely fifteen minutes east and west from his home and office, he could slip away early to shoot a few September doves or December mallard ducks.

Bowler ultimately spent six decades in a legal practice dedicated to passing along the West's natural heritage in trust undiminished. Not only wild country—wilderness and free-running rivers—merited Bowler's appreciation. He also made environmental law to conserve the health of cultivated acres, among which nested upland birds, as well as Idaho's "working rivers," on the vast reservoirs of which rested thousands of ducks and geese during their biannual migrations. And much as he cared for Idaho's pristine glacial peaks and bracing high desert, Bowler sought justice under law primarily to protect the well-being of his neighbors and their children. Citizens shielded by law from industrial pollution could better enjoy Idaho's boundless opportunities, their rights to health and beauty armored against the political indifference that wasted the state's inheritance.[6]

Fifty-two when he testified to the House water pollution subcommittee, Bowler labored late nights over environmental legal work for little compensation. Unconcerned about his professional prestige, he never joined a country club to golf and swim, never paid dues to lunch and drink at Boise's elite all-male Arid Club, never sought or held a leadership post in the Idaho State Bar. Instead, Bowler lawyered to discharge a newer version of what once was every attorney's civic duty: safeguarding his community's future by using his professional skills to seek justice.

Bowler reveled in the easy fraternal camaraderie he enjoyed among

Idaho's outdoorsmen, but did his best to democratize the conservation movement. In 1966, he marked his Pacific Northwest Sierra Club Chapter executive committee ballot to endorse a gender-balanced ticket: Emily Haig, an elderly Seattle resident, and Janet McLennan, a younger Club activist from Portland, along with Paul Wiseman and James Henriot.[7]

Bruce Bowler and his friendly Idaho Wildlife Federation clients—Ernie Day, Alvard "Al" Kiler, Kenneth "Bill" Reynolds, Franklin Jones—used environmental law already on the books, in the Idaho Code, United States Code, Code of Federal Regulations, and reported decisions of courts state and federal. And Bowler's strategizing and advocacy helped these grassroots recreation activists make law when their objectives demanded it. Advised and represented by Bowler, as the 1950s became the 1960s, the Idaho Wildlife Federation, "hook-and-bullet" traditionalists in a state far outside the corridors of national power, made new environmental laws to secure traditional conservation goals: cleaner waters, healthier game fish and bird populations, and unimpeded access to the state's millions of acres of federally managed public lands.[8]

Underlying much of their lawmaking success before 1970 was Bowler's keen appreciation that environmental lawmaking depended on politics. By engaging conservationists in public life, he helped translate their demands into political agendas. By helping traditional outdoor recreationists articulate newer yearnings for environmental health, IWF's lawyer ensured a louder voice in the state's councils for the druggist, grocer, and realtor. Their fishing license fees, tanks of gas, and boxes of shotgun shells helped transform their communities' economies. Their undimmed joy at being outdoors, confronted by ugly evidence of ecological sickness and political arrogance, fueled environmental lawmaking after the mid-1950s.

Bruce Bowler played neither a unique nor unprecedented part in American environmental law's invention during the postwar era. Other attorneys, representing other clients, were modifying older rules to attain the newer purposes that Americans embraced with vigor as the sixties began. Bowler's law practice reveals legal change happened in many places across a lengthy span of years after 1945. Before "environmentalist" became first an honor badge, and then an epithet, Bowler and his clients—an extraordinary lawyer and his ordinary citizen-clients who recreated outdoors—formed key ranks in lawmaking's vanguard.

Even before Congress began writing a new federal water-quality statute in the early 1960s, conservationists in Idaho and throughout the Northwest had been agitating, litigating, and politicking to make environmental law to attain specific goals. Bowler's legal work between the early 1950s and late 1960s helped secure salients that defined the new field: citizen standing to participate in administrative and judicial proceedings; national pollution control standards enforced by state action; natural resource agency democratization; "public interest" broadened to encompass environmental objectives; mass media scrutiny of environmental issues; and a political movement that crossed state lines, stretched partisan boundaries, and blurred older economic and ethnic divisions. The following sketches in this legal history isolate environmental law changes caused by Bowler's efforts to serve clients' needs. A focused view like this must neglect influences exerted on the process of legal change by his adversaries, allies, and the various ultimate decisionmakers Bowler sought to persuade and influence. Still, scrutinizing one lawyer's work illustrates larger patterns by isolating and illuminating the historic gears that drove legal change.[9]

CITIZEN STANDING

Environmental law texts often pinpoint a landmark 1965 federal court ruling, *Scenic Hudson Preservation Conference v. FPC*, as the touchstone that secured citizens' right to be heard before government agencies transformed the natural world.[10] Socially prominent, wealthy New Yorkers, assisted by elite legal counsel in Manhattan and Washington, D.C., fought this signal battle to stop a hydropower project at Storm King Mountain on the Hudson River. *Scenic Hudson* deserves appropriate attention, to be sure, but a new view down Idaho rivers offers a crucial perspective in appreciating environmental law's long, complex emergence. Almost a decade before New Yorkers began litigating issues posed by federal dam licensing, ordinary Northwestern anglers and their local environmental lawyer fashioned many of the innovative legal procedures that opened agency hearing rooms.[11]

Between 1954 and 1957, Idaho conservationists developed new legal procedures by intervening in federal administrative decisions to oppose damming Idaho's Snake, Salmon, and Clearwater Rivers. Between 1957 and 1960, Bruce Bowler invented and then applied new legal techniques that enabled his clients' new public interest views to shape these crucial Northwestern environmental decisions. By 1967, his legal advocacy and political acumen helped secure the important principles of public participation and judicial scrutiny, doctrines that lawyers call "standing."

The Hells Canyon and Echo Park controversies, decade-long debates about dams and rivers after World War II, clarified Idaho conservationists' thinking about environmental ends and legal means. These grinding battles convinced Bowler's IWF clients to act independently in their civic capacity and exercise their legal rights and political influence to protect rivers they cherished. Idaho activists determined they could no longer safely rely on government agencies, acting without sustained citizen involvement, to defend the public interest in running water and living fish. Neither state nor federal conservation agencies had formally intervened in Idaho Power's Hells Canyon Federal Power Commission case. Not knowing they had the legal right to do so, neither had organized conservationists. Citizen activists now vowed to participate more fully in future dam-licensing administrative cases.[12]

The IWF's January 1954 annual meeting voted to "flatly oppose without qualification" Penny Cliffs and Bruces Eddy, proposed Army Corps of Engineers dams on north Idaho's Clearwater River. Lewiston forester Mort Brigham charged the dams would "be the worst possible example of butchering fish and game on the altar of power." Bowler fanned his IWF comrades' ire by denouncing the Corps' November 1953 "public fact-finding" hearings in Orofino as neither. Sounding a little like John Foster Dulles, he dismissed the meetings as "undemocratic dupes," contaminated by "arbitrary and unfair procedures" that permitted "factual misrepresentations [to be] made." The Army Engineers had "not conducted them on principles of fair play," Bowler reported, because "they were trying to lull us into a false sense and I think it was deliberate." Flawed legal procedures ensured bad substantive decisions, he insisted, because government agencies using biased testimony usually acted "without consideration of wildlife values involved."[13]

A decade before Storm King broke along the Hudson, Bowler filed the first citizen-conservationist pleading to argue that the Federal Power Commission (FPC) should weigh ecological, cultural, esthetic, and recreational values when deciding whether to license dams. IWF's March 1954 Protest informed the FPC that "eighty organizations functioning within the State of Idaho . . . which have a total membership of 20,000 persons make this

protest on behalf of the public interests involved in the wildlife and its habitat." New reservoirs on the Clearwater would flood big game habitat, accelerate logging in "now inaccessible and remote timber regions . . . depreciate
and destroy . . . unique wilderness that has very great scenic and recreational
values," and choke migratory fish runs by "seriously depleting a valuable
sport fishery."[14]

In 1956, Bowler secured enactment of further IWF resolutions that authorized intervention to oppose two new Hells Canyon dams—Lower
Canyon on the Salmon River and Nez Perce at the Salmon/Snake confluence—menacing the all-important Salmon River watershed, in which two-
thirds of the Northwest's dwindling salmon and steelhead trout spawned.
IWF members debated the merits of consistency and pragmatism, Mort
Brigham still urging full-throttle opposition to all new dams while Bowler
counseled tactical realism that appreciated political geography. Lawyerly
caution persuaded IWF to deem a third new proposed Hells Canyon dam—
Mountain Sheep—both politically inevitable and ecologically acceptable.
Federation salmon experts—men who fished for pleasure and guided others
for pay—knew Mountain Sheep would only block the Snake *above* its confluence with the all-important Salmon River. Keeping the Clearwater and
Salmon lifelines open enabled conservationists and their attorney to concentrate lobbying and litigating on the most ecologically, and hence legally, vulnerable dams. IWF member Jack O'Connor, who had taken Brigham's
losing side in the debate with Bowler, cheerfully saluted his faction's good-
natured defeat by "passing the hat to get funds for a Clearwater Dams Fund
to defray expenses of their fight."[15]

In November 1960, Interior Secretary Fred Seaton announced his department's formal opposition to *any* new dams, private or federal, in the Snake,
Salmon, and Clearwater Basins. National support, albeit from the outgoing
Eisenhower administration, bolstered IWF's three-year-old regional alliance
with Oregon and Washington activists against Bruces Eddy and Penny Cliffs
on the Clearwater and any new dam—regardless of name—that blocked fish
migration into the Salmon drainage.[16]

Interior's moratorium vindicated Bowler's decision early in 1960 to intervene formally in the Clearwater dams' administrative process. Then he boot-
strapped his IWF clients into the FPC's Snake case by filing a new formal
protest against the proposed Nez Perce Dam in Hells Canyon. That high
dam at the Snake-Salmon confluence would, IWF contended, "block forever

all salmon and steelhead runs into most of Idaho." Bowler's deft stroke and bold tactics carried IWF into uncharted legal territory that the Scenic Hudson Preservation Conference would not enter until three years later in Storm King. His IWF clients endorsed their counsel's recommendation to fight both Clearwater and Salmon dams simultaneously before the FPC. Winning a wide two-front legal and political battle "will probably require a fight and a campaign such as we have never had before," IWF president Theodore H. "Theo" Wegener warned members.[17]

Bowler's IWF friends, Boise realtor Ernie Day and famed outdoor writer Ted Trueblood, helped their counsel refine legal tactics to secure environmental objectives by assessing ecological risks against political dynamics. Though their sophisticated and cold-blooded approach reflected 1960s realities, later environmental lawyers and clients would emulate IWF's analysis in future environmental law crises even when public opinion and cultural values shifted after 1970. Three low dams that Idaho Power was already building in Hells Canyon had doomed upper Snake River fish, the IWF sadly realized. A home-state political ally like Idaho senator Frank Church could not oppose all new dams for fear of being caricatured as a hopeless extremist. Powerful regional politicians like Washington senator Henry Jackson might become friends, but would certainly become enemies, if Idaho conservationists ignored the Columbia Basin's dependency on cheap public hydropower. Another Hells Canyon dam above the Salmon—High Mountain Sheep—would thus cost little ecologically but pay IWF big political dividends.[18]

So along the Salmon, damn the political costs, Idahoans would fight. Waters long held sacred by Indian people became central to conservationists' new conception of Idaho's environment. On the Salmon battle line, Bowler and IWF deployed their legal resources to keep the river running free. Trueblood's Field and Stream article asked two million readers in October 1960, "Must the Salmon River Die?" Nez Perce Dam, blocking the Salmon's outlet to the Snake, "would end forever the runs of steelhead and salmon in the Salmon River . . . but fortunately there is an alternative. . . . High Mountain Sheep would be built upstream from the mouth of the Salmon. If it is built, Nez Perce won't be."[19]

IWF's subtle politicking complemented Bowler's innovative legal tactic: vindicating the public's right to be heard in federal dam-licensing cases. This tactic served his client's environmental strategy to make scientific, recreational, and esthetic evidence part of the licensing record, thus expanding the Federal Power Act's test for determining "the public interest." By intervening before the FPC, Bowler used and made law to attain IWF's central environmental purpose: to keep the worst dams out of the best watersheds by forcing government decisionmakers to hear ecological evidence from citizen conservationists and native people.

When an unsympathetic Boise *Idaho Statesman* editorialized about IWF "hypocrisy" in challenging only dams proposed by private companies, Bowler's October 1960 reply clarified long-range strategy by explaining short-term tactics: "We favor construction of the private power dam . . . at High Mountain Sheep site above the mouth of the Salmon River which, like [Idaho Power's] Hells Canyon [dams], would not block the Salmon River. [We] oppose the public power dam at Nez Perce, being below and blocking the Salmon River, which has yet a great fishery future for salmon and steelhead." Day and Trueblood sent their own long letters to the *Statesman* that same week, further detailing conservationists' mixture of political calculation and legal acumen.[20]

Between 1947 and 1957, when Idaho Power Company clashed with federal public power agencies over the Snake in Hells Canyon, ecology was still a legal afterthought. The region's state conservation agencies hugged the periphery of the issue throughout the Hells Canyon controversy. Idaho, Oregon, and Washington agency lawyers acted as if federal administrative law entitled their clients only to spectate from the FPC's sideline. They gratefully took only what they thought environmental law then gave by negotiating dam-license conditions that obligated Idaho Power to try—unsuccessfully, as it turned out—to conserve migratory fish. Bowler's aggressive lawyering, backed by Northwestern conservationists' creative politicking, stiffened bureaucratic spines in Boise, Salem, and Olympia. Bowler's FPC case received a powerful boost when joint testimony from the Idaho, Oregon, and Washington fish conservation agencies backed High Mountain Sheep but blasted Nez Perce on ecological grounds. "We are unequivocally opposed," the state agencies declared, "to the construction of Nez Perce Dam because it would be the most severe blow the Columbia River fisheries have suffered since Grand Coulee Dam" closed in 1940.[21]

Read nearly fifty years later, Bowler's legal memoranda stand as precursors for environmental lawyering at the highest level. After polishing another lengthy brief to the FPC, he made sure to update Frank Church about conservationists' legal strategy and tactics, hoping that the senator's legislative work would complement IWF'S environmental objectives. "I feel confident," Bowler wrote the senator in June 1960, "that an adequate record of evidence of the reasons why we cannot now risk the Salmon River with Nez Perce, properly made to the Federal Power Commission, should result in denial of that application." FPC staff attorneys were quietly encouraging the conservation intervenors by telling Bowler "a good record can be made on the real substance that exists in the fisheries resources in the areas of controversy concerning the pending application." Although Bowler understood the difficulty of making new law, he appreciated effective legal advocacy's customary value. Likely appellate review of any licensing decision by the FPC, Bowler stressed to Church, boosted both the administrative and litigation value of "an adequate record of real evidence on the significance of the Columbia River fishery, which is more and more being recognized as a big thing." Alert to how environmental law was made politically in various competing arenas, the senator's one-time East Boise neighbor urged Church to press ahead with his legislative plan to enact a federal statute to preserve the entire Salmon as a "fish sanctuary." Bowler bravely encouraged the senator, "It looks to me like this is the time to do the big job."[22]

In spring 1962, Bowler reported with evident relief that he had concluded the first, primarily administrative, phase of IWF's legal campaign against Nez Perce Dam. As a good lawyer should, he leveled with his eager conservationist clients about the slow pace of the justice system. "With appeals and official red tape, regardless of who wins," Bowler told the group's annual meeting, "it will still be 2 or 3 years until a decision will be reached." Environmental lawyering must shift battlefields, as legal counsel once more became conservation rabble-rouser. Over 3,000 Americans, motivated by Ted Trueblood's 1960 *Field and Stream* article, had written to him, offering their support to "save the Salmon." Bowler reported that IWF volunteers around the region "are now in the process of addressing envelopes to these people appealing to them to write to the Federal Power Commission and advising them how to do it." His own efforts to rally Idahoans remained unstinting. Bowler urged "each sportsman in Idaho to do his part by writing a letter and if any question arises, please notify him, and he will advise on how to do it."[23]

While Bowler warned his IWF clients in 1962 that "the battle is still far from won," by 1967, they had won it. As recounted earlier in Chapter Four, the FPC satisfied none of the adversaries along the Clearwater, Snake, and Salmon. In 1964 the commission approved High Mountain Sheep Dam on the Snake as a private project, rejecting the Interior Department's new proposal to build it instead, and disapproved licensing Nez Perce Dam as a public project. The administrative record included Northwestern conservationists' full participation. FPC's decision devoted twenty pages to weighing environmental testimony from IWF and its allies. Though the commission had licensed another Snake River dam in Hells Canyon, its split decision accepted Bowler's political and ecological calculations by rejecting conservationists' worst nightmare, a giant new dam athwart the Salmon River.[24]

Bowler still had to preserve his clients' victories, but a respondent's chair in a federal courtroom sits a little more comfortably beneath appellate counsel. When Interior Secretary Stewart Udall as well as public power forces appealed FPC's Nez Perce denial, the Boise lawyer enjoyed the inestimable advantage of playing defense on all the points he had labored so hard to make during trial. As the administrative case proceeded up the federal appellate court ladder, Bowler had simply to preserve what he had already won, an easier task than persuading judges to reverse the FPC on points his advocacy below had failed to win. And, in due course, the federal appeals court that reviewed the Salmon/Snake dam-licensing case sustained Bowler's arguments in 1966.[25]

The Department of Interior then appealed, Secretary Udall arguing to the United States Supreme Court that Interior's Reclamation Bureau should get another bite at Hells Canyon's apple by building Nez Perce. As Bowler and conservationists again played defense, parallel federal court wins two thousand miles east, along the Hudson and Potomac, strengthened their Salmon River position. During the Snake-Salmon case, the influential Second Circuit Court of Appeals' *Scenic Hudson* decision vindicated conservationists' right to challenge FPC's Storm King license on environmental and esthetic grounds. And just before one three-judge panel of the District of Columbia Circuit Court of Appeals affirmed Bowler's Nez Perce/High Mountain Sheep win, another panel of the same court extended *Scenic Hudson's* reach. *United Church of Christ v. FCC*, authored by future Chief Justice of the United States Warren Burger, construed the APA's guarantees of due process and judicial review to afford citizen intervenors broad rights to be heard before federal agencies made important decisions under various regulatory statutes.[26]

As the Snake-Salmon controversy reached the Supreme Court, *Scenic Hud-*

son and *United Church of Christ* gave Bowler reason for cautious optimism. Justice William O. Douglas's 1967 *Udall v. FPC* opinion immediately underscored how much ground Bowler's legal innovations had gained, citing the new lower-court decisions as reasons that conservation intervenors belonged in the High Mountain Sheep administrative case. For more than fifteen years, the only Supreme Court justice from the Pacific Northwest had tried to persuade his brethren to take ecological science seriously. Douglas, a lifelong conservation activist in various activities off the bench, had also long endorsed Bowler's core legal beliefs: citizens had basic constitutional rights to participate in administrative decisionmaking, and appellate judges had a constitutional duty to scrutinize agency rulings to safeguard democratic values. The Snake-Salmon controversy gave Justice Douglas his opportunity, and he took it.

Udall v. FPC startled even Bowler by awarding his clients more than they had dreamed of asking. Douglas's opinion recurred to the audacious argument that Mort Brigham and Jack O'Connor had first advanced during heated IWF debates in the mid-1950s. *Udall* ordered the FPC to start its new administrative review of fish versus dams in Idaho by asking a fundamental question that Bowler had tactically dropped in 1960: "Should *any* new dam be built" on the Snake in Hells Canyon or at the mouth of the Salmon? The Supreme Court's decision ruled that the conservation intervenors, all 27 of them, were proper legal parties to present ecological and esthetic evidence on that existential issue. And it ordered the FPC thereafter to assume that the Federal Power Act's "public interest" test required carefully weighing all relevant environmental evidence, as well as the usual cost and engineering factors long thought to be the only dispositive administrative issues. *Udall's* sweeping reach prevented federal agencies and courts from ever answering "yes" to Ted Trueblood's anguished question, "Must the Salmon River Die?"[27]

Bowler's pioneering legal work on Northwest dam-licensing cases helped stimulate a national reappraisal of administrative law's relationship to environmental quality. His representation of the IWF before the FPC and in federal appellate courts recast a long legal tradition that confined administrative lawmaking to economic factors. In 1965, Congress enacted the Anadromous Fisheries Act, declaring a new national sense that dam-building too often destroyed the environment. The next year, the Supreme Court began reconsidering an FPC dam license in the Snake Basin. And in 1967, for the first time ever, the Court overturned an FPC dam license and directed the agency to.solicit environmental evidence about the wisdom of letting a river run. Bowler's environmental advocacy made these developments happen. Applied aggressively and skillfully across the country, they presaged further environmental lawmaking in the later sixties and seventies.

NATIONAL STANDARDS/STATE ENFORCEMENT

Bowler's 1963 testimony, putting IWF on record for strengthening federal clean water laws, commended the House subcommittee for visiting polluted areas in the Northwest. As he told the subcommittee, "To see and smell is something to behold." He pointed out how silver mining and lead smelting had fouled the Coeur d'Alene River Basin in northern Idaho's Panhandle. Food-processing waste, exacerbated when irrigation depleted water flows, was choking the Snake River in eastern Idaho. Dredge-mining spoil still occasionally obliterated Central Idaho's high-mountain fish-spawning gravels despite a state statute enacted by popular initiative in 1954. Bowler drafted the law on behalf of a conservationist alliance that included both outdoor recreation enthusiasts and public health experts. IWF provided crucial organizing and publicity to secure voter approval after miners, in league with irrigators and stock-grazers, had twice stifled the Idaho Legislature's efforts to enact a dredge-management bill.[28]

Bowler's House testimony maintained that Congress should enact national clean water standards for two reasons. First, federal power would strengthen enforcement of Idaho's 1959 water quality statute. Bowler, a charter member of the state Water Pollution Advisory Council, had to operate as its de facto attorney. Until 1965, a single, quite young deputy attorney general in the Fish and Game Department performed most of the state's environmental law administration and enforcement, ranging from water quality litigation to poaching prosecutions.[29] Idaho's weak enforcement powers required more demanding federal standards to tackle what Bowler termed the "serious pollution problem of the Middle Snake River." Minimally treated municipal wastes from eight of the state's twelve largest cities, mixed with potato peels and onion tops from the burgeoning food-processing industry, were choking Idaho's biggest river, killing millions of fish and tainting drinking water.[30]

Secondly, federal action would stimulate environmental lawmaking's all-important political dimension. By enacting and enforcing clean water standards under the Constitution's Interstate Commerce Clause, Congress could demolish what Bowler termed "the silliest argument . . . so often utilized by industrial polluters, . . . that water pollution is a local matter." Bowler criticized both rural irrigators and their industrial customers in the Snake River Basin for insisting they "owned" Idaho water. "To take a broad look," Bowler advised the Pollution Advisory Council in 1962, "I would say that nobody *owns* the water. . . . When we talk of 'ownership' of water, we are speaking of a temporary use of water, before it goes on to somebody else." His 1963 congressional testimony recurred to this argument, deemed heresy by Idaho's "water bulls" in the agribusiness sector and their attorneys. "Nothing is more transitory than water," he mused. "It is basically interstate in character and the federal government properly concerns itself accordingly with pollution at its source."[31]

Bowler's testimony grasped Western politics' electrified "third rail." He doubted irrigators' invocation of prior appropriation's mantras—"first in time is first in right" and "use it or lose it"—could permanently preempt public use of Idaho water for sewage treatment, recreation, and other environmental values. Prior appropriation, irrigator-style, ignored two other equally valid legal rules rooted in both the state constitution and seventy-five years of practice: all the people owned all the state's water, and beneficial uses justifying appropriation also included supporting urban life, outdoor recreation, and ecological quality.

"A grave part of the Idaho problem," Bowler testified in November 1963, "results from the historic laws of appropriation and the false concept that water has only one legal beneficial use, and that is to irrigate crops." A quarter-century's practice in a state that still required all Bar aspirants to pass a test about prior appropriation had taught Bowler a great deal about water law. A boyhood spent along headgates and lateral ditches, amid potato patches adjoining sagebrush plains, exposed him early on to water law's deep economic, political, and cultural roots. Bowler's postwar environmental lawyering persuaded him that the battle for legal reform, though a lifelong crusade, had to be waged on many fronts.

Bowler's Water Pollution Council experiences convinced him that federal quality standards could challenge prior appropriators' legal supremacy. Nine of southern Idaho's most influential water users, managers, and lawyers came to Boise in December 1962 to answer charges that their upstream manipulation of the Snake River forced downstream citizens to try flushing away city sewage and industrial effluents with a mere trickle of water. Council chairman Herbert Derrick politely framed the issue as "a problem involving many people including those who determine the amount of flow in a river for dilution of wastes." The Council's vague legal powers led him only to hope "some agreement might be reached as to increased water flow in the future in order to avoid fish kills, algae kills, and other health and nuisance problems."

Henry Eagle, Watermaster of District 36, listened stonily to Derrick's pieties. Employed by both state and federal governments as well as private irrigators who farmed the vast region between the Tetons and Magic Valley, Eagle reminded Idaho's novice water pollution administrators the traditional law of water gave government managers "no other alternative but to fill the reservoirs" above Twin Falls. "The farming industry is very important also and the water rights have been adjudicated going back to 1883 and these are rights belonging to individuals." Only Idaho Power Company, which also owned a state-law right to a minimum flow past Milner Dam, could expect winter-time water in scant snow years: "This flow is released and the remainder is stored until the reservoirs are filled." Farmers who owned water rights, organized since 1919 as the Committee of Nine, and the Bureau of Reclamation, which served their claims by building dams and reservoirs, sympathized with riverside residents. However, Eagle informed the Water Pollution Council, "the Committee of Nine or the Bureau of Reclamation . . . are obligated to abide by the decrees and adjudications of law and have no area of negotiations."

Bowler promptly rejoined, "The most important water is the glass of water to sustain life." Twin Falls, for example, drew all its drinking water from the foul Snake. State and federal water managers had "unknowingly allowed something to happen that has already cost the taxpayers too much, in allowing the irrigation companies and power companies to impound water which normally belongs to the people of the State." Watermaster Eagle, unmoved by urbanites' plight, shot back, "There would be no need for cities if no irrigation was done in the country." A northern Idaho wood products manager wondered, "How much more reclamation is needed to reclaim a little [water] for the rest of us—in addition to living up to these laws that were made in 1883?" Another council member asked the irrigators, "If we are to maintain any semblance of a river in the Snake River bed, and it appears to the people of the State that we need to have a flow of 1400 second feet [triple what then escaped down the Snake in winter], couldn't the State of Idaho demand this flow?" Prominent southern Idaho water lawyer Cliff Fix warned, "Not without depriving some of the people who have water rights under the State's own constitution."

Blunt declarations of property's customary preeminence led environmental lawyer Bowler to gently remind both hostile witnesses and his pollution control colleagues of law's capacity to effect change in social as well as environmental relations: "If the river is going to disappear between dams, the people will have to make a decision that they don't want a river or a decision that they do want a river. It appears to be something that can't be reached through cooperation but only through means of a law change." After irrigators and water managers were excused after three testy hours of debate and bluster, Bowler advised the Water Pollution Council to move carefully. Irrigators and their hydropower and food-processing allies commanded enormous economic and political power. The infant environmental regulatory agency had to consider all its legal options. "In light of the discussions held today with the recent visitors," he suggested, "it might be well to reserve judgment for a time and see what develops, for any action at this time might precipitate a fight which might be best avoided." A savvy environmental counselor, Bowler urged regulators to fortify administrative patience and political calculation with a long-term determination to fight a complex legal battle: "If court action becomes necessary, it will be discussed at a future meeting of the Council."[32]

Bowler's frustrations with making state water quality law informed, in a small way, enactment of one of the postwar era's most significant environmental statutes, the innovative 1965 Water Quality Act. President Lyndon Johnson praised its "positive controls over the discharge of pollutants into our interstate and navigable waters." Johnson's February 1965 "Special Message on Conservation and Restoration of Natural Beauty" summoned Congress to enact even more statutes to strengthen federal power in order to protect the nation's natural environment. Johnson explained the "new conservation's . . . concern is not with nature alone, but with the total relation between man and the world around him." Like Bowler, the president thought effective laws had to cross state boundaries: "Large-scale pollution of air and waterways is no respecter of political boundary lines, and its effects extend far beyond those who cause it."[33]

Bowler applauded the Water Quality Act's invocation of federal constitutional power to make "the cost of doing business . . . include the adequate
handling of wastes so they do not spoil this countries [sic] waters." Federal
rules would remove competitive incentives to pollute water, even if "it must
be a forced thing by government regulation." The Water Pollution Advisory
Council helped draft Idaho governor Robert Smylie's June 1966 letter that
approved the new federal statute and initiated state rulemaking to devise
"water quality criteria for interstate waters and to develop a plan for implementation and enforcement of the criteria." When Governor Smylie told Interior Secretary Udall that Interior's new *Guidelines for Establishing Water
Quality Standards for Interstate Waters* "coincided with Idaho's program for water pollution control . . . adopted in May 1959," he acknowledged Bowler
had been helping invent environmental law for some time.[34]

DEMOCRATIZING RESOURCE AGENCIES

Since the early 1950s, when stage-managed "fact-finding hearings" had provoked his righteous indignation, Bruce Bowler found that natural resources
agencies often interpreted their legal duties as a way to favor traditional consumptive users. Citizens with no direct economic stake in public lands and
waters lacked access and enjoyed little influence. IWF intervened in FPC
dam-licensing cases to vindicate Bowler's conviction that more information
and diverse views made good environmental decisions more likely. Well before the public began clamoring to democratize natural resource agencies in
the later 1960s, this small-town environmental lawyer was using political
leverage to effect administrative reform. With federal agencies managing
two-thirds of their state, Idahoans rode the crest of postwar public-lands
controversy. And the Interior Department's Bureau of Land Management
(BLM), which supervised half of Idaho's public lands, offered Bowler an easy
target.[35]

Two months after the New Frontier opened, Secretary Udall and new BLM
director Karl Landstrom warned public-range stockmen to expect change. A
March 1961 National Wildlife Federation special bulletin updated Bowler
about Udall's new priorities: "multiple use" rules would broaden BLM's
mandate to "watershed protection, outdoor recreation, minerals and timber,
urban development and not just livestock production"; customary advisory

groups of cattle-grazing permittees "should be broadened to include representation from all users (not just grazers)"; and "BLM personnel will not be expected to compromise on the accuracy of their decisions designed to protect the range (give in to pressures)." Bowler praised Udall's "refreshing public interest position," thanking him "very kindly" for "administering the public lands for the benefit of all the people . . . who actually own the land which you husband in the public interest."[36]

Bowler's growing reputation as a skilled environmental advocate and resourceful activist recommended him to Udall's quest for "balanced usage of public lands consistent with the public interest." Certainly, the Idahoan's political courage must have impressed the Arizonan. Each practiced environmental politics in states with un-reapportioned legislatures that accorded each county equal representation in at least one house. "Old bulls" from rural counties still led both houses of the Idaho legislature from their back seats on "Sirloin Row." Their unchecked power, Bowler told Udall in April 1961, bred arrogance. "For too long many stockmen in Idaho have acted like they owned the public lands on which they have been permitted to graze." Political and economic clout "sponsor[ed] a completely wrong idea that the Government, by its land management agencies, should be their wet nurse."[37]

To shake up the cozy administrative system that perpetuated agriculture's legal hegemony, Udall and Landstrom named a dozen new members to BLM's National Advisory Board Council (NABC) in 1962. Bowler eagerly answered Udall's call to "enlarge the Idaho advisory board to include representation of interests in addition to livestock and wildlife." The only council member selected strictly because of his environmental law reputation, Bowler welcomed his official duty to reform an agency grappling with cultural change, not only in the public-land West, but in the nation as a whole. Bowler hoped conservationists could use BLM's institutional crisis to help environmental law better govern public lands.[38]

From 1962, when Bowler attended his first NABC meeting in Las Vegas, to 1965, conservationists tangled constantly with Judge Dan Hughes, the Montrose, Colorado, rancher who chaired the council. The judge helped his congressional patron, Representative Wayne Aspinall, skillfully parry agency reform, wielding power conferred by the sophisticated political-economic apparatus that linked Western stock-raisers to national food processors and grocery chains. Udall's new assistant lands secretary, John A. Carver, Jr., rode herd on the newly fractious council. Formerly one of Frank Church's senior aides, Carver warned the NABC that New Frontiersmen intended to treat past as prologue. In Las Vegas, the assistant secretary outlined the challenge of modernizing the agency's 1934 Taylor Grazing Act mandate to include "values which do not easily have an economic base attached to them . . . some types of recreation value, certain types of outdoor experiences, . . . and certainly the wildlife values." Director Landstrom echoed his boss, telling the council that "public land management reflects broader considerations than domestic livestock grazing alone."[39]

Bowler's work on NABC to democratize public land management through the middle 1960s reflected conservationists' growing political power and legal sophistication. By changing how agencies discharged their duties, conservationists sought substantive legal reform. Procedural change could redirect BLM and the Forest Service toward ecological, as well as economic, objectives. Ranchers resisted agency democratization by trying to secure a form of legal tenure to graze public lands that more resembled fee ownership than permitted leasing. With tenure, ranchers hoped to maintain their customary authority despite changes in BLM personnel and mission.[40]

Bowler also exploited the legal fluidity that Aspinall stirred by having Congress authorize a Public Land Law Review Commission. The 1960 Multiple Use/Sustained Yield Act had provided the Forest Service a new "organic" act. Udall, Carver, and Landstrom hoped the NABC, invigorated by reformers like Bowler, would endorse a similar statute to update BLM's practices and recalibrate its mission. They intended the new law to widen the Taylor Act's single-minded focus on grazing by opening land management decisions to citizen input and directing BLM to manage Western ranges for ecological health.[41]

Tenure debates wracked the BLM's advisory council in Bowler's first three years. During their 1963 annual meeting, most councilors listened in stone-faced silence, though a handful applauded loudly, when Izaak Walton League president L. C. "Jack" Binford critiqued ranchers' tenure push. "Now it is said that the stockmen want a better deal than they now have," he observed. "What can the permittee gain? There isn't much more to give him except the legal title." If ranchers—a tiny numerical minority even in the public-land West—insisted on pursuing their chimerical notion, "186 million people, the folks who own the public lands . . . will eventually demand your abolition and the creation of a comprehensive advisory group." As "we have so much in common—the recreationist and the livestock man," Binford pleaded, "let me urge you to abandon any efforts to secure a change in tenure." Instead, he vowed the "Ikes" would rather "help you develop a sound, long-range program that gives consideration to all uses and users."[42]

Binford, a Portland, Oregon, lawyer, wrote his combative speech with Bowler's help. He thanked his fellow Northwesterner for teaching him "a great deal about the Bureau of Land Management, the lands they manage, the laws that control, and the problems of the livestock user." Bowler returned the praise, thanking Binford for "your splendid paper on this important subject." He also accepted the president's offer to join the "Ikes," whose membership traditionally centered in the Midwest and Northeast. Bowler's $5 annual fee helped forge a national alliance that paid valuable dividends; Western conservationists would rally national allies whenever Aspinall tried to use the Public Land Law Review Commission to shield the public lands' preferred, traditional customers.[43]

Aspinall's rancher allies exploited the controversy they stirred around the tenure debate. NABC chair Hughes defended ranchers' proposal to secure tenure as the minimum protection they needed "if our public domain is taken from us." Pouncing on BLM's abortive effort to raise grazing fees, cattlemen also forced Udall to jettison his first BLM Director in the spring of 1964. Compromise replacement Charles H. "Chuck" Stoddard himself soon found the post precarious. Not much later, he joined the unfortunate Landstrom in a lengthening line of BLM directors who lost their political balance when newly emboldened and more numerous conservationists clashed with resentful ranchers and their congressional patrons.[44]

Udall, still stinging from the Landstrom debacle, addressed the National Advisory Board Council in March 1964. Hughes and Aspinall had already bested him twice, a humiliation in Washington's feral political world. Aspinall's Land Law Commission bill was sailing toward final enactment that summer, so Udall sought some influence over its final composition and objectives by conciliating the powerful Coloradans. A confidential memorandum for stockmen, which Bowler somehow obtained, reported that "Udall asked that the Council keep discussions on a scientific basis and above passionate controversy." Assistant lands secretary Carver "flattered the Council on the type and scope of the advice they gave."

Udall closed his NABC address by advising councilors "to avoid a big controversy that can only cause damage to every one concerned." He told them what by then they certainly knew: conservationists like Bowler, riding a tide of public interest, were encouraging Congress to remodel the Taylor Act. "I think," the secretary observed, "there is more and more of a focus of interest in our public lands, not only interest in the mineral values or in outdoor recreation or in wildlife, but an interest in these lands as part of our public estate."[45]

Aspinall hoped the Land Law Commission could channel, or even blur, that new multiple-use focus. While Udall hoped Congress would enact a new BLM organic act modeled on the Multiple-Use/Sustained Yield Act, traditionalists fought back to maintain their prerogative to define "multiple use." By packing sympathizers onto the new six-member Land Law Commission and its twenty-five-member Advisory Council, Aspinall and Hughes wanted to give ranchers, miners, and economic concessionaires leverage in the constant struggle to interpret broad admonitory language such as "multiple use."[46]

Aspinall's handpicked Commission chair, a partner in a major Denver law firm that advised the cattle industry, was limiting attendance at planning sessions to secure members that IWF president Bill Reynolds dismissed as "chamber of commerce, mining, cattlemen, sheepmen and timber users." Bowler's political judgment, national experience, and own growing influence shaped conservationists' counterstroke to influence the Land Law Commission. He drafted Reynolds's 23 October 1964 letter to Hugh Wilson, president of the Idaho Chamber of Commerce. Congratulating him on his opportunity to meet Aspinall and the Land Law Commission chair in Denver, Reynolds warned Wilson that "fish and game and recreational uses have not been very prominent in the preliminary planning for this conference." He recommended that Wilson propose Tom Kimball, National Wildlife Federation executive director, for membership on the commission "to add balance." Knowing Aspinall believed public lands management concerned primarily the West, IWF extolled Kimball's Western roots and frequent visits to Idaho, where "he expressed himself each time in awe and admiration for our wonderful natural resources."[47]

Chuck Stoddard, BLM director for barely a year, apologetically opened his first formal presentation to NABC in Denver the week before Thanksgiving in 1965. BLM's new draft land-sale rules required viewpoints not wearing cowboy hats to be heard, Stoddard allowed. "These regulations are considerably different from the original proposal . . . that you saw at your last meeting [because] multiple use means, in effect, a lot more people are interested in the land and the Bureau is in the middle . . . in trying to find ways of reconciling or dovetailing these various interests and uses." Various interest groups that now claimed a right to manage the public's lands made "all of this difficult for us," he wearily concluded, "because we are trying to do these things with the same manpower as we have always had. We have to do the same job with more responsibility . . . [and] we are concerned with overloading our people beyond the point of things that can be taken care of." Making multiple use a legal reality, Stoddard admitted, felt like repairing an airplane engine in flight.[48]

Later that morning, as Stoddard tried to clarify the practical implications of applying "multiple use/public interest" perspectives, the director's halting explanation sparked a fierce debate between Bowler and Judge Hughes. Their duel—one Western lawyer against another— illustrated the deep resistance that conservationists provoked by pushing agency reform. "As the single recreational interest on the Council," the Boisean began, "I perhaps technically represent a pretty large segment of the people who actually own this BLM land that we are talking about." Forage-pricing and water-leasing rules now interested more than cattle-owners. Ranchers had to "recognize the economy of a changed social system over [sic] which we operated when the laws now governing this public land first became effective." Beef production filled bank accounts in Idaho, to be sure, but "in Idaho . . . our recreational industry is $160 million annually . . . and that is number two to the agricultural industry in all of Idaho's economic operations and growing fast."[49]

Judge Hughes exploded, "How much of this $160 million goes to the Federal government? . . . None of it is paid direct to the government for the use of the public land. . . . They hunt on the public domain free of charge, I know. . . . We pay plenty of taxes." Another rancher took up where Hughes left off, demanding that Bowler agree that "anyone spending money for recreation could not have spent it unless that dollar or $10 or $100 was first developed and produced as new wealth in a basic industry . . . such as your agriculture, your minerals, or wherever it is derived from." Bowler acknowledged, "We are all in this boat together," but made no apologies for his Idaho friends, the conservationists who funded his lonely advocacy: "They call us fish folks sometimes, or fishheads, or wildlifers, but nevertheless we are your neighbors, and we are the grocers and druggists and even the farmers, and all the people that make up the economy that like to get upon these lands. . . . It is a big form of exchange [and] we have a common base of a great resource here to work and preserve these public lands more fruitfully for multiple and beneficial uses."[50]

Bowler pursued public-land law reform for fifteen more adventurous years on BLM's National Advisory Board Council. By the "environmental decade" of the 1970s, he had helped a diverse range of citizens earn the legal right to force governments to explain how they planned to convert natural forces into economic resources. Public agencies made decisions after giving scientific evidence about ecological relations nearly as much consideration as economic predictions about technological change. Natural features and forces, held in trust by Americans for the benefit of generations yet unborn, enjoyed a measure of care sufficient to allow their agencies to operate more unmediated by human intervention.[51]

MASS-MEDIA SCRUTINY

Conservationists, even in a largely rural state like Idaho, were quickly adapting sophisticated media relations tactics to shape a political climate conducive to environmental lawmaking. Bruce Bowler's files reveal that the IWF, as early as the mid-1950s, was subsidizing local wildlife photographers and filmmakers. The state's wild beauty and heart-stopping adventure opportunities offered rich pictorial fare. And the media productions employed by conservationists opposed to a dam in Dinosaur National Monument doubtless inspired emulation.[52]

Articles in the outdoor sports press and *Audubon Magazine* alerted conservationists in the mid- and later 1950s to growing concerns about the environmental impacts of DDT and other chemicals. Five years before *Silent Spring* brought the issue to the nation's attention, Bowler buttonholed the supervisor of the Boise National Forest on a Boise street to quiz him about DDT spraying in the mountains north of the city. Outfitters had alerted the Boise lawyer "that the recent spray job . . . had resulted in complete elimination of fish life." K. D. "Ken" Flock, the Boise Forest supervisor, immediately wrote to the Idaho Fish and Game Department, assuring him that managers of both national forests north of Boise were concerned about the reports. He pledged the Forest Service's cooperation if Fish and Game wanted to "work together . . . to investigate thoroughly to find out what the facts might be."[53]

Two months before Bowler's 1963 testimony urged the U.S. House to enact stricter federal water quality laws, Idaho's biggest TV station broadcast "The Big Thirst," an hour-long documentary. Jarring images jammed the black-and-white special: dead fish floating at the base of Magic Valley dams, steaming sewage disfiguring rural sloughs downriver from Boise, and milk-white sulfides pouring out of paper mills into the inaptly named Clearwater River in north-central Idaho. The reporters who prepared the program for Boise's KBOI, Rick Raphael and Dick Kassan, had quizzed Bowler throughout the summer of 1963 to learn which municipal officials and state health department regulators could lead them to the most graphic samples of Idaho's aqueous filth.[54]

ENVIRONMENTAL LAW'S POLITICAL PREDICATES

Idaho conservationists understood environmental lawmaking went hand-in-hand with environmental politicking. Bruce Bowler's files reveal an environmental lawyer who blended research, advocacy, and public relations. One part of his political work aimed to capture public opinion and, if necessary, to reshape it toward conservationists' objectives. Another part tried to keep old allies in government, and to make new ones as times changed. Bowler observed no scrupulous disdain for the rough world of Idaho natural resources politics. He worked as hard, and as effectively, as his adversaries in the timber, cattle, mining, and agricultural industries.

During the summer of 1954, Bowler helped IWF cooperate with the state's AFL-CIO to lobby Idaho's congressional delegation to pass bills dedicating a fixed percentage of U.S. Forest Service timber-sale receipts "to improve wildlife and recreational facilities in our national forests." Sensitive to rural people's hopes to balance better hunting and fishing with job growth and community stability, Bowler drafted an IWF questionnaire sent in summer 1954 with union funds to all state legislative candidates, asking their views on restoring the state Fish and Game Commission's independent status. That fall, his efforts to build broad constituencies secured voter passage of an initiative limiting dredge mining.[55]

Bowler also reached across ethnic as well as class lines to build environ-

mental coalitions. He enlisted Seattle attorney Joseph T. Mijich to help innovate a multistate, multiracial citizens' intervention into the FPC dam-licensing case. Bowler and Mijich advanced two novel claims in their May 1960
Petition for Leave to Intervene. They contended any FPC license violated the
Federal Power Act because "Nez Perce [Dam] would . . . destroy approxi-
mately 43 per cent . . . of the salmon and steelhead" migrating up the Columbia-Snake system. And, for the first time in an administrative-law case
about dams, rivers, and fish, Northwesterners demanded formal intervention *as citizens*. Previous Northwestern FPC dam-license cases, along the Deschutes and Cowlitz Rivers, had pitted Oregon's and Washington's state
conservation agencies against dam-builders. Bowler and Mijich, by contrast,
asked FPC to hear testimony and legal arguments from white and Indian
people because "no other party or organization appearing before the Commission will adequately represent the interest of your petitioner." Having
seen government fish agencies fail to protect Northwestern ecological values
since the postwar dam-building offensive commenced, twenty-seven organizations—from commercial fishers on the Pacific Coast to sport anglers in
eastern Idaho—signed the petition.[56]

Racist bickering and ethnic condescension had hamstrung conservationists' and Indians' ability to coordinate their energies during the Hells
Canyon controversy. In 1960, by contrast, Bowler and his IWF clients gratefully entered the Clearwater/Salmon dam cases accompanied by four Indian
nations inhabiting Oregon and Washington reservations. Ernie Day traveled
to Washington, D.C., with Bowler in February 1961 to testify before the FPC
against Nez Perce Dam. The Idaho realtor took the witness oath alongside
fellow intervenor-witnesses Wilfred Petite of the Chinook Nation, Quentin
Markishtum of the Makahs, and Alex Saluskin of the Yakima Nation.[57]

Shifting public opinion created new opportunities for environmental
lawmaking. In November 1962, Idaho conservationists secured a crucial political objective by helping reelect their strongest national ally and state's
most powerful Democrat, United States Senator Frank Church. Bowler knew
the erstwhile Boise attorney well: during the senator's own brief private
practice his young family had lived four blocks from the Bowlers while
Church rented an office three blocks from Bowler. They socialized in the
same small legal fraternity; only one woman belonged to Boise's bar in 1952,
when Church lost his first political campaign as Republicans again retained
all of Ada County's legislative seats.[58]

Bowler's dual role as IWF counsel and Ada County Fish and Game League's incoming president complemented the close political relationship he forged with Church confidante Ted Trueblood, the famed *Outdoor Life* writer from Nampa. Quiet partnership between the lawyer and the journalist, undoubtedly known to Church's advisers, delivered conservationists' 1962 senatorial endorsement. Bowler and Trueblood mounted a campaign both sophisticated and blatant. Idaho's electorate numbered barely 400,000, so most politically active people knew who was writing press releases and creating special-purpose "citizen groups." In February 1962, the Ada County Fish and Game League bestowed on Church its 1961 Conservation Award. The senator's thank-you letter to "Dear Bruce" elicited Bowler's chatty "Dear Frank" reply. Bowler commended the senator for "having done the things meriting this award," especially "making firm friends of Republicans as well as Democrats on your sincere, forthright stands . . . taken in the genuine public interest in wildlife matters." No doubt mindful of Church's risky decision to endorse a wilderness bill, Bowler reassured him, "I think it will be proved that there are lots of people who appreciate these things, that normally do not get the attention of those in high public office."[59]

Trueblood then announced the formation of "Outdoorsmen for Better Government," a committee he chaired, as the 1962 senatorial campaign intensified in autumn. "Dedicated to the support of those political candidates who believe in the practices of sound conservation," OBG promptly endorsed Church. The state's now senior senator (Republican Henry Dworshak had just died) "demonstrated political courage of the highest order when he carried the Wilderness Bill on the floor of the Senate." Trueblood's thirty-year career in print journalism equipped him to put into words what "all Idahoans who enjoy the outdoors, who delight in green forests and clean streams" felt: "this generation has an obligation to pass on to future generations its heritage of lands, forests, water, and wildlife in as healthy condition as it found them." Church not only showed rare courage when he won overwhelming Senate passage of the first Wilderness bill, Trueblood wrote, but the young politician knew how to balance risk and reward. Even as he courted political oblivion in his home state by backing federal wilderness, Church cannily played a three-handed poker game. He got the Senate to authorize a new Clearwater River dam and name it for his late Republican colleague Dworshak, told conservationists beforehand he was deserting them, but then salved their Clearwater wounds by introducing a counterpart bill to declare the undammed Salmon River drainage a "sanctuary" to protect "60 percent of the remaining migratory fish in the entire Columbia Basin."

Trueblood sent Bowler an undated version of the OBG endorsement bearing his confidential note: "Frank Church, despite his [Clearwater dam] position, is still the best senator Idaho has ever had from the standpoint of the sportsman, conservationist, and lover of the outdoors. WE WILL NEVER HAVE A PUBLIC OFFICIAL WHO IS WITH US ON EVERY ISSUE."[60]

Shrewd federal political calculations—Church's narrow November 1962 reelection commenced three more Senate terms—paralleled conservationists' successful state strategy the same year. Bowler and Wildlife Federation president Ernie Day and secretary Bill Reynolds agreed to nominate an IWF member to Governor Robert Smylie's purely advisory Committee for Natural Resources in Idaho. The moderate Republican, seeking an unprecedented third term, wanted to convey the impression that he, too, cared about conservation. Reynolds's 24 February 1962 letter told Smylie that the IWF appreciated the governor's courtesy and recommended Day, whose real estate acumen made him acceptable to Smylie and one of Senator Church's closest hometown allies. Reynolds flattered the egotistical chief executive, assuring Governor Smylie "many kind and gratifying remarks were made about you in regard to your interest in our State's natural resources" during IWF's annual January meeting in Pocatello. Bowler helped engineer the entreaty to Smylie: his copy bore Reynolds's scribbled note, "I think this is the type of letter you had in mind."[61]

Reynolds and Bowler guessed right when Smylie won a healthy reelection in November 1962. The governor quickly appointed Day to his new Natural Resources Committee and got University of Idaho president Donald Theophilus, the committee's chair, to invite the Wildlife Federation to hold its annual December meeting in Moscow at the UI campus. Smylie also endorsed one of IWF's chief objectives for the 1963 legislative session: a state parks system. IWF approved an ambitious conservation agenda for the legislature that convened in Boise a month later: "better state parks, a strong pollution bill," and restoration of the Fish and Game Commission's independent status, a casualty of Smylie's Republican predecessor in 1953. "For the future," secretary Reynolds's minutes noted, "President Ernie stated that we must work hard. . . . We must play the game the way we find it and fight hard for the things that are right."[62]

President Theophilus reciprocated the Federation's enthusiasm, interpreting Smylie's reelection as the catalyst for environmental lawmaking. Welcoming IWF to his campus, he told members that the governor had tasked the Natural Resources Committee to "effectively draw up and recommend legislation . . . for the protection and effective use of our state's natural resources." He hinted that Smylie would press both his legislative majority and agency directors to develop "a coordinated plan because the people of this state want to see our natural resources handled in a proper manner. If we do not do it today, the future of these resources will be very bleak tomorrow." After hearing Theophilus' encouraging words, IWF delegates unanimously made legislative creation of a state park system, a roadside park plan, and a roadless lakeside park in north Idaho their top three political priorities for 1963. Restoring the Fish and Game Commission's independence was number five, just behind congressional enactment of "a strong, national wilderness bill."[63]

IWF, taking Day's advice to play the game as they found it and to play smart and act strong, was gaining political power to make more and better environmental law. Idahoans needed to make new laws and revise old for, as the Minutes phrased it, "time is running out" to conserve "rare and precious natural resources" because "such areas once lost can never be restored to their original state." For too long, IWF declared, "too many individuals in public office have placed politics and their own personal gain above the public welfare." Now, however, with "our exploding population creating ever-growing pressure and demands for fishing, hunting, and outdoor recreation areas," lawmakers had to "work together without thought of personal gain or political advantage" to safeguard the place for which they cared so deeply.[64]

New president Bill Reynolds proudly closed the minutes on Ernie Day's eventful year at IWF's helm by noting "the 1962 convention was one of the best ever." He attested to one new source of the growing influence that "sportsmen" were wielding in environmental lawmaking and politics: "The program especially arranged for the delegates' wives was very much appreciated by them and they all stated that they would never miss an annual meeting of the Idaho Wildlife Federation." During its first twenty-five years, IWF's winter annual meeting had been a stag affair. In the year of *Silent Spring*, though, Bowler, Day, and Reynolds felt warmer winds blowing in a new wave of citizen activism.[65]

Conservation's political climate continued warming when legislators assembled in Boise to hear Smylie's State of the State address in January 1963. Bowler enlisted a new, young member of the Idaho Bar, Scott Reed of Coeur d'Alene, to help write proposed legislation and develop testimony for committee hearings. Like most part-time state legislatures that convened for only several months every other winter, the Idaho legislature maintained no legislative counsel's office to help members write bills. Lobbyists and their retained lawyers, along with local and state agency officials, performed that crucial function. Bowler and Reed often used lawyer-legislators—ambitious, hard-charging Boisean William "Bill" Roden and methodical, quiet Harold "Hal" Ryan of Weiser—to pass IWF's recommended bill drafts to sympathetic, influential legislators.[66]

Early in the 1963 session, Reed copied Bowler and Day with his letter to the Democrats' floor leader in the House of Representatives, enclosing drafts of bills to create a state park system and to restore the Fish and Game's commission status. Reed told Representative Herm McDevitt, a Pocatello lawyer, "I have tried to put the bills in some kind of final form, [but] my guidebook is dated and my experience is nil. Presumably introduction through committee would be proper, but you will know what is best." Indicative of conservationists' zeal, Reed asked McDevitt to "call upon me for anything of further assistance," volunteering to drive over 400 miles of icy, two-lane mountain roads in mid-winter to Boise to testify "before the committee on the parks bill if you feel it useful." For a young attorney with two small children trying to establish a solo practice in a small town, Reed's offer carried a hefty price tag: at least three days away from the office, and thus away from billing regular clients, and the enmity of at least some powerful business interests. Smylie, however, redeemed his State of the State pledge to sign bills that would create a state parks department, toughen the state's water quality laws, and restore commission status to the Fish and Game commission.[67]

Senator Church reciprocated IWF's crucial 1962 support by cooperating closely with Bowler and Trueblood to enact the first version of what would, by 1968, become the Wild and Scenic Rivers Act. Bowler read with satisfaction Ted Trueblood's 22 April 1965 testimony before the Senate Interior Committee, which reflected the environmental lawyer's careful thinking over many years about communities' power to make new law by readjusting rights to use water. This legal problem, freighted with Western history and enmeshed in regional economics, had occupied Bowler since Idaho's battle over dredge mining during the fifties.[68]

Trueblood told senators that Church's Wild Rivers bill "would stak[e] a claim for all the people, on a narrow strip of land along these rivers, and in the rivers themselves, so that all Americans will have the right to enjoy them in their unspoiled state." He prudently reminded the committee, dominated by Westerners, that traditional water and land laws in the public-domain West had indeed "been chiefly beneficial." The son of a father who had "grown up with a strong belief in the right of an individual to stake his claim, build his home, and rear his family on the land from which he wrested a living, whether with rocker and sluice box or with plow and harrow," the Outdoor Life author framed the legal changes promised by S. 1446 as an integral, evolutionary part of Western history. By recognizing a new legal right to leave water flowing down undammed rivers, the Wild Rivers Act would simply write another chapter in the law's steady adjustment to changing social circumstances. Of the 3,000 Americans who had answered his call five years earlier to "save the Salmon," Trueblood considered a letter from a Kansas City teenager the most eloquent. "When I grow up, I want to see a river running," the young Midwesterner had written him, so Trueblood asked senators to pass the Wild Rivers bill to "insure for all Americans, for all time, this privilege."[69]

Bowler also shared Trueblood's shrewd assessment of how political realities constantly shaped environmental lawmaking. Church was by now their firm mutual friend and the journalist copied his letter to the senator's close boyhood friend, Boise photographer Stan Burns, so his report about exciting, hopeful days testifying in Washington and hunting big-city financial support the next weekend in New York City could help Burns and Bowler fine-tune their Idaho lobbying. Much as Trueblood and his IWF cohort Franklin Jones had enjoyed their committee appearances and urban prospecting, they foresaw daunting obstacles ahead of the Wild Rivers bill that were as big as any boulders frothing the wild Salmon River. Wyoming senators on the Interior's committee, for example, imported a solid phalanx of opponents to testify: "the governor, the president of the cattleman's association, and other cowboy and chamber of commerce types." And Idaho's other Democratic member of Congress, Compton I. White, Jr., looked ready to fight even if Church navigated S. 1446 through the Senate to the House of Representatives.

Trueblood's and Jones's long visits with national conservation activists and sympathetic Interior and Agriculture administrators suggested a tactic for Idahoans trying to overcome White's resistance. "You can't argue with him," Trueblood conceded, but IWF should emphasize how they helped Church draft his bill so wild-river status "can't hurt mining, lumbering, etc." These primary industries employed thousands of White's constituents in the rural district through which ran the Clearwater and upper Salmon, key watersheds that Church sought to preserve. "Maybe we can say, in effect, 'Here's your chance to get on the conservation bandwagon,' and maybe he'll go along. Anyway, it's something to try," Trueblood mused.[70]

Even if Church earned Senate passage of the Wild Rivers bill, Trueblood worried about its fate in the House Interior Committee, on which "Comp" White sat. His colleagues would surely defer somewhat to a member whose constituents would have to learn to log, mine, and live along "forever wild" rivers. But Trueblood and Jones spotted an even bigger obstacle looming ahead like a ten-ton boulder blocking Wild Rivers' float trip to statutory permanence: House Interior's chair—formidable, intelligent Wayne Aspinall, Democrat from rural Colorado's Western Slope. "The problem will be in Aspinall's committee," Trueblood told Bowler. The Boise lawyer's own forays into public-land law reform had already introduced him to Wayne Aspinall's power. No New Frontiersman, the Coloradan resented President Johnson's efforts to recast the "old conservation" into newer forms of "environmental law."[71]

On the Monday evening before Christmas 1965, Bruce Bowler sat in the smoky ballroom of Boise's Owyhee Hotel, an honored guest at a banquet honoring an even more illustrious postwar environmental lawmaker, Frank Church. Republicans joined Democrats, and government employees mingled with private citizens. All applauded as the senator— still the Senate's youngest Democrat after eight years of service—accepted IWF's "Bald Eagle Award" as State Conservationist of the Year. Midway through the second of what would become his record-setting four Senate terms, Church had earned IWF's plaudits by working to enact landmark statutes that established environmental law on solid foundations a half-decade before the "environmental decade" opened in 1970: the water quality and clean air acts in 1965, new restrictions on pesticides under the Federal Insecticide Act (FIFRA), and the 1964 Wilderness Act, a monument of utmost importance to Idahoans who cherished the recreational and ecological values bestowed by public lands covering two-thirds of the state's area.[72]

Church earned the IWF's award because "with genuine statesmanship [he has] concerned himself with man's responsibility to his environment." The environmental lawmaking burst of the early 1960s would continue; IWF noted the senator was still trying to win final congressional approval of the Wild Rivers bill to enshrine "the highest and best use for the Clearwater and Salmon Rivers," home to the Northwest's embattled salmon and steelhead trout. The Bald Eagle Award reflected how environmental lawyers like Bowler had pushed the process of legal change. In words that would not have been out of place in 1975 or even 2005, IWF saluted Church for "demonstrat[ing] his appreciation for the components of a quality environment that needs diligent husbandry before irresponsible damage is done."[73]

"PUBLIC INTEREST" ENVIRONMENTAL LAWYERING

A Harvard man from Massachusetts, Dr. Charles H. W. Foster, told a seminal 1969 environmental law conference near Washington, D.C., how he had used lawyers during "several decades of personal experience in public and private affairs." A Johns Hopkins biologist who gravitated into policy-making, Foster had worked in the immediate postwar years on the staffs of the Conservation Foundation and Nature Conservancy, national groups of long standing. Foster's salary came from budgets funded with generous legacies endowed by some of America's richest families. Their scions, themselves men of successful distinction, managed these conservation groups with the same care and wisdom they applied to private business and philanthropic endeavors. Foster moved smoothly from nonprofit conservation into public office, serving seven years under Governor Francis Sargent as the Boston Brahmin's hand-picked director of Massachusetts' Natural Resources Department. While Bruce Bowler of Boise litigated the Nez Perce/Mountain Sheep case by working alone late at night after handling paying clients' work, Foster was getting legal advice from big-firm lawyers in major cities who were professionally trained at Harvard, Yale, and Columbia. Dr. Foster truly appreciated professional services donated pro bono to their shared mission. "Conservation's basic credibility," he told the Airlie House conferees, "lies in the volunteer nature of its participants and [their] lawyers—like physicians, scientists, or businessmen—should be willing to donate time to the cause."[74]

Foster's experiences, recollected in 1969, understated the financial and logistical challenges that "counsel for the concerned" faced a decade before. Conservation fund-raising had always been desperate, its groups scrimping along on budgets meager by comparison with its legal adversaries. Pioneer environmental lawyers such as Bowler might nonetheless have envied the resources Foster and his Eastern cohorts enjoyed. In December 1960, to "help defray the cost of our intervention in the Federal Power Commission hearing in Washington, D.C., in regards to the opposition of Nez Perce Dam," the Idaho Wildlife Federation solicited each of its 80 member-clubs "$25.00 or *more.*" Federation secretary Bill Reynolds praised Bowler's home club: the Ada County Fish and Game League "has already started the ball rolling with a check for $100.00." Reynolds's enthusiasm could not conceal Bowler's huge personal, uncompensated investment in IWF's cause. To help fashion environmental precedents which Charles H. W. Foster and the Airlie House conferees—lawyers educated in and employed by the nation's preeminent law schools—gratefully saluted in 1969, the Boise attorney underwent tribulations of which few of them could conceive.

"Through the joint efforts of Bruce Bowler, Ernie Day, Franklin Jones and others," Reynolds told IWF members in December 1960, legal briefing had been completed "at no cost to us." Had the research and writing "been done professionally, it would have cost us over $25,000." Reynolds's unintentional slight to his friend's legal skills could not conceal IWF's pride in its crusade, nor in its counsel's professionalism. "The project [Bowler and others] have completed is something I wished every sportsman in Idaho could see," Reynolds crowed. "It will absolutely be the first time testimony from us 'fish folk' will be heard by the FPC, and if it doesn't open their eyes as to how we regard our Salmon fishing in Idaho, nothing else will."[75]

"A FIELD SO VARIED AND RAPIDLY CHANGING"

AMERICAN LAW SCHOOLS DISCOVER
ENVIRONMENTAL LAW

8

The simplified tale of environmental law locates its "heroic moment of conception" in the "environmental decade" that opened with the enactment of the National Environmental Policy Act on 1 January 1970. Norman Vig and Michael Kraft, for example, have described environmental policymaking as springing forward "in almost unprecedented fashion [as] a new environmental policy agenda was formulated [and] implemented throughout the 1970s." Environmental lawmaking generated an "outpouring of new federal legislation in the next decade [that was] truly remarkable." Twenty years after Vig and Kraft, Nancy Kubasek and Gary Silverman were still advising readers in their 2003 American environmental law primer that "the area of law you are now beginning to study is one of extremely recent development." Into the early 1970s, they insisted, "there would not have been any law school or undergraduate or MBA courses in environmental law because there was no such cohesive body of law."[1]

The field of environmental history historicizes environmental law by complicating its past and stretching its origin across decades. Incremental legal change, more nuanced and contingent than heroic and remarkable, restores the field's historic context. Thus, when written historically, environmental law's origins challenge the conventional paradigm—presented in nearly all contemporary law school textbooks—that the "environmental decade" opening in 1969–1970 created environmental law. Professionally trained lawmakers, allegedly present at the field's creation, recognized that legal change during the quarter-century before 1970 had shaped the exciting political developments going on around them. They gave due weight to established legal principles operating before Earth Day. They placed the rapid legislative lawmaking underway in Washington, D.C., into context as just one tributary among environmental law's many sources. Congress and the president made important environmental law in the 1970s, they understood, but neither made the first nor only laws reshaping Americans' relationship to their natural world.

Commentators on and practitioners of environmental law, writing in the heady atmosphere around the first Earth Day in April 1970, appreciated their field's deep, spreading intellectual roots. Their work reflects environmental law's environmental history. By listening to how these lawmakers thought, talked, and wrote about their field's past and prospects, its incremental development becomes apparent. Witnesses to its birth as an official subject in law school curriculums in the late 1960s and early 1970s, pioneer practitioners and scholars testified to environmental law's lengthy gestation.

As exciting and even radical as environmental law may have seemed in 1971, its conventional legal heritage reassured Harvard Law School professors Louis Jaffee and Laurence Tribe. This eminent senior scholar of administrative law and brilliant young constitutional law expert, respectively, felt comfortable editing their new *Environmental Protection* casebook because, after all, it presented "traditional questions of law and politics which have assumed heightened significance in a society increasingly influenced by science and technology and increasingly concerned with the quality of its natural environment." Even frontline practitioners, usually lacking the historical perspective afforded by law teachers' distance from courtroom and conference table, appreciated their field's deep past. "It is only within the last year or two that the term 'environmental law' has come into common usage," Friends of the Earth litigators Norman J. Landau and Paul D. Rheingold advised in their 1971 *Environmental Law Handbook*. "At the same time there is actually very little new law in the field of environmental law."[2]

David Sive, a longtime New York City civil litigator, ardently hiked in his city's surprisingly vast green spaces. He had earned his law degree from Columbia University after World War II service in Europe as a foot soldier. By the time he reached early middle age, the native Brooklynite had helped his more senior partners build Winer, Neuburger & Sive into a reasonably successful mid-sized law firm on the Upper East Side of Manhattan. Firm lawyers handled a range of civil matters for prosperous individuals and small business clients. While Sive preferred advocating clients' positions in courtrooms and administrative agency hearings, his partners specialized in dispensing office advice about wills and trusts, businesses and unions, families and children. Successful in his chosen profession and settled in the community he dearly loved, Sive recalled with pleasure his father's dedication during the late 1930s and early 1940s in educating his son about the pleasures of engaging the natural world on its own terms whenever possible.[3]

In the early 1960s, a handful of citizen conservationists sought to defeat plans by New York City's major private electric utility to divert the Hudson River into a massive reservoir carved into Storm King Mountain, upstream near West Point. They soon learned that their efforts would become as much a legal slugfest as a political crusade. Crucial to the power company's plans was securing a Federal Power Commission (FPC) license to divert the Hudson's waters to spin electricity-generating turbines at the reservoir's base. Consolidated Edison's longtime law firm, LeBoeuf & Lamb, boasted a platinum "book of business." Its clients included some of the nation's most powerful corporations: utilities, investment banks, manufacturers. Used to staffing big matters with big teams, and paying for the talent with exceedingly big billings, LeBoeuf tasked a half-dozen lawyers, and many more paraprofessional staff, to the licensing proceeding. Sive agreed to represent the conservationists in challenging ConEd's FPC license although he knew he would have to discount his fees severely to match the volunteers' limited checkbooks.

His clients, affiliated by the mid-1960s into the Scenic Hudson Preservation Conference, ultimately secured a series of federal court rulings that stopped Storm King.[4] Reflecting in 1970 about their tortuous, costly legal campaign to overturn a federal agency's power plant permit, Sive wryly noted "the *ad hoc* citizens group or regional or national conservation organization, the typical plaintiff, has little money and no paid legal staff." Government agencies, and the businesses that needed their approval to transform the natural world into profit, enjoyed "virtually unlimited or at least ample means." By contrast, on the opponents' side, penury encouraged creativity and required professional generosity. "Every product and service that goes into a substantial litigation—lawyers, typists, photostats, expert witnesses—must generally be wholly or substantially donated."[5]

Sive contributed a scholarly analysis of the Storm King case to a special *Columbia Law Review* issue in 1970 that was dedicated to topics in environmental law. He stressed important practical challenges that conservationists—by then coming more and more to be known as "environmentalists"—faced when they entered the agency conference room or courthouse: unequal monetary means, the pressure of time, and the need to elicit crucial evidence from adversaries less than willing to disclose proprietary information. What troubled Sive less was the caliber and quantity of lawyers capable of representing environmental groups. "The adequacy, in numbers, talent and dedication, of the supply of lawyers is already assured, in the opinion of most nature loving lawyers and law professors (sometimes referred to as 'environmental lawyers' or 'environmental law experts')." Nor did the new legal experts lack theoretical discipline or creativity: "Courses in environmental law are proliferating at the law schools [and] many schools now have organized environmental law societies." And even the firepower disparity was narrowing with the steady proliferation in the late 1960s of "organizations whose function, in whole or in part, is supplying legal services for environmental causes." He listed, on both coasts, Natural Resources Defense Council, Environmental Defense Fund, Center for Law and Social Policy, and the Conservation Law Society.

"So much for lawyers," Sive concluded. "What about the law?" Writing just months after the 1969 National Environmental Policy Act took effect, this pioneer environmental lawyer happily noted "the explosion of concern for the environment, at every private and governmental level, [that] is the great political phenomenon of the last twelve months." He speculated this "great movement of the Seventies" might portend as much cultural significance as the civil rights revolution, which had been underway for at least two decades. Yet this practicing lawyer believed all the impressive political and social passions unleashed by the "environmental decade" only accelerated the environmental lawmaking process that had been underway for some time. "There is no doubt now that 'environmental law' is a separate field," Sive concluded in 1970. "It has its own courses, teachers and students. Within a few months at most it will have its own texts and casebooks."

As a maturing legal field engaged in projects of great significance, environmental law presented problems that Sive believed needed more study "in order for courts and litigating lawyers to play a significant role in the environmental movement." Among the tasks was one he defined as "the most difficult and baffling problem on the civil side of this 'environmental litiga-tion,' namely, judicial review of administrative rulings in the field of environ-mental law." Though the judicial review problem vexed practicing lawyers who wanted to "win cases to neutralize the effluents of affluence," this clas-sic administrative law issue had deep roots in twentieth-century legal soil. Nearly all of the authorities—case decisions, law teachers' books and arti-cles—that Sive reviewed to develop his preferred solution to the judicial re-view problem had appeared during the preceding thirty-five years but scholars and practitioners, politicians and judges, had been debating vari-ous approaches to this administrative law chestnut since the 1920s. For fifty years, legal professionals had been wrestling over "the manifold response of government to the forces and needs of modern society," a process then-Har-vard Law School professor Felix Frankfurter called "The Task of Administra-tive Law." Sive modestly admitted he was not quite the "tramper in new snow or new fields of law" he fashioned himself in 1970. He acknowledged environmental law's "boundaries are vague [as] it is really still a hodge-podge of rules of administrative law, constitutional law, torts, conflicts [of law], civil procedure and property law."

The year before his alma mater's law review published its special environ-mental law edition, Sive had traveled to Warrenton, Virginia, near the foot of Willis Robertson's beloved Shenandoah Valley, to join over seventy-five prac-ticing lawyers, law professors, conservation-group activists, and politicians in a two-day conference on law and the environment. Richard Lazarus, among others, has traced environmental law's birth to this mid-September 1969 "Airlie House" conference. Sive and his colleagues, though, would have demurred at ordination as the field's founders. Airlie House cohosts Richard H. Goodwin, president of the Conservation and Research Foundation, and Sydney Howe, president of the Conservation Foundation, observed in their "Foreword" to the published proceedings that environment and law had been influencing each other for some time. Indeed, they had invited partici-pants to Warrenton to "assess evolving legal techniques for protecting and enhancing the quality of the environment and . . . the prospects for greater application of the law to conservation efforts."

The rising pace of environmental lawmaking on Capitol Hill exhilarated these key legal academics, conservation activists, and officeholders. Yet they rarely talked as if they were witnessing the origin of a distinctively new legal field nor did they act like legal inventors. Rather, they frankly confessed, and took proud pains to point out, how much they, their clients, and students were doing—and had been doing for some time—that was already distinctively legal. And among Airlie House's adversaries—the counsel and lobbyists and publicists who worked on behalf of polluting industries and the governments that facilitated their actions—few doubted that, for some time prior to 1969–1970, citizens had been deploying lawyers and exercising their own legal sovereignty to protect the earth from their fellow Americans' insatiable appetites.

Malcolm F. Baldwin and James K. Page, Jr., two environmental lawyers who edited the Airlie House proceedings for publication in 1970, already held jobs in the field as the Conservation Foundation's litigation and lobbying directors. So deep was their field's heritage in Americans' longtime efforts to safeguard natural processes, Baldwin and Page wrote, that environmental law practitioners could have defined the field's characteristics a decade earlier. They confirmed the notion of an evolving but extant legal order and they agreed that further environmental lawmaking depended on politicking, courtroom litigation, legal education, and attracting practitioners to the "business" of lawyering in a capitalistic economy. Environmental law's currently "primitive stage," Baldwin and Page believed, reflected less the field's infancy than its dependence on rapidly shifting public opinion, spiritual knowledge, and scientific inquiry. Law, after all, derived from "social, economic, and political thought," indicating just how "limited the traditional scope of a lawyer's inquiry may be."[6]

A fifth of the Airlie House conferees were law school teachers. Among them were scholars who would, by 1980, have built national reputations by systematizing and systematically critiquing environmental law in their prolific writings, constant teaching, and far-flung lecturing: Joseph Sax, of the University of Michigan; Donald Carmichael, of the University of Colorado; Louis L. Jaffee, of the Harvard Law School; N. William Hines, of the University of Iowa; James Krier, of the University of California-Los Angeles; and A. Dan Tarlock, of the University of Indiana. As the conference closed on 11 September 1969, these conferees, along with practicing lawyers, citizen conservation activists, and a handful of former and current elected officials, adopted "specific recommendations for action."

Few Airlie House recommendations assumed environmental law was a newcomer. Most presumed the field already existed and, as the beneficiary of growing public interest, was entering a period of rapid change. Only two recommendations urged enactment of new substantive law: one for national land-use planning, and another for a national "environmental trust fund" to buy future resource development rights from present owners using new national taxes on polluting industries. Airlie House's major action items instead confirmed that the field was in practical transition, buffeted by a new surge in popular passion: publication of a specialized environmental law reporter to keep pace with lawmaking across the country; creation of another national environmental law organization, modeled on the ACLU; internships for energetic law students with practicing lawyers and government agencies; and closer alliances with ambitious politicians who saw environmental conservation as an election-winning tactic.

Discussions among the legal academics at the conference exposed differences about the best methods of training new lawyers to practice environmental law, but even the disputants understood that law teachers and the profession had been arguing for decades about the optimum law school experience's components. In Professor Sheldon J. Plager's bemused estimate, "Legal education has been generally accepted over the years. We have been able to fake it very well because of what lawyers have been doing over these years. . . . We taught them to recite the litany and the myths that are a part of the trade. . . . The truth is, of course, that we don't know what makes a good lawyer." He wondered if the sudden rage for clinical and multidisciplinary teaching was anything more than "the latest attempt to kid the students into thinking that they are really getting something they can use." When public interest environmental lawyer James Moorman gently chided the assembled legal academics for being "too modest," Plager's senior colleague, Professor James MacDonald of Wisconsin, suggested that law schools' traditional methods of teaching legal analysis were even more apposite amid the present political activism: "All of us are aware that a large percentage of Congress, the state legislatures, and people in a policy-making position in the administrative agencies throughout the country are lawyers. If we can give them some insight into problem solving in the environmental area and make them aware of what the present law is and is not able to accomplish, maybe they can in the long run do as much through awareness as we do through litigation or through attempting to influence legislation."[7]

None of the law faculty defined an environmental law problem that needed their solution as the absence of law to be taught and analyzed. "Bill"

Hines, the Iowan, played the "aw-shucks" Midwesterner, apologizing that "our local issues perhaps are not as dramatic as they are in the wilder country or on the coasts." Perhaps because "our students are mostly Midwesterners, usually no more than one generation removed from the farm, . . . as yet, we have not really experienced the phenomenon taking place on the West Coast where militant students are actually taking up the conservation issue as a cause." Nevertheless, Hines had already begun introducing first-year law students to environmental quality under the guise of "resource planning," since "subject matter really doesn't count for very much in law school, that actually what we are teaching is process, so you can do it in one context about as effectively as you can in another."[8]

Jim Krier had just joined the UCLA Law School faculty after clerking for California's influential chief justice Roger Traynor and getting two years' national experience with Washington, D.C.'s most prominent law firm. A 1966 graduate of Wisconsin Law School, he studied in Madison while J. Willard Hurst was still teaching how workaday, often mundane social circumstances shaped both the substance and practice of law. For Krier in 1969, the problem was not one caused by a dearth of trained, motivated counsel: "I don't think there is a legal-service supply problem. . . . The law schools have already done far more than their share to create a demand for the supply they are producing." Nor was the challenge one of inventing law to meet perceived environmental needs: "I think environmental law is a big enough field so that one is generalizing enough if he specializes in environmental law." To Krier, the problem facing environmental lawmaking was simply dollars and cents, mismatched to student aspirations and client needs: "You have to give these people something to live on, because lawyers do make their living practicing law. They do a lot of it at night for which they don't get paid. . . . I can't pay you $25,000 a year. Okay. But a lot of students today don't want to go work on Wall Street. They don't want to go work for big Washington firms and for conglomerates. They really want to take on a lot of these interests and they can do it very, very well."[9]

By the dawn of the "environmental decade," citizen litigants and their attorneys had already realized courts' potential to halt both public and private projects that threatened environmental quality. Organized activists, often advised by counsel, had learned to concentrate public pressure on their elected representatives and on the agencies that executed statutes. Businesses that bore the brunt of new regulations and public scrutiny concurred with the Airlie House estimate. Environmental law had not just arrived, it had been gaining political, social, and economic traction for at least a decade before the "environmental decade" dawned.

In February 1970, *Fortune*—which billed itself as "America's leading business monthly"—devoted its entire fortieth anniversary special issue to "The Environment: A National Mission for the Seventies." As "the final authority on the companies that shape the nation and the world," *Fortune* believed that "business needs to be aware of changes, whether of danger or opportunity, outside itself." The editors told their corporate readers that "conservationists are on the march." Their "burgeoning movement" was enlisting "a growing number of Americans." "Environmental anxieties have coalesced [into] a permanent part of the American awareness, part of the set of beliefs, values, and goals within which U.S. business operates." Environmental activism's power "is being felt in the courts, in politics, and in the boardrooms of the nation's top corporations."

Six months after the Airlie House conferees agreed that environmental lawmaking's pace was accelerating, *Fortune* senior editor Max Ways concurred. He informed readers that "public concern over the physical environment crept forward during the first half of this century. In the Fifties anxiety began to quicken. In the Sixties the environment became one of the major topics of American discussion." Immediately after Ways's opening essay, associate editor Gene Bylinsky's lead article discussed water pollution and the legal and technological efforts to reduce and manage it. The "war on water pollution" was a "limited" one, *Fortune* told its audience, but one with a legal history. Appropriate for readers who named the Vietnam War one of their top four worries, the "limited war" analogy, like the war itself, traced its roots to the postwar years. "The nationwide campaign to clean up ravaged rivers and lakes" began in 1956, Bylinsky observed, when the federal government began funding municipal water treatment plants. Legal change accelerated in the early and middle 1960s, as did industrial and governmental spending, when Congress enacted major new water quality statutes in 1965 and 1966. Two full years before the 1972 Clean Water Act took effect, polluting businesses and local governments had already spent $15 billion building and installing new pollution control equipment at 7,500 separate point sources.[10]

Fortune's final special article noted that "Conservationists at the Barricades" were being reinforced by lawyers. The oldest conservation organizations, such as the Sierra Club and National Audubon Society, were "bringing their goals up to date to fight a broader 'environmental' battle." Lawyers who represented Sierra Club chapters and members were pursuing fifty-five lawsuits. They had already bested the new Nixon Administration by enjoining Forest Service approval of a ski resort proposed by the Disney entertainment empire. Skeptical of government agencies' commitment to environmental protection, citizen and organizational litigants "are deliberately seeking stormy confrontations," Fortune reported. "The front line of this war is in the courts." Joseph Sax told the magazine that "the courts are going to have to respond to this new perspective" and the article also reported that UCLA law professor James E. Krier was urging attorneys to redeploy ancient common-law concepts of nuisance and waste to accommodate broader citizen interests in "beauty, history, peace and quiet, wildlife, and trees and plants."[11]

Fortune deemed two 1960s lawsuits in New York emblematic of the new environmental lawyering. In both instances, federal courts had construed existing statutes, regulations, and case law to establish citizens' rights to intervene in agency and judicial proceedings to assert non-economic interests. In 1965, after more than five years of administrative fact-finding and judicial review, the Second Circuit Court of Appeals' Scenic Hudson decision barred the FPC from permitting a power plant along the Hudson River. It also ruled that agencies' statutory duty to serve "the public interest" required weighing alternatives to assess the environmental impacts of proposed actions.[12]

Farther down the Hudson, citizens opposed to a state freeway plan had won an injunction from a federal district judge in New York City after a five-week trial in 1968. The judge rejected the Army Corps of Engineers' and New York Transportation Department's arguments that their decisions were immune from judicial review that was initiated by citizens. And, reaffirming its Scenic Hudson precedent, the appellate court covering New York held that citizens, both as individuals and as members of associations, had "standing to sue" in order to challenge administrative agencies' interpretation of congressional statutes.[13]

"Young lawyers see in the conservation battle an opportunity to work in a higher cause," Fortune observed. Its environmental law article profiled attorney Roderick Cameron, "the personable young" executive director of the new Environmental Defense Fund. Formed in the late 1960s by "some young lawyers and scientists" in the New York City area "to pool the expertise in taking environmental cases to court," EDF was litigating in state and federal courts to "incorporate modern science into public policy." Environmental litigation was already "achieving precedents that should change court and government procedures," *Fortune* concluded. After *Scenic Hudson*, for example, Congress specifically blocked new Hudson River power plants that did not preserve the watershed's environmental quality.[14]

Activists and attorneys interviewed by *Fortune*, including Sax, saw litigation as the first step toward attaining legislative enactment of statutes that required comprehensive, long-range environmental planning. Prominent members of Congress were already dueling to pass bills that would create the Environmental Protection Agency while state and federal governments, stung by adverse court decisions, were beginning "to reorient the system a little."[15]

Both President Richard Nixon and Democratic Senator Edmund Muskie authored articles for *Fortune*'s special 1970 issue on the environment. Both deemed environmental protection a challenge of surpassing national urgency. "Perhaps no single goal will be more important in our future efforts to pursue the public happiness," Nixon wrote, "than that of improving our environment." Echoing his hero Theodore Roosevelt, Nixon believed "strong governmental action will be required to materially improve our environment." Muskie urged "an environmental policy which is designed to correct the abuses of the past, to eliminate such abuses in the future, to reduce unnecessary risks to man and other forms of life, and to improve the quality of our design and development of communities, industrial units, transportation systems, and recreational areas." He pointed to various federal statutes—"Air and Water Quality Acts, the Solid Waste Act, and the Environmental Quality Act"—as "a base on which to build." Muskie wanted federal agencies to more vigorously enforce existing laws that sought to protect natural systems. He vowed to use Congress's traditional appropriating power to boost public spending in order to reduce water and air pollution, restrict the sale of harmful products, and promote sound urban planning. Both the president and the senator agreed, however, that government could only do so much. Citizens and their organized expressions—businesses, associations, political parties, educational institutions—would have much to do as well.[16]

One of the country's most powerful organizations, the American Bar Association (ABA), soon got involved by establishing its first Special Committee on Environmental Law in spring 1970, initially to assist the more established Atomic Energy Law special committee formulate advice on nuclear power plant siting procedures. Environmental Law chairman David F. Maxwell reported to the ABA's 1971 annual meeting that his committee's work had quickly broadened. Most lawyers who belonged to the country's preeminent professional association practiced in the customary fields that produced problems and advanced solutions that were suitable for environmental lawmaking. Long-standing ABA sections that dealt with administrative law, business corporations, insurance and negligence, local governments, natural resources, and judicature quickly recognized the new environmental committee's value by appointing liaisons to work with Maxwell and establishing their own environment subcommittees. By mid-1971, established fields' enthusiastic embrace of his new enterprise caused Maxwell to realize that "the subject of environmental law covers a spectrum as broad as the environment itself."

The ABA continued its Environmental Law special committee at its 1971 annual meeting. Maxwell told the assembled delegates, "The American Bar Association has a clear responsibility in this area and it can be of genuine service to the public." Of course, solving the new scientific and moral problems that generated environmental conflict "is beyond the scope . . . and competence of the legal profession." What lawyers had always done, though, was make rules for solving conflicts. ABA's members had extensive experience in counseling clients in making and using rules to achieve their objectives. "It is not the purpose of the [special committee's] project to determine how much or what kinds of pollution can be tolerated," Maxwell assured the delegates, "but rather to describe the legal procedures which can be used in making such determinations." Neither members' private clients, nor the public at large, benefited from "the absence of such procedures."[17]

Like their professional colleagues in the private bar, legal scholars were already working methodically on materials present in the legal system. By the early 1970s, their environmental law courses and textbooks began appearing in American law schools.[18] "Law school courses that deal specifically with environmental protection and control are a phenomenon of the past two or three years," an early teacher wrote in 1971.[19] Course catalogs and law publishers' notices said little about how their subject cohered within the American legal system, but careful early environmental law teachers acknowledged preparing a syllabus or writing a textbook did not themselves cause law to happen. As Frank P. Grad observed about environmental law in 1971, "The field is now sufficiently developed to have acquired a generally agreed upon core content, and the time seems right to put forth teaching materials that seek to impose—or to reflect—a structured approach."[20]

Enough scholarship had appeared during these years to support the first American legal periodical devoted to environmental law, which appeared in spring 1970. *Environmental Law,* published by faculty and students at Lewis and Clark's Northwestern College of Law in Portland, Oregon, responded to the Airlie House conferees' recommendation. "The purpose of our new law journal," chief editor Ann Morgenstern wrote, "is to make lawyers aware of legal remedies to protect the environment." She and faculty adviser Bill L. Williams believed "the future of life itself is at stake," but took some comfort in the existence of laws capable of repairing "ecological imbalance." In spite of lax enforcement, "a careful search of statutes in every state will turn up laws that apply, or can be applied, to this area." Rising public pressure would supply one type of pressure. Litigation—advancing private claims for nuisance and trespass and deploying mandamus writs, some of the oldest Anglo American remedies—would be another. Fortunately, the editors of the periodical observed, "Conservation groups have achieved standing in the federal courts [and] can insist that federal agencies follow required procedures and consider all factors affecting the environment." Though "much of the damage to the earth still continues," *Environmental Law's* second editor sadly observed, "during the last decade the public as a whole has really become aware of the irreparable harm that has been and is being caused by the various forms of pollution."[21]

Litigators Norman J. Landau and Paul D. Rheingold published *The Environmental Law Handbook* under the auspices of a new citizen activist group, Friends of the Earth. *The Handbook's* 1971 cover might surprise legal scholars and historians who date invention of environmental law to the decade after 1970. In bold black letters it proclaimed, "The Legal Remedies In Existence Now [can] Stop Government and Industry From Destroying Our Environment."[22] While "it is only within the last year or two that the term 'environmental law' has come into common usage," Landau and Rheingold observed, "there is actually very little new law in the field of environmental law. It is more a conglomeration of legal doctrines which had their start in other fields of law and have existed for a long time."[23]

Landau and Rheingold urged citizens to direct their lawyers to file lawsuits and administrative appeals in order to stop environmental damage caused by both governments and private actors. Ample law existed in 1970 to justify these suits because "an extensive set of powers and interests have been given to the administrative branches of our federal government in the environmental area by Congress, especially by legislation passed in the last decade." *Environmental Law Handbook* listed key environmental problems that activists and their advocates could tackle with existing federal law: water and air pollution, pesticide misuse, radiation releases, and solid waste reduction and management. And in the places where Americans actually lived, in their states and communities, "to even attempt to list by names or legal citations all of these laws [on environmental protection]—or even the chief ones at the state level—would be foolhardy." Many of the largest states—California, New York, New Jersey, and Michigan—"have comprehensive laws on pollution control, sometimes more extensive than the federal laws themselves."[24]

Governments, even before enactment of the major 1970s federal environmental statutes and their state counterparts, possessed ample power to enforce existing prohibitions against pollution and habitat destruction. "It has been our point throughout this book," Landau and Rheingold contended, "that the primary obligation to bring actions to eradicate pollution rests with the government." Florida, Ohio, New York, and New Jersey were already litigating and winning cases against polluters. The United States had successfully prosecuted criminal cases under the 1953 Outer Continental Shelf Leasing Act against oil drilling. Working together, the Army Engineers and Justice Department had won civil monetary damages under the 1899 Rivers and Harbors Act (or Refuse Act) against land developers who filled wetlands without permits.[25]

University of Michigan Law School professor Joseph L. Sax mapped many of environmental law's earliest routes around pro-development precedents. He taught one of the first—possibly the very first—regular law school courses in environmental law, beginning in 1969. In 1970, the Michigan legislature enacted a pioneering statute that Sax drafted to give "any citizen the right to bring a private environmental action in court."[26] Mixing scholarly research, classroom teaching, and litigation counseling, Sax was identifying leading principles that supplied doctrinal coherence to the laws Americans were using to change and protect nature. He found these principles already established by judicial decisions, legislative statutes, and administrative rules. His 1970 book, *Defending the Environment: A Strategy for Citizen Action,* outlined the central legal problems, charted what lawyers and their clients had already accomplished, and announced a manifesto for future action.[27]

"The heart of the matter," Sax contended, was the need for "a fundamental realignment of power" so that the citizen became "an active initiator with authority to tip the balance of power." Various ideas to "reform" the administrative process that required environmental impact statements before agencies acted, extended public hearing duties, and created new independent agencies to assess the wisdom of projects, all suffered from "a fundamental misconception" that "the administrative agency must continue to be our central institution for environmental decision-making."[28]

Defending the Environment presented case studies that demonstrated how citizens who challenged proposed environmental changes had successfully litigated to delay, and occasionally halt, state and federal agency action. His book targeted courts and agencies because "the problems of environmental quality management . . . require a repudiation of our traditional reliance on professional bureaucrats." Too often, he claimed, "a decision reflect[s] the agency's response to its political necessities—its insider perspective about the public interest." These agency professionals have "shunted aside [the citizen] as a busybody or a crank." Since the New Deal, with its worship of administrative experts and its fear of judicial activism, "a central problem of government lies in the vast area of administrative 'discretion' that often masks submission to the demands of powerful interest groups."

To defend the environment, Sax argued, citizens needed to exercise their constitutional right to go to court. A well-chosen lawsuit, presented by competent counsel, could persuade judges to wield their constitutional power to "bring important matters to legislative attention, to force them upon the agendas of reluctant and busy representatives." Judicial decisions would revive "the ancient notion of the public trust," whereby "the citizen, as a member of the public, must be recognized as having rights enforceable at law, equal in dignity to those of private property owners." Once "adapted to contemporary problems," public trust lawsuits will put "concern with preservation of environmental quality . . . on a footing with the interest in its exploitation."[29]

Career politicians, like Nixon and Muskie, understood that law, albeit imperfectly, reflected popular needs. So, too, did activist citizens who had been, since 1945, organizing at all governmental levels to promote environmental values as good public policy. Their efforts helped guide a new corps of activists, many of whom participated in the civil rights and antiwar movements of the 1950s and 1960s, into the challenges of environmental lawmaking in a complex democracy. Political protest encouraged reformers to pursue environmental law campaigns in many public arenas.[30] They quickly understood that even the best lawyer composes only one-half of the advocacy equation. Clients form the other half. A lawyer without a client quite likely violates ethical rules by suing in court or intervening in administrative agency proceedings. And even the essential lawyer-client relationship forms only one-third of the environmental law triangle. Courts that decide cases form another leg, while lawmaking entities—legislatures and executive agencies that administer statutes—constitute the third.

Even before the "environmental decade" of the 1970s got rolling, thoughtful citizens understood lawyers' limitations did not prevent legal change. In 1971, organizers of the first Earth Day published *Earth Tool Kit*. Its editors hung distinctively professional tactics—lawsuits and administrative appeals—on a broad rack of legal tools to reduce pollution and protect human and environmental health. Lawsuits fit within "the whole gamut of nonviolent protest—from lobbying and lawsuits to boycotts, picketing, strikes and harassment."[31] Citizens should consult a lawyer as much for strategic advice as for filing a lawsuit. Tony Roisman, an early Washington, D.C., environmental attorney, advised activist clients to use their legal counsel as "a strategist, a doctor of social problems, . . . an important preliminary advisor to an environmentally concerned group, suggesting what people to contact, in what order, at what time."[32]

Earth Tool Kit echoed Dr. Spock's postwar advice to anxious new mothers. "You know more than you think you do," the good doctor had written. In the same vein, *Earth Tool Kit* reassured citizen activists about their own sovereign competence to make legal change. "Environmental lawsuits are expensive for citizens to pursue, require extensive preparatory research and frequently take years," the book warned. Litigation is a stylized game played by experts. Citizens often lose interest, even if they understand the technical issues. "For these reasons suits should never be the first or only concern of citizen environmental groups. . . . Citizens' efforts, then, should really be directed to all those steps preceding the lawsuit where public opinion and public action may be strong enough to convince a polluter to change his attitude and methods before a lawsuit becomes necessary. This is where a lawyer can serve his most important purpose."[33]

9

*Laws are coldly reasoned out and established upon what the lawmakers believe
to be a basis of right. But customs are not. Customs are not enacted, they grow
gradually up, imperceptibly and unconsciously, like an oak from its seed. In the
fullness of their strength they can stand up straight in front of a world of
argument and reasoning, and yield not an inch. . . . Customs do not concern
themselves with right or wrong or reason. But they have to be obeyed; one may
reason all around them until he is tired, but he must not transgress them, it is
sternly forbidden. . . . Laws are sand, customs are rock. Laws can be evaded and
punishment escaped, but an openly transgressed custom brings sure
punishment.*
—Mark Twain, "The Gorky Incident" (1906)

Americans use environmental law to structure their individual
and social relationships with the natural world. American environmental law, like all legal rules, also enables people to order
their relationships with each other, with those yet unborn, and
with people in other countries. Even though people govern
themselves by making environmental law, its commands both
affect and reflect nonhuman ecological imperatives. Natural
features and forces have, therefore, also made environmental
law. The philosophical convention that confines sovereignty—
the capacity to make binding rules—only to people needs revi-
sion in light of the natural world's own imperative commands.
Environmental law's environmental history reveals that both
American citizens and the natural world exercise complementary sovereignties that changed (and still change) the legal order. Their dual historic agency not only helps explain American
environmental law's emergence, but its structure, scope, and

purposes. Dual sovereignty also illuminates where and why environmental law has failed to attain some of its founders' most ambitious goals. Triumphalists claim that environmental law tells a twentieth-century American legal order "success story." Evidence spread on history's jury table suggests a less hopeful verdict.[1]

"The central principle of our legal order [is] that law exists for the benefit of people and not people for the benefit of law," J. Willard Hurst observed in 1955.[2] Property and contract thus supplied nearly all the environmental law needed for the first three hundred years after Europeans reached North America's shores. These ancient rules defined nature as "resources," enabling people to convert it into private property or national assets. After founding their new nation, Hurst argued, Americans then used law for more than a century to unleash their energies. "The promise of a steeply rising curve of material productivity" supplied "the dynamic of a new kind of society." Across the North American continent and beneath its neighboring oceans, "unclaimed natural abundance together with the promise of new technological command of nature dictated that men should realize their creative energy and exercise their liberty peculiarly in the realm of the economy."[3]

By around 1900, according to Hurst, gross property disparities produced so much political inequality that it destabilized the nineteenth-century legal order. Vivid scenes of environmental waste highlighted unequal access to property that was created when individual liberty commanded natural wealth. Americans then tried to restore a measure of economic and political equality by reordering their relationships with the natural world as the twentieth century began. Citizens began using law to restrain individual freedom to acquire and use property. Lawmakers sought to protect human health by requiring property owners to respect their neighbors' rights as well as their own. By using law to restrain the power conferred by property ownership, citizens hoped to reinvigorate political democracy by restoring economic opportunity.[4]

At the middle of the twentieth century, widespread public health problems and esthetic anxieties intensified Americans' reappraisal of their long national quest to own nature. Their legal order had treated the natural world merely as property, which encouraged them to foul their surroundings as they accumulated wealth. By commodifying nature and exalting liberty, Americans bequeathed their progeny a precarious legacy: polluted air and water, denuded forests, vanishing species, and diminished recreational opportunities. Environmental law emerged as a response to these problems. New legislation and judicial decisions, coming quickly after 1945, recast legal precedents into new methods to accomplish new goals. Americans began using law to slow the rate, and ameliorate the ecological consequences, of handling nature mostly as resource and property.[5]

Environmental lawmaking flourished throughout the United States during the quarter-century after World War II. Citizens both biological and corporate, clients and legal counsel, elected legislators and executives, and appointed judges and administrators all combined their distinctive shares of sovereignty. In cities, states, and at the federal level they crafted new rules governing private and governmental conduct. Diverse lawmakers aimed to adjust some important, long-standing relationships that linked Americans to the natural world. Of course, their new laws could not displace fundamental physical and scientific principles through which nature shaped humanity; legislatures cannot amend the law of conservation of energy, and judges cannot enjoin photosynthesis. Neither did lawmakers repeal popular convictions nor abolish personal beliefs. Citizens and their public servants preserved national independence, encouraged personal consumption, and celebrated private mobility. Instead, Americans' new rules tried to better align human relationships with the natural world by adjusting how people dealt with one another. Nearly all the legal changes recast rules of the political realm, where citizens—in groups, as individuals, and artificially as business corporations—encountered the state.

Environmental lawmaking in the postwar era established five core principles before 1970. Citizens could participate in making many, though not all, governmental decisions that altered nature. Courts stopped reflexively deferring to governmental agencies' plans to alter natural features and remodel natural forces. The individual's liberty to transform private property became a legitimate matter of public debate and state regulation. Legal counsel learned techniques to assert their clients' right to challenge public and private actions that threatened to disorder nature. And public regulation of private activity that degraded the earth's environment overstepped formal boundaries that separated governmental jurisdictions.

By 1970, many lawmakers' combined labors had created new means to enforce public policies, outlined contours of a new jurisprudence, opened a recognizable new field for attorneys to practice, and invented a subject that warranted specialized instruction in American law schools. Such prodigious legal creation warranted a new label. Before the later 1960s, lawyers and those who wrote about law had not used the term "environmental law." After 1970, as lawmakers shifted from creating new principles to applying and routinizing them, the phrase became commonplace.[6] Before the early 1970s, law publishers included environmental topics within books under the traditional categories of "Natural Resources Law," "Local Government," or "Torts." By 1977, West Publishing Company of St. Paul, Minnesota, the nation's leading lawbook publisher, offered students and teachers four separate volumes on pollution and environmental law.[7]

Environmental law emerged when it did and developed as it did because a distinctive human society, encountering nature's sovereign power, adapted traditional rules during a particular time. Americans during the decade after World War II debated the meaning of freedom amid a string of environmental crises generated by the long national onslaught against nature.[8] Citizens beset by pollution and shamed by the ugliness of a damaged environment concluded that old legal rules—property, contract, nuisance, tort—often prevented them from enjoying their hard-earned prosperity. The "problem" of abundance seemingly having vanquished the fear of scarcity, laws that traditionally handled nature as property were plainly worsening environmental problems by impeding their solution.[9]

Postwar environmental lawmaking blended practical solutions to problems with penetrating self-criticism. New environmental laws that were intended to secure Americans' place within nature also dramatized their new place in the Cold War world. In various international forums following World War II, American diplomats were trying to discipline nationalism to respect international order. Many understood that even the most powerful country could never enjoy security if the whole world feared war. In like fashion, American lawmakers endeavored to trim property's prerogatives to better serve community needs. If future generations were to live prosperously and well within functioning ecosystems, they needed environmental law to maintain individual liberty by conserving its natural preconditions. Conservation activists thus began scrutinizing freedom's toll on public health, personal safety, and natural beauty. Liberty and property, they argued, must promote security and opportunity, fortifying the nation from within to surmount challenges from abroad. National security depended on environmental health as well as on military strength and economic might.

Americans after World War II ultimately turned to federal environmental lawmaking because, first, their municipalities and then their states proved unable to safeguard either public health or natural systems on which human life depends. Nascent environmental sciences revealed how human alteration of biotic systems triggered impacts that made lines on political maps meaningless in any legal or ecological sense. Even when local or state governments overcame political resistance to enact stronger controls on enterprise, a single jurisdiction could not effectively manage environmental threats, like air and water pollution, that ignored boundaries.

National markets, created and served by the great industries that arose after the Civil War, facilitated environmental law's growth after 1945. Ecological damage, like the economic enterprises causing it, crossed state lines with impunity. Congress, encouraged by generous Supreme Court interpretations during the New Deal, extended national law to the very limits of the Constitution's Interstate Commerce Clause (Article I). When federal law encountered conflicting state and local rules, the Constitution's Supremacy Clause (Article VI) ensured federal primacy. Constitutional boundaries to Commerce Clause environmental lawmaking have only recently been suggested by a handful of Supreme Court decisions. Federal primacy to make environmental laws that shape human activity on the 700 million acres of public lands—national forests and rangelands, defense facilities, Indian reservations—has never been doubted, given the Constitution's expansive Federal Property Clause (Article IV).

Until the very end of the nineteenth century, courts that resolved private legal disputes about contracts and property through common-law adjudication made most legal decisions about nature. After 1900, Progressive reformers at both the state and national levels began grafting new branches onto private law's old roots: legislative statutes administered by expert civil servants in executive branch agencies. The Great Depression, New Deal, and World War II all cemented this new "administrative state" into American law's framework between 1930 and 1950. Administration became the preferred legal method to handle complex problems that were caused by harnessing private action to serve public needs. Measured by their sheer output, administrative agencies—some directly responsible to the executive branch and others formally independent—have since the late 1970s made the most influential, and problematic, environmental law. For example, the Environmental Protection Agency regulates how farmers apply pesticides to their fields, the National Park Service determines how tourists use motorized vehicles to traverse our public lands, and the Bureau of Land Management superintends millions of cattle that each year munch their share of the public domain.[10]

Even before Congress enacted such keystone statutes as the Clean Air Act and Clean Water Act around 1970, the administrative law process was making environmental law. The most important environmental law Americans have never heard of, the 1946 Administrative Procedure Act (APA), established a rough but flexible workbench on which much lawmaking took place. The APA's authors intended to ensure that elected representatives made basic policy choices, professional administrators executed those choices in everyday matters, and federal judges protected constitutional rights to liberty and property by reviewing both agency action and congressional statute writing. Nearly every celebrated environmental legal dispute now turns on application of the Administrative Procedure Act. A federal agency makes rules to apply a congressional statute to tackle real-world problems. A regulated government entity, business, or individual decides how or whether to observe the rules. And a judge resolves a lawsuit that challenges the agency's action. Despite its formal title, the APA makes as much environmental as "procedural" law. Many "little APAs" have exerted equally significant impact, over time, on the shape and consequences of state-made environmental law.

Environmental law's postwar growth highlights how lawmakers have veered through contested intersections between power and principle. The Constitution's power-sharing structure guaranteed not only tensions among the three federal branches, but between the national government and the states. Creative opportunism flourished when blunt economic leverage and shrill rhetoric infused the careful, even mundane, routine of rule-parsing. Legal professionals have jousted with scientific experts. In spite of popular misconceptions that law is for lawyers, ordinary citizens—whether a state legislative committee drafting a pollution bill or a federal court jury weighing a takings claim for money damages—have frequently had to decide the meaning of the nation's foundational legal document, the United States Constitution.

Federal enforcement of national statutes has dominated environmental law headlines for the past three decades, but all fifty states and nearly every size and type of local government have contributed to making the complex body of rules that adjust citizens' relationships to land, air, water, and non-human life forms. All of the keystone federal pollution control statutes, with the exception of the 1969 National Environmental Policy Act, require substantial state and local lawmaking. American federalism, an uneasy and often unpredictable blend of national authority with residual state (and local) sovereignty, therefore requires lawyers and citizens to heed environmental law made and enforced beyond Washington, D.C.

Environmental law's state and local heritage invests federalism with more influence than most environmental law histories have understood. Local and state law still bear a powerful, though often unrealized, potential to recast human relationships with each other and with nature. American law was once English common law, for the most part. Common law embedded the "police power" deep within the fabric of Anglo-American law. Police power entitles state and local governments to restrain private liberties such as property ownership and individual action to protect the public welfare. For more than three centuries, local and state governments have deployed their police powers to keep drinking water pure, make workplaces safer, and abate landowners' nuisance behavior that menaces both neighbors' rights to enjoy their own property and the public's right to live in healthful peace. Liberty and property occupy sanctified status in American law. Yet the police power's coercive capacity to restrain private conduct can still protect environmental quality in the ordinary places where people live and work.[11]

Essentials of Environmental Law, a handbook written in the mid-1990s "to present the basics of American environmental law so that anyone can understand them," catalogued the field's primary features. Chief among them are

Federalism—the division of legal authority between the national government and the fifty states

Politics—the continuous making, and remaking, of law by contests among interested actors seeking advantage over adversaries

Administration—the execution of laws enacted by elected representatives through expert efforts by appointed public employees

Property—the state's delineation and protection of citizens' possession and control of tangible nature through intangible instruments such as corporations and deeds

Liberty—the bedrock political right to act without restraint, secured by the United States Constitution's deep historical links to property ownership

Technology—the paired biases of an environmental law system that favors continuous private innovation of productive means while depending on that very innovation to regulate humans' impacts on nature

Reaction—law's inherently conservative tendency to preserve existing situations until urgent natural crises or political demands require coercion to regulate human conduct

Professionalism—the reliance on expertise, whether legal, technical, managerial, or political, instead of citizens' intervention to effectuate law's purposes

Routine—the preference for rules that maintain ingrained norms and systems of thought and practice instead of relying on invasive coercion to stimulate change

Nationalism—the limited application of most laws to United States territory coupled with disdain for international rules enforced by supranational institutions[12]

Modern environmental law reflects the circumstances of its postwar emergence. Though many commentators have praised environmental law's fluidity as evidence of Americans' genius for marrying politics to principle, original flaws in the new system of legal restraints have only widened under pressure. Environmental law's postwar makers didn't use government power to coerce individuals. They rarely challenged corporate power. They never promoted a new public ethos that condemned irresponsible consumption by saluting cautious conservation. Whenever opponents captured the political initiative to renew the debate between liberty and security, environmental law proved mutable—which aided its persistence—and unstable. Environmental law's instability has, especially after 1980, limited its capacity to help enforce the balance that its creators sought to establish. Human communities' demands have consequently outrun the natural environment's capacities. [13]

"The legitimate monopoly of force is a distinctive mark of the law," J. Willard Hurst observed in 1956. Divided authority, timid enforcement, expert deference, and political vulnerability have often rendered environmental law more rhetorical than forceful. Born amid postwar federalism's power struggles, environmental law's joint state and federal heritage produced unending disagreements over its most basic purposes. Political negotiations between economically unequal parties subjected environmental law to perennial uncertainty. Wealthy actors, both public and private, learned to elude its commands, which has undermined the predictability that sustains a legal field's legitimacy. Environmental law enforcement has often encountered fierce popular resistance to state restraints on economic liberty because it emerged well after political conservatives had euthanized whatever crusading zeal once fired the New Deal. The Cold War stimulated citizens to wonder aloud about the meaning of liberty and security, but vicious anticommunist paranoia stigmatized the very concept of popular dissent against corporate influence and expert leadership.[14]

Environmental law emerged amid the nation's most voracious economic expansion. Capitalistic incentives so permeated environmental law that its mild restraints have generally impeded only the grossest displays of Americans' consumptive impulses. Americans in the 1950s preferred experts' opinions to adjust social problems, so their new environmental rules diluted citizen criticism of government or business. Rudimentary postwar ecological science, often generated and managed within a cozy government and business duopoly, left regulators long ignorant about technological change's accelerating environmental impacts. Environmental law thrived on technological adaptation of productive processes because regulators believed that engineers could solve pollution problems. Content to let capitalists design their production systems, Americans declined to make new rules that redirected innovation toward more benign goals. Scientific ignorance encouraged reactive, crisis-mode law enforcement. Environmental law has thus proven mostly powerless to diagnose, let alone avert, long-term injuries that prevent Earth from healing itself.

"Life is not a melodrama," J. Willard Hurst observed. "Law consists more in policy developed out of rather routinely handled instances than in policy developed in moments of drama." Environmental law emerged incrementally and responsively, unfolding like any complex system created in human time to meet human needs. Law evolves slowly, as legal change organically preserves precedent. Environmental rules might therefore have been especially well-suited to match the long, slow unfolding of natural processes. Yet so frequently have American lawmakers revisited the perennial debate between liberty and security that political instability has often knocked environmental law out of any possible synchronization with the natural systems it was supposed to guard.[15]

The 1980 Reagan landslide marked American environmental law's transition from adolescence to middle age. The creative lawmaking era that opened after 1945 had largely sputtered out during the decade of the 1970s. Obscured by political smoke and fury in the early 1980s, but now visible a quarter-century afterward, Reaganism exposed environmental law's unrealized promise. Despite the creative fizz bubbling around its youthful exuberance, environmental law's apparent vigor yielded more administrative form than legal substance. Its early architects compromised with individual liberty and corporate political power. The price that citizens and natural systems paid for compromise came due by the end of the twentieth century. Accelerating suburban sprawl accompanied, and perhaps unleashed, frenzied private mobility. Unchecked market capitalism intensified global heating by promoting expanded use of fossil fuels for indoor comfort and exterior mobility. Profound climate change was already measurable by 2000. Healthy ecosystems continue to decline across the globe. Basic problems that inspired the founders of environmental law have stubbornly defied both international cooperation and domestic cure.[16]

Fierce partisan struggle for the presidency at the end of the 1970s subjected environmental law to tremendous political pressure. Presidential candidate Reagan and his Republican allies criticized much of the "environmental decade's" legal output. Backed by many small and large businesses that resented restraints imposed by new laws enacted since the latter 1960s, Republicans sought public endorsement, and Jimmy Carter's defeat, by promising to repeal or at least amend many new statutes and rules. Reagan decisively defeated Carter while Republicans captured a Senate majority in 1980. Both independent commentators and partisan combatants attributed some of the outcome to combative conservatives' critique of environmentalism and environmental law. Conservative Republicans attacked taxes and civil rights laws' enforcement and equated environmental protection with oppressive, expensive government controls on business initiative and individual liberties.[17]

Law displays properties of momentum as well as inertia, so the growth of environmental law did not simply stop with Reagan's January 1981 inauguration. Agencies made new law—volumes of it—by adopting regulations. Courts, by interpreting statutes and rules to resolve hundreds of disputes, applied extant law in new ways. The president and Congress each year shaped the executive budget to enable dozens of agencies to pursue environmental objectives that were previously assigned. As spending power enables positive law to affect real life, annual appropriation bills made new law each year. Of course, in the fifty states, counterpart institutions in the three branches performed similar lawmaking functions. Contemporary observers, both supporters and enemies, generally forecast more legal growth.

American environmental law nevertheless entered adulthood after 1981, and soon reached middle age in the 1990s. With Congress and the president increasingly concentrated on guidance, political representatives and the people who elected them preferred maintenance to creation. Lawmakers mainly oversaw administration of laws enacted during the preceding twenty years. During its precocious adolescence, environmental law became a productive system, capable of regeneration by sinking roots, growing branches, bearing fruit. As it entered middle age, however, its enthusiasts in public life turned to consolidating gains and refining methods. Activists out of doors rarely rallied to demand new rules, usually preoccupied with waging rearguard actions to resist fundamental ideological challenge.

Environmental law's distinctive emergence during the three decades after World War II weakened its capacity to realize its creators' hopes. A quarter-century after its creative period ended during the 1970s, environmental law's inbred disabilities hadn't prevented Americans from heating the earth's atmosphere to ecologically dangerous levels, consuming a disproportionate share of the earth's irreplaceable resources, patronizing industries that moved their pollution to poorer nations, and ignoring national policies that condemn the world's poor to lives threatened by scarce water, poor nutrition, and unequal power to shape nature's fate.[18]

Environmental law's character flaws confound political, social, and economic efforts to discipline American citizens. Rarely stopping, scarcely discouraging people from doing the very things that degraded natural systems in the first place, environmental law preserved customary freedoms and accepted economic and political structures. Environmental law enabled citizens to drive big private cars, subdivide open green spaces, build huge houses that require vast amounts of energy to heat and cool and light, entertain themselves with devices powered by rising electricity demands, patronize businesses that transform natural resources into consumer goods on a global scale, and demand an ascending level of material comfort. Instead of making Earth's health every American's duty, the structure of environmental law has attenuated civic responsibility. Few citizens today make personal choices and take collective action to stop global warming; and even fewer act as if they believe doing so will matter. Rather than using law to discipline themselves, Americans hope their governments will somehow devise solutions. Time and again, however, citizens have failed to empower their governments to impose the restraints they themselves fail to observe.[19]

Americans began building a complex environmental law system shortly after World War II ended. Compromising all along the line with liberty and power, environmental lawmakers constructed an unsteady system that appeared more impressive, measured by volume, than it proved effective, measured by results. By settling for what they could get during foreshortened electoral cycles, its makers purchased incremental gains at the price of declining public attention and deepening ecological crisis. A staggering quantity of written law packs the shelves and glows on lawyers' and clients' computer monitors. Cohorts of environmental law teachers and phalanxes of practitioners write, talk, and convene. Hopeful rhetoric hails each new iteration or application of precedent. In spite of this evidence, environmental law's trajectory during the twenty-first century's first decade has traced doctrinal stasis and intellectual limbo. Dimly recalled, when not largely ignored, its creators' hopeful ambitions may slip into any legal field's ultimate purgatory: monotonous irrelevance, routine application, marginal effects, intangible outcomes, and popular media and political indifference.

Environmental law at the outset of the twenty-first century resembles labor law during the last decades of the twentieth. This historic legal field, now grown dull and prosaic, once crackled with life, struggle, and consequence. Between corporate capital captained by privileged wealth and rude labor inspired by eager agitators, a fierce struggle for the soul of America's economy once raged. Rules that negotiated the battle's truce, formalized into labor law after 1935, succeeded beyond its conservative opponents' wildest dreams in dulling organized labor's political sting. During the quarter-century that linked the Great Depression to the Eisenhower presidency, labor law offered workers a life raft. By the sixties, labor law had become a party boat, lively and comfortable for those lucky enough to sail, but less relevant than ever with each passing season because a dwindling number of unionized passengers boarded. After the 1970s, American labor law became the *Flying Dutchman*, unable to navigate, let alone anticipate accelerating currents that transformed modes of production and distribution. Once-hot boilers banked, crew listless, its purpose simply to remain afloat, labor law has drifted aimlessly during the last quarter-century, placidly riding the deep, still waters that eventually characterize all established, arcane legal fields.[20]

Labor law's fate may foreshadow what will happen to environmental law if the environment's fate recedes from public concern, no longer a defined "problem" to be addressed by governmental action. Even as environmental scientists attained a level of sophistication by the 1980s that emboldened them to speak with far greater urgency than they had in the 1960s, environmental policy slipped off citizens' agendas. After Reagan's 1980 election, crime and public safety commanded local TV news programming and newspaper headlines in all the places, large and small, where Americans lived. Breathless reports, redolent of decaying order and spreading disorder, dominated national print and electronic journalism. Popular interest, reflected and magnified in the mass media, fanned a sort of collective dread, and even hysteria. Sensational news coverage may not have reflected an actual increase in crime during the 1980s but it certainly nurtured the decade's focus on criminal law. Bombarded by media accounts of crime, citizens increasingly told pollsters they wanted criminal law changed to match their changing beliefs. Uppermost in the public mind were linked convictions about the American criminal law system: first, that old laws defining and punishing criminal behavior had grown inadequate; and second, that lawmakers—politicians, judges, and law enforcement officers—should make new law.

The "problem" of crime, between 1980 and 2000, generated a flurry of lawmaking at all governmental levels, from village hall to the United States Supreme Court. Buffeted by nervous, insistent citizens, elected and appointed officials directed an intense political movement that remodeled the law of crime and punishment. By the mid-1990s, the campaign to make more criminal law and to raise its profile within the American legal order had succeeded. State and federal statute books carried thousands of new pages of laws. Legislators both criminalized conduct that previously went unregulated and imposed new penalties on existing criminal acts. Police enforced new laws and filed millions of new criminal charges. Courts not only applied these new laws to convict and sentence; they increasingly revisited older decisions to make arrest, conviction, and punishment under existing statutes easier. Executives and legislators cooperated to raise taxes and reorder priorities, spending hundreds of billions of dollars, at all governmental levels, to build thousands of new jail cells. And legions of new offenders filled these cells, incarcerated by the American state at all levels, from city jail to federal penitentiary.[21]

Criminologists and public officials still disagree, a decade later, whether new criminal laws enacted and enforced between 1980 and 1995 actually slowed rising rates of criminality or simply reflected new public frustration with behavior previously deplored but not prosecuted. No observer, then or now, doubts how intensely Americans wanted to build a new criminal law structure and how richly they rewarded its key governmental architects.

The public face of the anticrime, pro-order crusade became a staple of TV news programs and pictures above the fold of newspapers across the country. Stern-faced, clad in a dark business suit or police uniform, bathed in spotlights, commanding a podium bedecked with a seal of state or overseeing a table spread with drugs, guns, cash, or pornography, often flanked by underlings, stood an elected prosecutor or one of his telegenic deputies, a police chief, or a federal law enforcement officer. He delivered a no-nonsense message couched in heated rhetoric about the scourge of crime, the plague of the disorderly, and the community's determination to change the dynamic by taking quick, strong, visible, state action. Criminal law became again, as it had been so often in the twentieth century, "hot" and vital, the subject of kitchen-table chat and coffee-shop arguments. It was salient, productive and clearly alive, responsive to what nearly all responsible observers deemed to be the people's will that justice be done.

Contrast criminal law's face with that which American labor law presented after 1981. A handful of recognizable union officials occasionally garnered a few minutes of news time. A smattering of strikers sporadically appeared on TV, or in newspapers, punctuating the quiet business of labor and management relations with their signs, demands, and picket lines. No ordinary American could name the Secretary of Labor, the chair of the National Labor Relations Board, the vice presidents responsible for personnel at any of the biggest 100 American businesses, or the national leaders of any trade union except perhaps the AFL-CIO president. No American could name the previous year's key labor law cases decided in the federal courts. Hardly any could describe any significant labor legislation debated, or even enacted, by the federal government.

Labor law, so volatile and contested for the first fifty years of the twentieth century, had become routinized and bureaucratized. It receded from the national consciousness, becoming nearly invisible to all but the declining handful of citizens who worked in union-organized industries. Public officials whose daily job it was to manage the vast body of law, and legal professionals whose duty it was to implement and adjust it, worked mostly beyond ordinary people's understanding. Labor law had become part of the economic system, no more contested or political than settled rules of contract, agency, or trusts and estates.

Like labor law between 1930 and 1955, environmental law emerged between 1945 and 1970 as a contested creation amid vivid political and social struggles. Like labor law, environmental law reflects both new rules specific to the conditions of its birth and internal evolution of older legal principles. Still visible and vital, therefore, are environmental law's heritage in the law of property and contract, nuisance and tort, business corporations and municipal government. Labor and environmental law share another paradoxical trait: born amid strife as a means of restraining capitalism's relentless expansion, both kinds of law pacified early battlefields by turning political conflict into prosaic dispute resolution. Daily, routine practice by government agencies and regulated business has largely defanged environmental law's original critical bite. Even as its overriding objective of slowing the rate of human-caused change to the environment has become more imperative, American environmental law has gradually become less confrontational.

Legal academics James Krier and Edmund Ursin claimed in 1977 that environmental law's "dramatic" emergence "marked a sharp break with the past."[22] Like most easy conclusions, theirs has proved wrong. Americans did limit themselves by creating new rules, but the environmental law they made was not—nor did they intend it to be—a comprehensive legal system blending coercion and incentives to restructure citizens' relationship with the natural world. Instead, a quarter-century's perspective on its emergence reveals environmental law's persistent instability. Institutional weakness and intellectual contradictions, present from the creation, have preserved the very tendencies in American life environmental law might have reformed.

Most middle-aged, middle-class Americans, as the twenty-first century turns ten, appear at least as impulsive, materialistic, domineering, ignorant, and heedless as their parents and grandparents who helped make environmental law. Resentful of restraints on consumption, dedicated to maximizing their comfort, eager to wield ever-greater power over nature, twenty-first-century citizens seem unable to perceive their culpability in causing dangerous environmental changes. Despite their widespread acceptance of environmental law's existence, few Americans appear willing to mobilize either its coercive capacity or creative potential to promote public policies or private behaviors that promise to abate the serious challenges already besetting their society.

Should this lassitude persist, environmental law's future will track labor law's past. But if Americans once more recognize how actions have consequences, environmental law may again become a tool to help manage change. Revived, environmental law can perhaps attain its founders' hopes by becoming a vibrant mechanism of community-made rules to preserve the natural environment while striking better balances between private and public interests. In the midst of deepening global political and economic crises, measured by food scarcities and monster storms that leave utter devastation in their wakes, any other course of action consigns us to a fate far graver than courtroom litigation.

NOTES

PREFACE

1. Karl Boyd Brooks, *Public Power, Private Dams: The Hells Canyon High Dam Controversy* (Seattle: University of Washington Press, 2006).

2. Arthur McEvoy, *The Fisherman's Problem: Ecology and Law in the California Fisheries, 1850–1980* (New York: Cambridge University Press, 1986); Edmund Russell, *War and Nature: Fighting Humans and Insects with Chemicals from World War I to Silent Spring* (New York: Cambridge University Press, 2001).

3. All presentations during the 6–7 October 2005 University of Virginia conference, entitled "Environmental Letters, Environmental Law: A Cross-Disciplinary Conference Exploring the Impacts of the Humanities on Environmental Law," are reprinted in *Virginia Environmental Law Journal* 24, 3 (2005).

4. Richard J. Lazarus, *The Making of Environmental Law* (Chicago: University of Chicago Press, 2004).

5. Edmund Russell, "'Speaking of Annihilation': Mobilizing for War against Human and Insect Enemies," *Journal of American History* 82 (March 1996): 1505–1529.

6. Brooks, *Public Power, Private Dams*, extensively discusses these events and their legal and environmental implications.

7. Joseph Cone and Sandy Ridlington, eds., *The Northwest Salmon Crisis: A Documentary History* (Corvallis: Oregon State University Press, 1996); Michael C. Blumm, "The Northwest's Hydroelectric Heritage," in Dale D. Goble and Paul W. Hirt, eds., *Northwest Lands, Northwest Peoples: Readings in Environmental History* (Seattle: University of Washington Press, 1999).

8. Rodney P. Carlisle and Joan M. Zenzen, *Supplying the Nuclear Arsenal: American Production Reactors, 1942–1992* (Baltimore: Johns Hopkins University Press, 1996); Carl Berger, *B29: The Superfortress* (New York: Ballantine Books, 1970).

9. Department of Defense, "At Home on the Range," 4 April 2001, www.defenselink.mil/news/newsarticle.aspx?id=45051 (accessed 30 November 2007).

10. Paul Charles Milazzo, *Unlikely Environmentalists: Congress and Clean Water, 1945–1972* (Lawrence: University Press of Kansas, 2006).

11. J. Willard Hurst, *Law and Economic Growth: The Legal History of the Lumber Industry in Wisconsin, 1836–1915* (Cambridge, Mass.: Belknap Press of Harvard University, 1964).

CHAPTER 1. "TO THINK LIKE AN ENVIRONMENTAL LAWYER: MAKING
ENVIRONMENTAL LAW THROUGHOUT THE POSTWAR ERA

1. *Lawrence Journal-World*, 7 August 2003, 1B; City of Lawrence Dept. of Utilities, *The Water We Drink: 2003* [in author's possession].

2. *Lawrence Journal-World*, 29 April 2003, 8B.

3. *Kansas City Star*, 5 June 2003, B4.

4. "Wildlife Group Opposes . . . Dams," *Idaho Statesman*, 11 January 1954, 3/16/1, MS 721, Bruce Bowler Papers, Idaho State Historical Society. Materials from the Bowler Papers will be cited thus: [box number]/[folder number]/[series number], BP.

5. IWF Protest, FPC Project 2147 [Clearwater dams], 2 March 1954, 3/16/1, BP.

6. Bruce Bowler to Rep. Hamer Budge, 28 July 1954; Sen. Henry Dworshak to Bowler, 30 July 1954, enclosing Under Secretary of Agriculture True D. Morse to Dworshak, 28 July 1954, 21/11/2, BP; Theo. H. Wegener (IWF) to Mr. ____, 2 August 1954, 15/9/2, BP.

7. IWF Legislative Bulletin, 18 March 1957; IWF 1958 Annual Meeting Minutes, 3/17/1, BP.

8. K. D. Flock to Ross Leonard, copying Bowler, 10 September 1957, 15/9/2, BP.

9. Richard N. L. Andrews, *Managing the Environment, Managing Ourselves: A History of American Environmental Policy* (New Haven, Conn.: Yale University Press, 1999), 372; William H. Rodgers, Jr., *Handbook on Environmental Law* (St. Paul, Minn.: West Publishing, 1977), 1; Richard J. Lazarus, *The Making of Environmental Law* (Chicago: University of Chicago Press, 2004), 1.

10. William P. Cunningham and Barbara Woodworth Saigo, *Environmental Science: A Global Concern*, 5th ed. (Boston: WCB/McGraw-Hill, 1999), offers a useful introduction to the vast field.

11. Steven Stoll, *U.S. Environmentalism since 1945: A Brief History with Documents* (Boston: Bedford/St. Martin's, 2007), 10–12; Lazarus, *Making of Environmental Law*; and Ted Steinberg, *Down to Earth: Nature's Role in American History* (New York: Oxford University Press, 2002), 240–253, all offer representative chronologies.

12. Nancy K. Kubasek and Gary S. Silverman, *Environmental Law*, 3d ed. (Upper Saddle River, N.J.: Prentice-Hall, 2000), 123.

13. John Adams quoted in Alan Brinkley et al., *American History: A Survey*, 8th ed. (New York: McGraw-Hill, 1991), 111; Mark Hamilton Lytle, *The Gentle Subversive: Rachel Carson, Silent Spring, and the Rise of the Environmental Movement* (New York: Oxford University Press, 2007).

14. Adam Rome, "'Give Earth a Chance': The Environmental Movement and the

Sixties," *Journal of American History* 90 (September 2003): 525–554, argues environmentalism itself emerged as a powerful popular political current before 1970.

15. John-Mark Stensvaag, *Materials on Environmental Law* (St. Paul: West Group, 1999), v.

16. Samuel P. Hays, *A History of Environmental Politics Since 1945* (Pittsburgh: University of Pittsburgh Press, 2000), 5–35.

17. Karl Brooks, "'Powerless' No More: Postwar Judges and Pacific Northwest Hydroelectrification, 1946–1967," *Idaho Yesterdays* 45 (Winter 2001–2002): 11–26; and "Illuminating the Postwar Northwest: Private Power and Public Law in Hells Canyon, 1950–1957," *Western Legal History* 12 (Winter/Spring 1999): 49–75.

18. Andrews, *Managing the Environment*, 201–225.

19. *Hadley v. Baxendale*, 9 Exchq. Rptr. 341 (1854), in Lon L. Fuller and Melvin Aron Eisenberg, eds., *Basic Contract Law*, 3d ed. (St. Paul: West Publishing Co., 1972). Plaintiffs could not. That is, lost profits caused by weather were not "the natural consequences" of the carrier's inability to deliver the contracted part.

20. Stensvaag, *Materials on Environmental Law*, 140; Robert V. Percival, Alan S. Miller, Christopher H. Schroeder, and James P. Leape, *Environmental Regulation: Law, Science, and Policy* (Boston: Little, Brown & Co., 1992), 72.

21. Frank Grad, *Environmental Law: Sources and Problems* (New York: Matthew Bender Co., 1971), 2–43 to 2–222, skims through the pre-1971 water pollution laws in fifteen pages, then devotes 164 pages to the post-1971 statutory and regulatory framework.

22. Stensvaag, 2. So decisive was 1970 that Stensvaag entitled this part of *Materials* "Environmental Law Origins." Although he carefully acknowledges "modern environmental law was not created out of nothing," all the American evidence cited in his Chapter One postdates 1970, with the oldest from 1981. His only evidence about law and nature predating 1970 comes from medieval Italian city ordinances.

23. Percival, Miller, Schroeder, and Leape, *Environmental Regulation*, xxxii, 1, 6, 106.

24. J. Willard Hurst, *The Growth of American Law: The Law Makers* (Boston: Little Brown, 1950); *Law and the Conditions of Freedom in the Nineteenth-Century United States* (Madison: University of Wisconsin Press, 1956); and *Law and Social Process in United States History* (Ann Arbor: University of Michigan Law School, 1960).

25. J. Willard Hurst, *Law and Economic Growth: The Legal History of the Lumber Industry in Wisconsin, 1836–1915* (Cambridge: Belknap Press of Harvard University, 1964); Cunningham and Saigo, *Environmental Science*, 293–316, introduce the ecological relationships at work in forests.

26. Lloyd K. Garrison, "Willard Hurst: A Tribute," *Wisconsin Law Review* (1980):

1095–1097; Robert W. Gordon, "J. Willard Hurst and the Common Law Tradition in American Legal Historiography," *Law and Society* 10 (Fall 1975): 9–55.

27. John Opie, *Nature's Nation: An Environmental History of the United States* (Ft. Worth, Tex.: Harcourt Brace, 1998), 379–383; Donald Worster, ed., *The Ends of the Earth: Perspectives on Modern Environmental History* (New York: Cambridge University Press, 1988).

28. Lawrence M. Friedman, *History of American Law* (New York: Simon & Schuster, 1973), 595.

29. Ibid.; Kermit L. Hall and Peter Karsten, *The Magic Mirror: Law in American History*, 2d ed. (New York: Oxford University Press, 2009).

30. Arthur McEvoy, *The Fisherman's Problem: Ecology and Law in the California Fisheries, 1850–1980* (New York: Cambridge University Press: 1986); Theodore Steinberg, *Slide Mountain, Or the Folly of Owning Nature* (Berkeley: University of California Press, 1995); Lazarus, *Making of Environmental Law.*

CHAPTER 2. SEED-TIME: PLANTING ENVIRONMENTAL LAW IN THE POSTWAR YEARS

1. Charles H. Callison, "The Real Value of Wildlife," *Missouri Conservationist*, November 1945, 4.

2. Louis J. Halle, Jr., "Gabrielson," *Audubon Magazine* 48 (May–June 1946): 140–144.

3. E. Sydney Stephens, "Where Are We and What Time Is It?" *Transactions of the 11th North American Wildlife Conference* (Washington, D.C.: American Wildlife Institute, 1946), 24.

4. Interview with Robert McNeil, Mt. Vernon, Virginia, 20 June 2002 [in author's possession]. McNeil, trained as a Richmond journalist in the 1950s after graduating from Washington and Lee University in 1949, joined Senator Robertson's staff in 1960. He reported extensively during the 1950s on Robertson's move from the House to the Senate, where he became one of the body's leaders on legislation affecting international economics and banking.

5. McNeil's interview describes the 1946 Senate special election's intensity. Robertson maneuvered around the Byrd machine's favorite son during two steamy days of conventioneering in Richmond's "Mosque," without openly appearing to break with Governor Byrd. Biding his time, Byrd let Robertson win a full Senate term in 1948 but then tried and failed to force him out in 1954, when the senator again outfoxed him by secretly securing enough commitments from key county party chairs to foil the machine. For the Pittman-Robertson hunting excise tax, see Paul Tulenko, "The Federal-Aid Wildlife Program in Missouri," *Missouri Conservationist*, July 1946, 4.

For the fishing excise tax, see "Back the Robertson Bill," *Missouri Conservationist*, November 1946, i. *Biographical Directory of the United States Congress, 1774–1971* (Washington, D.C.: Government Printing Office, 1971), 1726, contains Robertson's basic biography.

6. National Research Council and The Wildlife Society, *Some Wildlife Jobs Awaiting Attention*, in House Select Committee on Conservation of Wildlife, *Hearings under H. Res. 75*, 79th Cong., 2d sess. (1946), 112–123.

7. House Select Committee on Conservation of Wildlife, *Report on Conservation of Wildlife*, H.R. Rept. 2743, 79th Cong., 2d sess. (1947), 97.

8. Ibid., 1–3, 96–97.

9. A. Willis Robertson ["AWR"] to M. D. "Mack" Hart, 3 January 1945; Hart to AWR, 4 January 1945, Drawer 128, Folio 38, A. Willis Robertson Papers, Special Collections Department, William and Mary College, Williamsburg, Virginia [hereafter "RP"].

10. Gwathmey to AWR, 22 July 1945, RP.

11. AWR Speech, Izaak Walton League National Convention, 25 March 1947, speech files, RP.

12. Ibid.

13. AWR to Oshkosh, Wisconsin, Conservation Dinner, 15 June 1946, speech files, RP.

14. James A. Austin to AWR, 18 June 1946; AWR to Austin, 19 June 1946, legislation files, 79th Cong., 2d Sess., drawer 3, folio 24, RP. AWR to John H. Gwathmey, 19 July 1945; Gwathmey to AWR, 22 July 1945, miscellaneous subject files: Commission on Game and Fish 1943–1945, Drawer 128, Folio 38, RP.

15. William Voigt Speech to Denver Rotary Club, 12 August 1948, folder 24, drawer 13, legislation files, RP.

16. I. T. Bode, "Wildlife Stake in Flood Control Planning," *Missouri Conservationist*, September 1945, 1.

17. G. B. Herndon, "Can We Expect Good Fishing in Big, Man-Made Lakes?" *Missouri Conservationist*, March 1946, 4.

18. Senate Agriculture and Forestry Committee, *Hearings on H.R. 6097*, 79th Cong., 2d sess. (19 July 1946), 5, 63.

19. H.R. 6097, 79th Cong., 2d sess., Public Law 732, 60 Stat. 1080, was finally enacted in July 1946, less than a week before the 79th Congress adjourned, and signed by President Truman in August. It largely repealed its toothless New Deal predecessor, the 1934 Coordination Act (Act of 10 March 1934, 48 Stat. 401).

20. *Hearings on H.R. 6097*, 13–15, 41, 63.

21. Ibid., 40.

22. *Congressional Record: Senate*, vol. 92 (17 July 1946), 9205.

23. Interview with Charles McDowell, 13 June 2002, Washington, D.C. [in author's possession]; McNeil Interview. McDowell was Washington correspondent for the *Richmond Times-Dispatch* during the latter part of Robertson's 1946–1966 Senate career.

24. *Hearings on H.R. 6097*, 37–38, 40. McNeil admired Robertson immensely, but acknowledged his boss's formal oratorical style surrendered in gravity what it won in earnestness. McNeil Interview.

25. AWR to Truman, 25 July 1946; Darling to Charles Ross, 14 August 1946; Stephens to Truman, 31 July 1946, official file 177, Box 793, Papers of the President, Truman Presidential Library, Independence, Missouri [hereafter Truman Library].

26. Leland Olds to Frederick J. Bailey (Bureau of Budget Assistant Director), 7 August 1946; Julius A. Krug to James E. Webb (Bureau of Budget Director), 7 August 1946, 14–16 August 1946, Folder, Box 23, White House bill file, Papers of the President, Truman Library.

27. Robert E. Patterson to Webb, 7 August 1946; Webb to Truman, 12 August 1946, Papers of the President, Truman Library.

28. Robertson to Truman, 15 August 1946; Michael T. Hudoba to Matthew Connelly, 7 August 1946, official file 177, Box 793, Papers of the President, Truman Library. The political cruise is discussed in David McCullough, *Truman* (New York: Simon & Schuster, 1992), 520–524, and documented in Daily Presidential Appointments, Apr. 1945-Aug. 1946, Folder 8, Box 1, Papers of Matthew J. Connelly, Truman Library.

29. 42 U.S.C.S. §§ 4321–4370d (NEPA); Congressional Quarterly, *Congress and the Nation: A Review of Government and Politics in the Postwar Years, 1945–1964* (Washington, D.C.: CQ Press, 1965), 1064–1065.

30. Hal K. Rothman, *The Greening of a Nation? Environmentalism in the United States Since 1945* (Ft. Worth, Tex.: Harcourt Brace, 1998), 15–20.

31. Lary May, ed., *Recasting America: Culture and Politics in the Age of the Cold War* (Chicago: University of Chicago Press, 1989), collected some of the best early scholarship about postwar America's creative tension. In *Beauty, Health, and Permanence: Environmental Politics in the United States, 1955–1985* (New York: Cambridge University Press, 1987), 15, 21; and *History of Environmental Politics since 1945* (Pittsburgh: University of Pittsburgh Press, 2000), 3, 22, 84, Samuel P. Hays developed the case for taking the postwar years seriously as a period of legal creativity.

32. "Nature Protection [in USA], for National Research Council," file folder

["FF"] 17, Box 8, Wildlife Management Institute Papers ["WMIP"], CONS 37, Denver Public Library, Denver, Colorado [hereafter DPL].

33. "Wildlife Conservation and Management [1945] for *Encyclopedia Britannica*," FF 3, Box 8, WMIP, DPL.

CHAPTER 3. FERTILIZATION: ENVIRONMENTAL LAWMAKING IN THE POSTWAR ADMINISTRATIVE STATE

1. Robert G. Kaufman, *Henry M. Jackson: A Life in Politics* (Seattle: University of Washington Press, 2000); *Biographical Directory of the American Congress, 1774–1971* (Washington, D.C.: Government Printing Office, 1971), 602 [Bland], 520 [Angell]; Karl Boyd Brooks, *Public Power, Private Dams: The Hells Canyon High Dam Controversy* (Seattle: University of Washington Press, 2006), 60–61.

2. Richard White, *The Organic Machine: The Remaking of the Columbia River* (New York: Hill and Wang, 1995); and Joseph E. Taylor III, *Making Salmon: An Environmental History of the Northwest Fisheries Crisis* (Seattle: University of Washington Press, 1999), introduce the vast literature about Northwestern anadromous fish and hydroelectricity.

3. Act of 14 August 1946, ch. 965, 60 Stat. 1080, codified at 16 U.S.C. §§ 666a–666c (1997) [FWCA]; Act of 11 August 1946, ch. 324, 60 Stat. 237, codified at 5 U.S.C. §§ 551–559, 701–706 (1997) [APA].

4. Karl Brooks, "'Powerless' No More: Postwar Judges and Pacific Northwest Hydroelectification, 1946–1967, *Idaho Yesterdays* 45 (Winter 2001–2002): 11–26; Karl Brooks, "Illuminating the Postwar Northwest: Private Power and Public Law in Hells Canyon, 1950–1957," *Western Legal History* 12 (Winter/Spring 1999): 49–75.

5. The Coordination Act required federal agencies to prepare "biological surveys," share them with Congress before seeking dam-building funds, and demonstrate that the surveys affected their construction plans. The FWCA and its biological surveys established the basic framework for the 1960 National Environmental Policy Act's environmental impact statements. NEPA's principal congressional sponsor, Senator Henry Jackson (D-Washington), had been one of FWCA's most ardent backers as a member of the 1945–1946 House of Representatives. Kaufman, *Henry Jackson*; Paul Charles Milazzo, *Unlikely Environmentalists: Congress and Clean Water, 1945–1972* (Lawrence: University Press of Kansas, 2006), 112–138.

6. Alan Brinkley's essay, "The Late New Deal and the Idea of the State," in *Liberalism and its Discontents* (Cambridge, Mass.: Harvard University Press, 1998), 37–62, argued that administrative agencies were "in decline" by the end of World War II, their task of ameliorating industrial capitalism's social tension now accomplished by fiscal policies that promoted sustained economic growth. Where growth required dis-

ordering the environment, though, administrative power and discretion expanded, as in postwar water and land policy. Lizabeth Cohen, *A Consumer's Republic: The Politics of Mass Consumption in Postwar America* (New York: Knopf, 2003), extends this point across society.

7. James M. Landis sketched the rise of the administrative state before 1950 in "The Administrative Process: The Third Decade," *American Bar Association Journal* 47 (February 1961): 135–139; Kenneth C. Davis, "Fiftieth Anniversary of the Administrative Procedure Act," *Administrative Law Review* 48 (Summer 1996): 307–398. Kenneth C. Davis and Walter Gelhorn, in "Present at the Creation: Regulatory Reform Before 1946,"*Administrative Law Review* 38 (Fall 1986): 511–533, offer useful accounts of the APA's drafting. Bernard Schwartz, in "The Administrative Procedure Act in Operation," *New York University Law Review* 29 (June 1954): 1173–1264, discusses the APA's legislative history during the War. Charles H. Koch, Jr., provides a more recent view in "James Landis: The Administrative Process," *Administrative Law Review* 48 (Summer 1996): 419–433.

8. "Administrative Procedure Act Report," House Rpt. 1980 (3 May 1946), U.S. *Code Congressional Service: 1946*, 1205; Section 10 of the APA is codified at 5 U.S.C.S. §§ 703, 551(b), 555(a).

9. 5 U.S.C.S. §§ 701–706, especially § 702; "APA Report," 1205–1206.

10. 16 U.S.C.S. §§ 825g(a), 825g(b); Kenneth Culp Davis, "Standing to Challenge and to Enforce Administrative Action," *Columbia Law Review* 49 (June 1949), 766–767.

11. Bernard Schwartz, "A Decade of Administrative Law: 1942–1951," *Michigan Law Review* 51 (April 1953): 791, 861; Nathaniel L. Nathanson, "The Administrative World of Felix Frankfurter," *Yale Law Journal* 60 (1957): 240–265, offers a critical contemporary view of judicial deference to agency action.

12. Schwartz, "Decade," 861–862; *Wong Yang Sung v. McGrath*, 339 U.S. 33 (1950); *Joint Anti-Fascist Committee*, 341 U.S. 123 (1950).

13. Sidney A. Shapiro and Robert L. Glicksman, "Congress, the Supreme Court, and the Quiet Revolution in Administrative Law," *Duke Law Journal* 1988 (November): 819–878, analyzes the lawmaking potential inherent in the tensions between regulated and regulators, mediated by elected representatives.

14. House Committee on Merchant Marine and Fisheries, *Hearings on Columbia River Fisheries*, 79th Cong., 2d sess. (14 August 1946), 8–9, 46.

15. J. T. Barnaby to Director, Fish and Wildlife Service, 5 April 1946, trip file 1946: June 6–19, box 17, C. Girard Davidson Papers, Truman Library.

16. USFWS Memo: Fisheries and Dam Construction, 31 May 1946, trip file 1946: June 6–19, box 17, C. Girard Davidson Papers, Truman Library; Milo C. Moore (Wash-

ington Fisheries Dept. Director) to Senator Warren Magnuson, 8 April 1946; Oscar L. Chapman (Undersecretary, Interior Dept.) to Rep. Hugh DeLacy, 11 July 1946, reading file: July 1–Aug. 31, 1946, box 104, Oscar L. Chapman Papers, Truman Library.

17. House Merchant Marine Committee, *Hearings on Columbia River*, 20, 40.

18. Ibid., 45–47.

19. Statement on behalf of the Department of the Interior, Pacific Northwest Coordination Committee, 23 June 1947, speeches/addresses, box 19, Davidson Papers, Truman Library.

20. "Transcript of Proceedings in the Matter of Conference on Wildlife, Recreation, and Related Problems," Dept. of Interior, 2 December 1947, 268–273, subject file: Conference on Wildlife/Recreation Problems, 2 December 1947, box 10, Davidson Papers, Truman Library.

21. Ibid., 285–290.

22. "Congress Holds the Key," *Outdoor America*, March 1948, file folder 24, box 15, Izaak Walton League Papers, CONS 41, DPL.

23. "Waltonians! Here Are Your Goals!" *Outdoor America*, April 1949, file folder 24, box 15, Izaak Walton League Papers, CONS 41, DPL.

24. W. B. Smith, "Note: Statutory Treatment of Industrial Stream Pollution," *George Washington Law Review* 24 (1955): 302–319, n. 59, lists state water pollution statutes enacted between 1945 and 1954; James E. Krier and Edmund Ursin, *Pollution and Policy: A Case Essay on California and Federal Experience with Motor Vehicle Air Pollution, 1940–1975* (Berkeley: University of California Press, 1977), Chapters 3 and 8, discuss state air pollution lawmaking between World War II and the early 1960s.

25. "Pollution Abatement Laws," *Engineering News-Record* [hereafter EN-R], 15 September 1949, 22–23; Don E. Bloodgood, "Effect on Stream Pollution Legislation and Control," *Papers on Industrial Wastes*, September 1948, 1048–1051; "California Pushes Clean Stream Drive," EN-R, 12 February 1948, 221.

26. Gwynne B. Myers, "Water Pollution Control," *Ohio State Law Journal* 12 (1951): 376–380.

27. John L. Laubach, Jr., and Sanford Mark Lampl, "Stream Pollution and the Allegheny County Sanitary Authority," *University of Pittsburgh Law Review* 10 (1949): 345–363.

28. J. C. Graul, "Pennsylvania's Clean Streams Program," *Public Works*, February 1949, 28–30. Graul directed the Sanitary Water Board's Public Relations office, which began publishing 80,000 quarterly bulletins, printing 500,000 color posters, and distributing a 64-page booklet "which will cover the entire program and the necessity for its promotion."

29. Seymour C. Wagner, "Notes: Statutory Stream Pollution Control," *University of Pennsylvania Law Review* 100 (1951): 225–241.

CHAPTER **4**. HARVEST HOME: ENVIRONMENTAL LAWMAKING AND POSTWAR FEDERALISM

1. Scott Hamilton Dewey, *Don't Breathe the Air: Air Pollution and U.S. Environmental Politics, 1945–1970* (College Station, Tex.: Texas A & M University Press, 2000), offers an excellent account of the postwar L.A. phenomenon.

2. Chris J. Magoc, in "The *Donora* Disaster and the Problem of Air Pollution," in *Environmental Issues in American History: A Reference Guide with Primary Documents* (Westport, Conn.: Greenwood Press, 2006), puts the Pennsylvania incident into national perspective.

3. "Air Pollution," *American Journal of Public Health*, January 1951, 30.

4. Ibid., June 1948, 761.

5. "Toughest Air Pollution Problem Yet Tackled," *Engineering News-Record*, 20 October 1955, 33; "Smog Fighters," *Chemical Engineering*, October 1948, 114; "Los Angeles Smog," *Steel*, 23 February 1955, 48.

6. William Deverell and Greg Hise, eds., *Land of Sunshine: An Environmental History of Metropolitan Los Angeles* (Pittsburgh: University of Pittsburgh Press, 2005), collect an array of articles that set the city's mid-century transformation into a long-term context.

7. "Note: California's Water Pollution Problem," *Stanford Law Review* 3 (1951): 649–666.

8. Ibid. The article analyzes the intent of CAL. WATER CODE §§ 13053, 13054, 13064.

9. "California Water Pollution Problem," 660–661.

10. Ibid., 657, 666.

11. Harold W. Kennedy and Andrew O. Porter, "Air Pollution: Its Control and Abatement," *Vanderbilt Law Review* 8 (1955): 854–877.

12. Ibid., 875–876.

13. Irving Stone, in a contemporary campaign biography, *Earl Warren: A Great American Story* (New York: Prentice-Hall, 1948), chronicles the postwar trajectory of California progressivism; and G. Edward White, *Earl Warren: A Public Life* (New York: Oxford University Press, 1982), supplies background on the California Republican Party from which Warren emerged to become a national figure.

14. *New York Times*, 5 December 1954, 78, and 22 February 1955, 9; "Los Angeles Smog," *Steel*.

15. *New York Times*, 22 February 1955, 9.

16. Kennedy and Porter, "Air Pollution," 864; Stanford Law Review, "California's Water Pollution Problem," 649.

17. Anthony J. Badger, *The New Deal: The Depression Years, 1933–1940* (New York: Hill and Wang, 1989); Paul S. Sutter, *Driven Wild: How the Fight against Automobiles Launched the Modern Wilderness Movement* (Seattle: University of Washington Press, 2002); and Sarah T. Phillips, *This Land, This Nation: Conservation, Rural America, and the New Deal* (New York: Cambridge University Press, 2007), introduce the vast literature about Roosevelt's natural resources initiatives. Donald E. Worster, in *Dust Bowl: The Southern Plains in the 1930s*, 25th anniversary ed. (New York: Oxford University Press, 2004), sets New Deal policies about nature and society into environmental history's broader perspective. Michael C. Blumm, "The Northwest's Hydroelectric Heritage: Prologue to the Northwest Electric Power Planning and Conservation Act," *Washington Law Review* 58 (April 1983): 175–244 ; and Karl Brooks, *Public Power, Private Dams: The Hells Canyon High Dam Controversy* (Seattle: University of Washington Press, 2006), focus closely on the Federal Columbia River Power system's postwar expansion throughout the Pacific Northwest.

18. Entry into the vast literature about two of the Supreme Court's towering twentieth-century figures should begin with G. Edward White's sketches in *The American Judicial Tradition: Profiles of Leading American Judges*, 3d ed. (New York: Oxford University Press, 2007).

19. Two volumes of memoirs recount Douglas's transcontinental journey, stellar academic career, and assiduous networking among the nation's powerful. See his *Go East, Young Man: The Early Years* (New York: Random House, 1974); and *The Court Years, 1939–1975: The Autobiography of William O. Douglas* (New York: Random House, 1980). Adam Sowards, "William O. Douglas' Wilderness Politics: Public Protest and Committees of Correspondence in the Pacific Northwest," *Western Historical Quarterly* 37 (2006): 21–42, previews his important forthcoming environmental-historical biography, *The Environmental Justice: William O. Douglas and American Conservation* (Corvallis, Ore: Oregon State University Press).

20. William E. Leuchtenburg, *The Supreme Court Reborn: The Constitutional Revolution in the Age of Roosevelt* (New York: Oxford University Press, 1995), expands his earlier treatment of New Deal judicial history in *Franklin D. Roosevelt and the New Deal, 1932–1940* (New York: Harper Colophon, 1963), 230–38.

21. William O. Douglas, "Stare Decisis," *Columbia Law Review* 49 (June 1949): 735–758.

22. Joseph P. Lash, ed., *From the Diaries of Felix Frankfurter* (New York: W. W. Norton,

1975), 83 [1947 Cardozo Lecture], 56 [Brandeis]. Leonard Baker, *Brandeis and Frankfurter: A Dual Biography* (New York: Harper and Row, 1984), assesses the older man's influence on his protégé.

23. Bernard Schwartz, "The Administrative World of Mr. Justice Frankfurter," *Yale Law Journal* 59 (June 1950): 1228–1265; Lash, *Frankfurter Diaries*, 53.

24. Schwartz, "Administrative World," 1230–1231, 1246, 1256, 1257.

25. Melvin I. Urofsky, ed., *The Douglas Letters: Selections from the Private Papers of William O. Douglas* (Bethesda, Md.: Adler & Adler, 1987), xvi–xvii.

26. Lash, *Frankfurter Diaries*, 61–63, 64, 66.

27. Ibid., 62, 73; Douglas, *Court Years*, 7.

28. *Frankfurter Diaries*, 52, 155, 230, 309.

29. Ibid., 276, 343.

30. Douglas, *Court Years*, 3, 8, 22–23, 33–34, 39, 244, 282–283, 289.

31. Ibid., 22, 55, 133–135, 391.

32. Mary Frances Berry, *Stability, Security, and Continuity: Mr. Justice Burton and Decision-Making in the Supreme Court, 1945–1958* (Westport, Conn.: Greenwood Press, 1978), 26–30, 38–39, 41–42, 47.

33. *Chapman v. FPC*, 345 U.S. 153 (1953), cited *First Iowa Hydro-Electric Cooperative v. FPC*, 328 U.S. 152 (1946), as the controlling precedent.

34. *Chapman v. FPC*, 345 U.S. at 175–182 (Douglas, J., diss.). Emphasis in original.

35. *State of Washington Dept. of Game v. FPC*, 207 F.2d 391 (9th Cir. 1953), *cert. denied*, 347 U.S. 936 (1954) (Cowlitz River); *State of Oregon v. FPC*, 211 F.2d 347 (9th Cir. 1954), reversed as *FPC v. Oregon*, 349 U.S. 435 (1955) (Deschutes River).

36. *In re Idaho Power Co.*, 14 F.P.C. 55 (1955), affirmed as, *National Hells Canyon Assn. v. FPC*, 237 F.2d 777 (D.C. Cir. 1956), *cert. denied*, 353 U.S. 924 (1957).

37. "Legacies of World War II," in Alan Brinkley, *Liberalism and Discontents* (Cambridge, Mass.: Harvard University Press, 1998), 94–110.

CHAPTER 5. THE PEOPLE OUT OF DOORS: POPULARIZING POSTWAR ENVIRONMENTAL LAW

1. John Opie, *Nature's Nation: An Environmental History of the United States* (Ft. Worth, Tex.: Harcourt Brace, 1998), 313–314.

2. Nancy K. Kubasek and Gary S. Silverman, *Environmental Law*, 5th ed. (Upper Saddle River, N.J.: Pearson Prentice Hall, 2005), 136; Steven Stoll, *U.S. Environmentalism since 1945* (Boston: Bedford/St. Martin's, 2007), 76; Linda J. Lear, *Rachel Carson: Witness for Nature* (New York: Henry Holt, 1997); Mark Hamilton Lytle, *The Gentle Sub-*

versive: *Rachel Carson, Silent Spring, and the Rise of the Environmental Movement* (New York: Oxford University Press, 2007), 186–191.

3. Aldo Leopold, *A Sand County Almanac* (New York: Oxford University Press, 1949) reissued with *Essays on Conservation from Round River* (New York: Oxford University Press, 1966); Curt Meine, *Aldo Leopold: His Life and Work* (Madison: University of Wisconsin Press, 1988).

4. Richard White, "'Are You an Environmentalist or Do You Work for a Living?': Work and Nature," in William Cronon, ed., *Uncommon Ground: Rethinking the Human Place in Nature* (New York: W.W. Norton, 1996), 171–185, provocatively assesses the recreation transformation that Samuel Hays, *Beauty, Health, and Permanence: Environmental Politics in the United States, 1955–1985* (New York: Cambridge University Press, 1987), best analyzed. A good recent treatment is Mark Harvey, *Wilderness Forever: Howard Zahniser and the Path to the Wilderness Act* (Seattle: University of Washington Press, 2005).

5. Penfold Obituary, 28 June 1973, file folder [ff] 38, box 12, Izaak Walton League Papers [IWLP], CONS 41, DPL

6. Penfold Oral History: ORRRC [undated, but about 1966], ff 48, box 12, IWLP, DPL.

7. Ibid.

8. Harold Titus, Conservation, *Field and Stream*, September 1960, 40.

9. Ibid., January 1956, 25 and November 1957, 48.

10. Frank Luther Mott, *A History of American Magazines*, vol. IV (Cambridge: Harvard University Press, 1957), 381; James L. C. Ford, *Magazines for the Millions: The Story of Specialized Publications* (Carbondale, Ill.: Southern Illinois Press, 1969), 54–55; John F. Reiger, *American Sportsmen and the Origins of Conservation*, rev. ed. (1975; Norman, Okla.: University of Oklahoma Press, 1986).

11. Penfold Oral History: ORRRC, ff 48, box 12, IWLP, DPL.

12. Ibid.

13. Mark W. T. Harvey, *A Symbol of Wilderness: Echo Park and the American Conservation Movement* (Seattle: University of Washington Press, 2000), xxii.

14. Ibid., xvi, xix. To the burgeoning historiography of American wilderness that started with Roderick Nash, *Wilderness and the American Mind*, 4th ed. (New Haven, Conn.: Yale University Press, 2001), and Samuel Hays, *Beauty, Health, and Permanence*, should be added Mark Harvey, *Wilderness Forever*; Michael Lewis, ed., *American Wilderness: A New History* (New York: Oxford University Press, 2007); and Kevin Marsh, *Drawing Lines in the Forest: Wilderness in the Pacific Northwest* (Seattle: University of Washington Press, 2007).

15. Penfold Oral History, ORRRC; Stoll, *U.S. Environmentalism*, 36–39.

16. Van Campen Heilner, "The First 60 Years of Field and Stream," FS, November 1955, 87; Harold Titus, "A Sixty-Year Fight Continues," in ibid., 68.

17. Titus, "Sixty-Year Fight," 70; Rachel Carson, *Silent Spring* (1962; Boston: Houghton Mifflin, 1994), 64.

18. Harold Titus, Conservation, FS, November 1953, 32; Titus, "Sixty-Year Fight," 70.

19. Titus, Conservation, FS, October 1951, 36, and June 1952, 27.

20. Titus, Conservation, FS, April 1953, 36 and September 1956, 18.

21. Titus, Conservation, May 1954, 33.

22. Ibid., May 1958, 52.

23. Paul Hirt, *A Conspiracy of Optimism: Management of the National Forests since World War Two* (Lincoln: University of Nebraska Press, 1994); Michael R. Fein, *Paving the Way: New York Road Building and the American State, 1880–1956* (Lawrence: University Press of Kansas, 2008).

24. Harold Titus, Conservation, FS, February 1952, 16, and September 1957, 38.

25. Titus, Conservation, FS, January 1958, 52, and May 1961, 36.

26. Joseph Penfold, "Recreation Needs in the Public Lands States," 9 September 1956, FF 38, Box 12, IWLP, DPL.

27. Elaine Tyler May, *Homeward Bound: American Families in the Cold War Era*, rev. ed. (New York: Basic Books, 1999); Adam Rome, *The Bulldozer in the Countryside: Suburban Sprawl and the Rise of American Environmentalism* (New York: Cambridge University Press, 2001); William H. Chafe, *The Unfinished Journey: America since World War II*, 6th ed. (New York: Oxford University Press, 2007), 117–119.

28. Sloan Wilson, *The Man in the Gray Flannel Suit* (1955; New York: Arbor House, 1983), 7, 10, 14–15, 39–40.

29. John C. Keats, *The Crack in the Picture Window* (Boston: Houghton Mifflin, 1956), xi–xii, 7, 49.

30. Ibid., xvi, xvii, 66; Froma Harrop, "Candidates Are Silent as City Sprawl Explodes," *Omaha World-Herald*, 16 August 2004, 7B.

31. Quoted in Rome, *Bulldozer*, 119–120.

32. Ibid., xi, 12–13; Hays, *Beauty, Health, and Permanence*, 3–5.

33. May, *Homeward Bound*; Chafe, *Unfinished Journey*.

34. Chafe, *Unfinished Journey*, 115–118.

35. FIFRA's purposes and methods are set out in House Committee on Agriculture, House Report 80–313, 80th Cong., 1st sess. (1947), accompanying Act of 25 June 1947, ch. 125, 61 Stat. 163–173, codified at 7 U.S.C.S. §§ 135–136y; Roger W.

Findley and Daniel A. Farber, *Environmental Law in a Nutshell*, 5th ed. (St. Paul, Minn.: West Group, 2000), 169–176.

36. *U.S. Code Congressional and Administrative News 1947*, 1205.

37. William H. Rodgers, Jr., "The Persistent Problem of the Persistent Pesticides: A Lesson in Environmental Law," *Columbia Law Review* (April 1970), 573. Rodgers's article furnishes the evidence for discussion of the 1954 Miller Amendment and 1958 Delaney Clause, as well as the 1958–1959 "cranberry scare."

38. Senate Report 83-1635 (1954) explained the Miller Amendment, codified at 21 U.S.C. §§ 346a(a)-(f).

39. Rodgers, "Persistent Problem," 589–590.

40. Dwight D. Eisenhower, *The White House Years: Waging Peace, 1956–1961* (Garden City, N.Y.: Doubleday & Co., 1965), 467–480.

41. House Rpt. 85-2284 (1958) and Senate Rpt. 85-2422 (1958) explained the Delaney Clause, now codified at 21 U.S.C. § 348(c)(3)(A).

42. House Committee on Inter-State Commerce, *Hearings on Color Additives*, 86th Cong., 2d sess., prepared H.R. Rpt. 86–1761 (1960), to explain the 1960 Color Additive Amendment, codified at 21 U.S.C. § 376(b)(5)(B).

43. Chafe, *Unfinished Journey*, 106–117.

44. John Keats, *The Insolent Chariots* (1958; New York: Fawcett Crest, 1959), 13, 110–111, 170.

45. Ibid., 18–19, 50–53, 63, 81–84, 161–163, 169.

46. Lary May, ed., *Recasting America: Culture and Politics in the Age of the Cold War* (Chicago: University of Chicago Press, 1989); Chafe, *Unfinished Journey*, 106, 119.

47. Richard H. Pells, *The Liberal Mind in a Conservative Age: American Intellectuals in the 1940s and 1950s* (New York: Harper & Row, 1985); Daniel Horowitz, *Vance Packard and American Social Criticism* (Chapel Hill: University of North Carolina Press, 1994), 9.

48. David Morris Potter, *People of Plenty: Economic Abundance and the American Character* (Chicago: University of Chicago Press, 1954); Dale Carter, ed., *Cracking the Ike Age: Aspects of Fifties America* (Aarhus, Denmark: Aarhus University Press, 1992).

49. Six of the top ten nonfiction books in 1956 discussed cooking, home improvement, or etiquette. Kerr's *Daisies* made the top ten for a second straight year in 1958, a year that also saw Pat Boone's gentle guide to awkward teens, *Twixt 10 and 20*, reach number two, on its way to number one in 1959. A. P. Hackett and J. H. Burke, *80 Years of Best Sellers, 1895–1975* (New York: R. R. Bowker, 1977).

CHAPTER **6**. ACROSS THE NEW FRONTIER: NATIONALIZING ENVIRONMENTAL LAW

1. Paul Charles Milazzo, *Unlikely Environmentalists: Congress and Clean Water, 1945–1972* (Lawrence: University Press of Kansas, 2006), Chapter 1, sets the 1961 bill into historic context. James Salzman and Barton H. Thompson, Jr., *Environmental Law and Policy*, 2d ed. (New York: Foundation Press, 2007), Chapter 5, summarizes federal clean water law.

2. William H. Rodgers, Jr., *Environmental Law* (St. Paul, Minn.: West Publishing, 1977), § 3.1, 207.

3. Richard N. L. Andrews, *Managing the Environment, Managing Ourselves: A History of American Environmental Policy* (New Haven, Conn.: Yale University Press, 1999), 200, 203, 205, 207–208.

4. House Committee on Public Works, *Hearings on Executive Session on H.R. 4036*, 87th Cong., 1st sess. (13 April 1961).

5. William H. Rodgers, Jr., "Industrial Water Pollution and the Refuse Act: A Second Chance for Water Quality," *University of Pennsylvania Law Review* 101 (April 1971): 761–822.

6. *Hearings on H.R. 4036* (18 April 1961).

7. Andrews, *Managing the Environment*, 227.

8. Richard J. Lazarus, *The Making of Environmental Law* (Chicago: University of Chicago Press, 2004), xv, 44, 66–69, 84, 79.

9. Ibid., xiii, 73–74, 78.

10. As will be shown more fully, both of these statutory monuments regulating air and water pollution amended existing federal law, meriting the quotation marks designating their popular titles as shorthand for a more complicated legal process.

11. Dwight D. Eisenhower, *The White House Years: Mandate for Change, 1953–1956* (Garden City, N.Y.: Doubleday, 1963); Stephen E. Ambrose, *Eisenhower*, vol. I (New York: Simon & Schuster, 1983), Chapters 26–27, and vol. II (New York: Simon & Schuster, 1984), Chapter 1.

12. Milazzo, *Unlikely Environmentalists*, 7, 19–23.

13. Ibid., 59–60; Dwight D. Eisenhower, "Veto Message of 22 February 1960: Water Pollution Bill," *Papers of the Presidency Project*, http://www.presidency.ucsb.edu/ws/?pid=12103 (accessed 30 May 2007).

14. Kennedy followed up his 1961 State of the Union with specific water-pollution proposals and generous budget requests in his "Special Message on Natural Resources Policy," 23 February 1961, *Public Papers of the President: John F. Kennedy* (Washington, D.C.: Government Printing Office, 1962), 115–117.

15. Milazzo, *Unlikely Environmentalists*, 29–33.

16. Rodgers, *Environmental Law*, § 4.1, 354, 356.

17. *Hearings on H.R. 4036* (18 April 1961).

18. Ibid. (12 April 1961), emphasis added.

19. Karl Brooks, *Public Dams, Private Power: The Hells Canyon High Dam Controversy* (Seattle: University of Washington Press, 2006); Kennedy, "Special Message on Natural Resources (1961)."

20. *Hearings on H.R. 4036* (13 April 1961).

21. A convenient compilation of the Federal Water Pollution Control Act, a.k.a. "the Clean Water Act of 1972," in *Selected Environmental Law Statutes: 1998–99 Educational Edition* (St. Paul, Minn.: West Group, 1998), 331, helpfully provides "Historical and Statutory Notes" to trace clean water law's genealogy: "The Federal Water Pollution Control Act, comprising [Chapter 26, Title 33], was originally enacted by Act of 30 June 1948, ch. 758, 62 Stat. 1155, and amended" *eleven more times* before 1972. Rodgers, *Environmental Law*, § 4.1, p. 354, correctly stresses clean-water lawmaking's postwar heritage.

22. James E. Krier and Edmund Ursin, *Pollution and Policy: A Case Essay on California and Federal Experience with Motor Vehicle Pollution, 1949–1975* (Berkeley: University of California Press, 1977), 4. Scott Hamilton Dewey, *Don't Breathe the Air: Air Pollution and U.S. Environmental Politics, 1945–1970* (College Station: Texas A&M University Press, 2000), offers a newer, wider view.

23. Krier and Ursin, *Pollution and Policy*, 3, 9, 11.

24. Ibid., 106–107.

25. Ibid.; Elmo Richardson, *Dams, Parks, and Politics: Resource Development and Preservation in the Truman-Eisenhower Era* (Lexington: University of Kentucky Press, 1973).

26. Krier and Ursin, *Pollution and Policy*, 108–110.

27. Ibid., 110, 169.

28. Ibid., 170.

29. Ibid., 172.

30. Ibid.; Dewey, *Don't Breathe the Air*.

31. Krier and Ursin, *Pollution and Policy*, 173–175.

32. Rodgers, *Environmental Law* § 3.1, 209–210.

33. Krier and Ursin, *Pollution and Policy*, 183; Rodgers, § 3.1, 208. "Historical and Statutory Notes" to the current version of the 1970 "Clean Air Act," now codified as U.S. Code, Chapter 85, Title 42, explicitly acknowledge its 1955, 1963, 1965, and 1967 ancestors. *Selected Environmental Law Statutes* (1998), 799–800.

34. Krier and Ursin, *Pollution and Policy*, 173.

35. Ibid., 175, 183.

36. Rodgers, *Environmental Law*, §§ 3.5, 4.8.

37. Andrews, *Managing the Environment*, ix–x.

38. Ibid., 227, 10.

39. Ibid., 28, 49.

40. Ibid., 49, 31.

41. Rodgers, *Environmental Law*, § 2.1, p. 100; § 1.1, pgs. 1–2; § 1.4, pgs. 14–15.

42. Lazarus, *Making of Environmental Law*, xii, 1, 15.

43. Ibid., 27–28.

44. Ibid., 179–180.

45. Andrews, *Managing the Environment*, 10–11.

46. Ibid., 11.

47. *Hearings on H.R. 4036* (18 April 1961).

CHAPTER 7: FROM THE FILES OF BRUCE BOWLER, POSTWAR ENVIRONMENTAL LAWYER

1. Bruce Bowler ["BB"] to Rep. Robert E. Jones, 21 November 1963, box 24, folder 15, series 2, MS 721, Bruce Bowler Papers, Idaho State Historical Society. Materials from the Bowler Papers will be cited thus: [box number]/[folder number]/[series number], BP.

2. This account of the day John Kennedy died, which was also the day Rep. Jones's House subcommittee convened in Seattle, draws from various published accounts of 22 November 1963. Its imaginative reconstruction of the subcommittee's morning draws from the author's professional legal experiences in various federal courthouses across the country, political experiences in various legislative committee settings in the Northwest, and congressional and judicial staff experiences in Washington, D.C.

3. This composite sketch of IWF's business affairs is drawn from materials in 3/14/1 to 10/15/1, BP.

4. The Bruce Bowler Papers' forty-one boxes cover only his environmental lawyering. Files from the rest of his practice, which he opened in Boise in 1938, remain confidential. The Papers' Finding Aid can be accessed through Northwest Digital Archives: www.nwda-db.wsulibs.wsu.edu.

5. Bowler's private law practice's dimensions are based on the author's personal knowledge of solo civil practice in Boise, Idaho, during the 1980s and 1990s, supplemented by "Biography," BP.

6. "Biography," BP; *Idaho Statesman*, 2 December 1962, p. 7, 1/5/1, BP.

7. Biographical Information, Pacific Northwest Chapter, Sierra Club, 12 November 1966, 12/12/1, BP.

8. IWF Legislative Bulletin, 18 March 1957, 3/17/1, BP; IWF twenty-fourth Annual Conference Minutes, McCall, 12–14 December 1958, 3/18/1, BP.

9. J. M. Neil, *To the White Clouds: Idaho's Conservation Saga* (Pullman, Wash.: Washington State University Press, 2005), sets IWF's postwar work into context.

10. 354 F.2d 608 (2d Cir. 1965).

11. James Salzman and Barton H. Thompson, Jr., *Environmental Law and Policy*, 2d ed. (New York: Foundation Press, 2007), 11; Richard J. Lazarus, *The Making of Environmental Law* (Chicago: University of Chicago Press, 2004), 21; Allen R. Talbot, *Power along the Hudson* (New York: Dutton, 1972).

12. Karl Boyd Brooks, *Public Power, Private Dams: The Hells Canyon High Dam Controversy* (Seattle: University of Washington Press, 2006); Mark W. T. Harvey, *A Symbol of Wilderness: Echo Park and the American Conservation Movement* (1994; Seattle: University of Washington Press, 2004); John Corlett, "Politically Speaking," *Idaho Statesman*, 12 January 1954, 3/16/1, BP.

13. "Wildlife Group Opposes . . . Dams," *Idaho Statesman*, 11 January 1954, 3/16/1, BP.

14. *IWF Protest*, FPC Project 2147 [Clearwater dams], 2 March 1954, 3/16/1, BP.

15. IWF 1956 Annual Meeting Minutes, 3/17/1, BP.

16. Interior Department Information Service, 22 November 1960, enclosing Elmer F. Bennett to FPC Chair, 21 November 1960, 4/20/1, BP; *Drumming Log: Voice of Dist. #1 IWF*, May 1957, 2/27/1, BP.

17. IWF Legislative Bulletin, 18 March 1957, 3/17/1, BP.

18. Sara Dant Ewert, "The Evolution of an Environmentalist: Senator Frank Church and the Hells Canyon Controversy," *Montana: The Magazine of Western History* 51 (Spring 2001): 36–51.

19. Ted Trueblood, "Must the Salmon River Die?" *Field and Stream* (October 1960), 10–12, 124–125, 28/24/3, BP [emphasis in original].

20. BB to Editor, *Idaho Statesman*, 25 October 1960; Trueblood to Editor, 30 October 1960; Day to Editor, 6 November 1960, all in 4/20/2, BP.

21. Harold D. Hughes, "Fish Group Criticizes High Snake River Dam," *The* [Portland] *Oregonian*, 14 June 1960; statement by Idaho Fish and Game Commission et al., FPC Projects 2173/2243 and 2273, 15 June 1960, 4/19/1, BP.

22. BB to Frank Church, 17 June 1960, 4/19/1, BP.

23. IWF Board of Directors, 29 April 1962, 3/18/1, BP

24. In re *Pacific Northwest Power Co./Washington Public Power Supply System*, 31 FPC 247, *rehearing denied*, 31 FPC 1951 (1964).

25. *Washington Public Power Supply System v. FPC*, 358 F.2d 840 (D.C. Cir. 1966).

26. Talbot, in *Power Along the Hudson*, discusses the 1965 Second Circuit Storm King decision in *Scenic Hudson*, and the 1966 D.C. Circuit opinion in *Office of Communication of United Church of Christ v. FCC*.

27. *Udall v. FPC*, 387 U.S. 428 (1967); Brooks, *Public Power, Private Dams*, 220–221, and William Ashworth, *Hells Canyon: The Deepest Gorge on Earth* (New York: Hawthorn Books, 1977), briefly discuss Udall.

28. *Idaho Statesman*, 11 January 1954, p. 2, 3/16/1, BP; IWF Legislative Bulletin, 18 March 1957, 3/17/1, BP.

29. Transcript of Reports . . . Concerning Water Pollution Problems, 19 January 1966, 24/18/2, BP; Statement by T. J. Jones III, Counsel for Idaho Fish and Game Commission, 4/19/1, BP.

30. Idaho Board of Health, Water Pollution Control Regulations, 11 May 1959; [Idaho] Department of Health, Report on Serious Water Pollution Problems, 8 February 1961; Water Pollution Control/Chapter 14, 29 May 1962; [Idaho] Department of Health, Water Pollution Council, 6 July 1962; Suggested Procedure for Enforcement of Pollution Control Deadlines, 13 July 1962, all in 24/14/2, BP.

31. BB to Jones, 21 November 1963, 24/13/2, BP; Water Pollution Control Advisory Council, 7 December 1962, 24/14/2, BP.

32. Water Pollution Control Advisory Council minutes, 7 December 1962, 24/14/2, BP.

33. The 1965 Water Quality Act, P.L. 89–234, is summarized in William H. Rodgers, Jr., *Environmental Law*, §§ 4.1, 4.2. (St. Paul, Minn.: West Publishing, 1977). Johnson's conservation message is in *Public Papers of the Presidents: Lyndon B. Johnson*, 1965, [54], 8 February 1965. Milazzo, *Unlikely Environmentalists*, 75–86, assesses the president's and key congressional members' attitudes about conservation, emphasizing Johnson's 1965 pledge to turn the "New Conservation" into positive law.

34. BB to Jones, 21 November 1963; Gov. Robert E. Smylie to Interior Secretary Stewart L. Udall, 2 June 1966; Udall to Smylie, 28 June 1966; [Idaho Health Department], Water Pollution Control Program, [n.d., probably summer 1966], all in 24/18/2, BP.

35. George Coggins, Charles F. Wilkinson, and John D. Leshy, *Federal Public Lands and Resources Law*, 3d ed. (Mineola, N.Y.: Foundation Press, 1993), offers the authoritative outline of the field.

36. NWF Special Information Bulletin, 20 March 1961, 18/1/2; BB to Stewart Udall, 3 April 1961, 18/1/2, BP.

37. Udall to BB, 21 April 1961; BB to Udall, 3 April 1961, both in 18/1/2, BP.

38. Joe T. Fallini (Idaho BLM Director) to BB, 30 March 1962, 18/1/2, BP.

39. NABC Proceedings, Special Meeting, Las Vegas, 15–16 November 1962, 18/2/2, BP; Interior Dept. Press Release, 1964 Conservation Service Award, 24 February 1964, 18/20/2, BP.

40. R. McGreggor Cawley, *Federal Lands, Western Anger: The Sagebrush Rebellion and Environmental Politics* (Lawrence: University Press of Kansas, 1993); Statement of Rep. Al Ullman (D-Ore.), NABC, 4 November 1963, 18/9/2, BP.

41. Karen R. Merrill, *Public Lands and Political Meaning: Ranchers, the Government, and the Property between Them* (Berkeley: University of California Press, 2002).

42. L. C. Binford, "Tenure and the Public Lands," NABC, 11 March 1963, 18/8/2, BP.

43. L. C. Binford to BB, 29 March 1963; BB to Binford, 7 May 1963, both in 18/8/2, BP.

44. Recommendations of Special Committee on Tenure, NABC, 3 November 1963, 18/9/2, BP. Bowler's copy bore his scribbled notes from Judge Hughes's explanation of the ranchers' preferred solution.

45. NABC Meeting, Washington, D.C., 18–20 March 1964, 18/19/2, BP.

46. Public Land Law Review Commission, *One-Third of a Nation's Land* (Washington, D.C.: Government Printing Office, 1970), presented the Commission's final report, which Merrill assesses in *Public Lands*.

47. Kenneth "Bill" Reynolds to Hugh Wilson, 23 October 1964, and Reynolds's handwritten note to "Homer," [n.d.], 18/21/2, BP, reveal both IWF's alarm and Bowler's part in devising a creative response.

48. NABC Proceedings, Denver, Colorado, 18 November 1965, 18/29/2, BP.

49. Ibid., 54–56.

50. Ibid., 56–58.

51. George Cameron Coggins, "Private Rights to Public Natural Resources," *Twelfth Inaugural Lecture*, University of Kansas (12 December 1984), helpfully collects a range of scholarship about public lands law.

52. Vernon McMikle (Ada County Fish and Game League) to Members, 12 June 1957, 1/4/1, BP.

53. K. D. Flock (Boise National Forest) to Ross Leonard (Idaho Fish and Game Director), copying BB, 10 September 1957, 15/9/2, BP.

54. *Idaho Observer*, 13 September 1962, p. 8, 24/14/2, BP.

55. BB to Rep. Hamer Budge, 28 July 1954; Sen. Henry Dworshak to BB, 30 July 1954; Theo. H. Wegener (IWF) to Mr. _____, 2 August 1954, all in 15/9/2, BP.

56. IWF Petition to Intervene, *In re Washington Public Power Supply System*, FPC No. 2273, 5 May 1960, 4/19/1, BP.

57. J. T. Mijich, Instructions for Intervention and [draft] Petition for Leave to Intervene, [n.d. but before 9 May 1960], 4/19/1, BP; BB to Jack Cook, 17 October 1960, 4/20/1, BP.

58. Leroy Ashby and Rod Gramer, *Fighting the Odds: The Life of Senator Frank Church* (Pullman: Washington State University Press, 1994).

59. Frank Church to BB, 27 February 1962; BB to Church, 8 March 1962, both in 27/17/3, BP.

60. BULLETIN-Outdoorsmen for Better Government, [n.d., probably Fall 1962], 27/17/3, BP.

61. Robert E. Smylie, *Governor Smylie Remembers* (Moscow, Id.: University of Idaho Press, 1999); Kenneth Reynolds to Gov. Robert E. Smylie, 24 February 1962, 3/18/1, BP.

62. Annual IWF Conference 1962 Minutes, 3/18/1, BP; IWF Board of Directors, 29 April 1962, 3/18/1, BP.

63. IWF Board of Directors, 29 April 1962.

64. Ibid.

65. Ibid.

66. Minutes of District #3 Wildlife Federation Meeting, 1 December 1950, 1/4/1, BP.

67. Scott W. Reed to Rep. Herman J. McDevitt, 21 January 1963, 15/11/2, BP.

68. James C. Simpson (Idaho Dept. of Fish and Game Fisheries Division Chief) to BB, 12 December 1956, enclosing American Fisheries Society Resolution, 11 September 1956, informed Bowler the continent's foremost fishery scientists and administrators had endorsed his view that prior appropriation doctrine had to accommodate ecological values to protect human health and aquatic life. Bowler thanked "Jim" for the "very interesting" resolution, which was "basic to the best interest of Western uses." BB to Simpson, 18 December 1956, 21/11/2, BP.

69. Ted Trueblood Testimony for IWF on S. 1446, 22 April 1965, 3/19/1, BP.

70. Ted [Trueblood] and Frank[lin Jones] to Bill [Reynolds], BB, [Stan] Burns, and [Alvard] Kiler, 29 April 1965, 28/24/3, BP.

71. Tim Palmer, *Endangered Rivers and the Conservation Movement*, 2d ed. (Lanham, Md.: Rowman & Littlefield, 2004), supplies an excellent account of the long struggle for the Wild Rivers Act. Randy Stapilus, *Paradox Politics: People and Power in Idaho* (Boise, Id.: Ridenbaugh Press, 1988), brings Idaho's First District, and "Comp" White into focus.

72. Ashby and Gramer, *Frank Church*, should be read with Sara Dant "Making

Wilderness Work: Frank Church and the American Wilderness Movement," *Pacific Historical Review* 77 (2008): 257–272.

73. State Conservation Awards Program, Idaho Wildlife Federation, 20 December 1965, 3/19/1, BP.

74. Charles H. W. Foster, "Counsel for the Concerned," in Malcolm F. Baldwin and James K. Page, Jr., eds., *Law and the Environment* (New York: Conservation Foundation, 1970), xii, 277–288.

75. Kenneth B. Reynolds/IWF Secretary to all Local Sportsmen Clubs, [n.d. but just before 9 December 1960], 4/20/1, BP [emphasis in original].

CHAPTER 8: "A FIELD SO VARIED AND RAPIDLY CHANGING": AMERICAN LAW SCHOOLS DISCOVER ENVIRONMENTAL LAW

1. Norman J. Vig and Michael E. Kraft, eds., *Environmental Policy in the 1980s: Reagan's New Agenda* (Washington, D.C.: CQ Press, 1984), 9, 14; Nancy K. Kubasek and Gary S. Silverman, *Environmental Law*, 5th ed. (Upper Saddle River, N.J.: Prentice-Hall, 2005), 127.

2. Louis L. Jaffee and Laurence H. Tribe, eds., *Environmental Protection* (Chicago: Bracton Press, 1971), vii; Norman J. Landau and Paul D. Rheingold, *The Environmental Law Handbook* (New York: Ballantine Books/Friends of the Earth, 1971), 12.

3. Sive's remarks are transcribed in Malcolm F. Baldwin and James K. Page, Jr., eds., *Law and Environment* (Washington, D.C.: Conservation Foundation, 1970); John Kieran, *A Natural History of New York City* (1959; New York: Fordham University Press, 1982).

4. The principal decision was *Scenic Hudson Preservation Conference v. FPC*, 254 F.2d 608 (2d Cir. 1965), *cert. denied*, 384 U.S. 941 (1966), although legal skirmishing sputtered on for five more years.

5. David Sive, "Some Thoughts of an Environmental Lawyer in the Wilderness of Administrative Law." *Columbia Law Review* 70 (1970), 618.

6. Baldwin and Page, *Law and Environment*, vii–xi.

7. Ibid., 356.

8. Ibid., 341.

9. Ibid., 351–353.

10. "Conservationists at the Barricades," *Fortune*, February 1970, 144–151.

11. Ibid., 146–47.

12. *Scenic Hudson Preservation Conf. v. Federal Power Commission*, 354 F.2d 608 (2d Cir. 1965), *cert. denied*, 384 U.S. 941 (1966).

13. *Citizens Comm. for the Hudson Valley v. Volpe*, 302 F. Supp. 1083 (S.D.N.Y. 1969), affirmed, 425 F.2d 97 (2d Cir. 1970); "Conservationists at the Barricades," 147.

14. "Conservationists at the Barricades," 150.

15. Ibid., 150–151.

16. "A Statement from President Nixon and Senator Muskie," *Fortune*, February 1970, 92–93.

17. American Bar Association, *Annual Report: 1970*, 255–256; ABA, *Annual Report: 1971*, 689–690.

18. Among the earliest textbooks were Frank P. Grad, ed., *Environmental Law: Sources and Problems* (New York: Matthew Bender, 1971); Louis L. Jaffee and Laurence H. Tribe, *Environmental Protection*; and Oscar S. Gray, *Cases and Materials on Environmental Law* (Washington, D.C.: BNA, 1970).

19. Grad, *Environmental Law*, iii.

20. Ibid.

21. "Editorial Comments," *Environmental Law* 1 (Spring 1970): iii–iv; "Editorial Comments, *Environmental Law* 2 (Spring 1971): v–vii.

22. Norman J. Landau and Paul D. Rheingold, *The Environmental Law Handbook*. Former Sierra Club executive director David Brower founded Friends of the Earth in 1969 to pursue political and legal advocacy that had been forbidden the Club by its income tax charitable exemption. Robert Gottlieb, *Forcing the Spring: The Transformation of the American Environmental Movement* (Washington, D.C.: Island Press, 1993), 144–148.

23. Landau and Rheingold, 12.

24. Ibid., 21–23.

25. Ibid., 48–49.

26. Ibid., 52.

27. Joseph L. Sax, *Defending the Environment: A Strategy for Citizen Action* (1970; New York: Alfred A. Knopf, 1971).

28. Ibid., 64.

29. Ibid., 60–61 (traditional reliance; insider perspective); xvii–xix (busybody; legislative attention; public trust).

30. Adam Rome, "'Give Earth a Chance,'" *Journal of American History* 90 (September 2003): 525–554, shows how environmental activism dovetailed with the sixties' leading protest movements.

31. Environmental Action, eds., *Earth Tool Kit* (New York: Pocket Books, 1971), i.

32. Ibid.

33. Ibid. 63.

CHAPTER 9. CONCLUSION: ENVIRONMENTAL LAW'S UNSTABLE LEGACY

1. Richard N. L. Andrews, *Managing the Environment, Managing Ourselves: A History of Environmental Policy* (New Haven, Conn. Yale University Press, 1999), 280–283.

2. J. Willard Hurst, *Law and the Conditions of Freedom in the Nineteenth-Century United States* (Madison: University of Wisconsin Press, 1955), 5.

3. Ibid.

4. University of Illinois law professor Eric Freyfogle's voluminous writings linking property rules, wealth acquisition, and legal change include *Bounded People, Boundless Lands: Envisioning a New Land Ethic* (Washington, D.C.: Island Press, 1998), which assesses historical struggles in trying to balance individual rights with property rules.

5. Ted Steinberg, *Down to Earth: Nature's Role in American History* (New York: Oxford University Press, 2002), 206–238.

6. Compare Richard J. Lazarus, *The Making of Environmental Law* (Chicago: University of Chicago Press, 2004), with Malcolm F. Baldwin and James K. Page, Jr., eds., *Law and Environment* (New York: Conservation Foundation, 1970).

7. William H. Rodgers, Jr., *Handbook on Environmental Law* (St. Paul, Minn.: West Publishing, 1977), iv–vi.

8. Richard H. Pells, *The Liberal Mind in a Conservative Age: American Intellectuals in the 1940s and 1950s* (New York: Harper & Row, 1985), and Lizabeth Cohen, *A Consumer's Republic: The Politics of Mass Consumption in Postwar America* (New York: Knopf, 2003), assess the postwar debates.

9. Samuel P. Hays and Barbara Hays, *Beauty, Health, and Permanence: Environmental Politics in the United States, 1955–1985* (New York: Cambridge University Press, 1987), provide a thoughtful environmental assessment of insights originally offered by David M. Potter, *People of Plenty: Economic Abundance and the American Character* (Chicago: University of Chicago Press, 1954).

10. Alan Brinkley, in *Liberalism and its Discontents* (Cambridge, Mass.: Harvard University Press, 1998), Chapter Three, thoughtfully considers the rise and postwar political implications of the administrative state.

11. "Symposium 1999: Land Use in the 21st Century—The Next Frontier for Environmental Law," *William and Mary Environmental Law and Policy Review* 23, 3 (Fall 1999), evidences local and state governments' police power lawmaking vitality.

12. Ray Vaughan, *Essentials of Environmental Law* (Rockville, Md.: Government Institutes, 1994), vi, 1–9, 143–155.

13. Lazarus, *Making of Environmental Law*, offers an eloquent, recent celebration. Robert Glicksman and George Cameron Coggins, "Federal Recreational Land Policy:

The Rise and Decline of the Land and Water Conservation Fund," *Columbia Journal of Environmental Law* 9 (1984): 125–161, typifies the skeptics' stance.

14. Hurst, *Law and the Conditions of Freedom*. Brinkley, *Liberalism and its Discontents*; Steve Fraser and Gary Gerstle, eds., *The Rise and Fall of the New Deal Order, 1930–1980* (Princeton, N.J.: Princeton University Press, 1989); and William H. Chafe, et al., eds., *A History of Our Time: Readings on Postwar America*, 7th ed. (New York: Oxford University Press, 2008), introduce the rich historiography of postwar America.

15. Hurst, *Law and the Conditions of Freedom*.

16. William P. Cunningham and Barbara Woodworth Saigo, *Environmental Science*, 5th ed. (Boston: McGraw Hill, 1999), 3–4, 8–22.

17. Jeffrey K. Stine, "Natural Resources and Environmental Policy," in W. Elliot Brownlee and Hugh Davis Graham, eds., *The Reagan Presidency: Pragmatic Conservatism and Its Legacies* (Lawrence: University Press of Kansas, 2003), 233–256, offers a measured introduction to the ongoing debate about Reaganism's effects.

18. James Gustave Speth, *Red Sky at Morning: America and the Crisis of the Global Environment* (New Haven, Conn.: Yale University Press, 2004).

19. Nancy Gibbs, "Global Warming," *Time* (24 September 2007), 17; and James Graff, "Fight for the Top of the World," *Time* (1 October 2007), 28–36, ably summarize the evidence.

20. Nelson Lichtenstein, *State of the Unions: A Century of American Labor* (Princeton, N.J.: Princeton University Press, 2002).

21. United States Sentencing Commission, *Annual Reports: 1995–2001* (Washington, D.C.: Government Printing Office), outline the era's developments. I became familiar with these studies during my service with the Sentencing Commission as a Supreme Court Fellow in 2001–2002.

22. James E. Krier and Edmund Ursin, *Pollution and Policy: A Case Essay on California and Federal Experience with Motor Vehicle Air Pollution* (Berkeley: University of California Press, 1977), 13, 10.

BIBLIOGRAPHY

ARCHIVES AND PAPERS

Bruce Bowler Papers. MS 721, Idaho State Historical Society, Boise, Idaho.

Izaak Walton League Papers, CONS 41, Conservation Collection, Denver Public Library, Denver, Colorado.

Kansas Collection, Spencer Research Library, University of Kansas, Lawrence, Kansas.

A. Willis Robertson Papers. Department of Special Collections, Swem Library, College of William and Mary, Williamsburg, Virginia.

Harry S. Truman Presidential Library, Independence, Missouri.

Chapman, Oscar L., Papers of

Conley, Matthew, Papers of

Davidson, C. Girard, Papers of

Official File, Papers of the President

White House Bill File, Papers of the President

Wildlife Management Institute Papers. CONS 37, Conservation Collection, Denver Public Library, Colorado.

INTERVIEWS

(All by author and in author's possession)

Carolyn Bowler, 8 January 2008

Charles McDowell, 22 June 2002

Robert McNeil, 20 June 2002

Scott Reed, 22 December 2007

William H. Rodgers, Jr., 14 May 2008

GOVERNMENT DOCUMENTS

House of Representatives

Agriculture Committee. *Insecticides Regulation*. H. Rept. 80–313. 80th Cong., 1st sess., 1947.

Conservation of Wildlife Select Committee. H. Rept. 79–2743. *Report on Conservation of Wildlife*. 79th Cong., 2d sess., 1947.

———. *Some Wildlife Jobs Awaiting Attention—Hearings Under H. Res. 75*. 79th Cong., 2d sess., 1946.

Interstate Commerce Committee. *Food Additive Regulations.* H. Rept. 85–2284. 85th Cong., 2d sess., 1958.

_____. *Hearings on Color Additives.* H. Rept. 86–1761. 86th Cong., 2d sess., 1960.

Judiciary Committee. *The Administrative Procedure Act.* H. Rept. 79–1980. 79th Cong., 2d sess., 1946.

Merchant Marine and Fisheries Committee. *Hearings on Columbia River Fisheries.* 79th Cong., 2d sess., 1946.

Public Works Committee. *Executive Session: H.R. 4036—Water Pollution Control Act Amendments.* 87th Cong., 1st sess., 1961.

Senate

Agriculture and Forestry Committee. *Hearings on H.R. 6097* (19 July 1946). 79th Cong., 2d sess., 1946.

Interstate and Foreign Commerce Committee. *Food and Drugs.* Sen. Rept. 83–1635. 83d Cong., 2d sess., 1954.

_____. *Food Additive Regulations.* Sen. Rept. 85–2422. 85th Cong., 2d sess., 1958.

Miscellaneous Congressional

Biographical Directory of the American Congress, 1774–1971. 92d Cong., 1st sess., 1971. Washington, D.C.: GPO, 1971.

Congressional Record. Vol. 92 (Senate, 17 July 1946).

U.S. *Code Congressional and Administrative News 1947,* 1205.

Executive

Department of Defense, U.S. "At Home on the Range." 4 April 2001. www.defense link.mil/news/newsarticle.aspx?id=45051.

Public Land Law Review Commission. *One-Third of a Nation's Land.* Washington, D.C.: GPO, 1970.

Public Papers of the Presidents of the United States: Dwight D. Eisenhower, 1956–1960. 5 vols. Washington, D.C.: GPO, 1957–1961.

Public Papers of the Presidents of the United States: John F. Kennedy, 1960–1961. 2 vols. Washington, D.C.: GPO, 1961–1962.

Public Papers of the Presidents of the United States: Lyndon B. Johnson, 1963–1968. 6 vols. Washington, D.C.: GPO, 1964–1969.

Judicial

United States Sentencing Commission. *Annual Reports*. Washington, D.C.: GPO, 1995–2001.

State and Local

City of Lawrence, Kansas. Utilities Department. *The Water We Drink*, 2003.

Statutes

Compilations and codifications of many of the federal statutes are in *Selected Environmental Law Statutes: 1998–99 Educational Edition*. St. Paul: West Group, 1998.

Administrative Procedure Act, 1946 (APA), 5 U.S.C, chapters 5, 7

Air Pollution Control Act, 1955 (APCA), 42 U.S.C., chapter 85

California Air Pollution Control Act, 1947 (Cal APCA)

California Water Quality Act, 1948 (Dickey Act), California Water Code §§ 13053 et seq.

"Clean Air Act," 1970 [and predecessors], 42 U.S.C., chapter 85

"Clean Water Act," 1972 [and predecessors], 33 U.S.C., chapter 26

Federal Insecticide, Fungicide, and Rodenticide Act, 1947 (FIFRA), 7 U.S.C., chapter 6

Fish and Wildlife Coordination Act, 1946 (FWCA). 48 Stat. 401 (1934), 60 Stat. 1080

Food and Drug Act, 1960 (Color Additive Amendment), 21 U.S.C. § 376(b)(5)(B)

Food and Drug Act, 1958 (Delaney Clause), 21 U.S.C. § 348(c)(3)(A)

Food and Drug Act, 1954 (Miller Amendment), 21 U.S.C. §§ 346(a)-(f)

National Environmental Policy Act, 1969 (NEPA), 42 U.S.C., chapter 55

Refuse Act, 1899, ch. 425, 30 Stat. 1152, 33 U.S.C. §§ 401–415

Safe Drinking Water Act, 1974 (SDWA), 42 U.S.C., chapter 6A

Court Cases

Chapman v. Federal Power Commission, 345 U.S. 153 (1953)

Citizens Committee for the Hudson Valley v. Volpe, 302 F. Supp. 1083 (S.D.N.Y. 1969), affirmed, 425 F.2d 97 (2d Cir. 1970)

Federal Power Commission v. Oregon, 349 U.S. 435 (1955), reversing *State of Oregon v. Federal Power Commission*, 211 F.2d 347 (9th Cir. 1954)

First Iowa Hydro-Electric Cooperative v. Federal Power Commission, 328 U.S. 152 (1946)

In re Idaho Power Co., 14 F.P.C. 55 (1955), affirmed as *National Hells Canyon Association v. Federal Power Commission*, 237 F.2d 777 (D.C. Cir. 1956), cert. denied, 353 U.S. 924 (1957)

Joint Anti-Fascist Committee v. McGrath, 341 U.S. 123 (1950)

Office of Communication of United Church of Christ v. Federal Communications Commission, 359 F.2d 994 (D.C. Cir. 1966)

In re Pacific Northwest Power Company/Washington Public Power Supply System, 31 FPC. 247, rehearing denied, 31 FPC. 1951 (1964), affirmed as *Washington Public Power Supply System v. Federal Power Commission*, 358 F.2d 840 (D.C. Cir. 1966), affirmed in part and revised in part as *Udall v. Federal Power Commission*, 387 U.S. 428 (1967)

Scenic Hudson Preservation Conference v. Federal Power Commission, 354 F.2d 608 (2d Cir. 1965), cert. denied, 384 U.S. 941 (1966)

State of Washington Department of Game v. Federal Power Commission, 207 F.2d 391 (9th Cir. 1953), cert. denied, 347 U.S. 936 (1954)

Wong Yang Sung v. McGrath, 339 U.S. 33 (1950)

NEWSPAPERS

Idaho Observer (Boise)

Idaho Statesman (Boise)

Kansas City Star

Lawrence Journal-World (Kansas)

New York Times

Omaha World-Herald

Oregon Journal (Portland)

Oregonian (Portland)

ARTICLES

"Air Pollution." *American Journal of Public Health*, June 1948, 761.

"Air Pollution." *American Journal of Public Health*, January 1951, 30.

Bloodgood, Don E. "Effect on Stream Pollution Legislation and Control." *Papers on Industrial Wastes*, September 1948, 1048–1051.

Blumm, Michael. "The Northwest's Hydroelectric Heritage." In *Northwest Lands, Northwest Peoples: Readings in Environmental History*. Ed. by Dale D. Goble and Paul W. Hirt. Seattle: University of Washington Press, 1999.

———. "The Northwest's Hydroelectric Heritage: Prologue to the Northwest Electric Power Planning and Conservation Act." *Washington Law Review* 58 (April 1983): 175–244.

Bode, I. T. "Wildlife Stake in Flood Control Planning." *Missouri Conservationist* 6 (September 1945): 1–3.

Brooks, Karl Boyd. "Illuminating the Postwar Northwest: Private Power and Public Law in Hells Canyon, 1950–1957." *Western Legal History* 12 (Winter/Spring 1999): 49–75.

———. "A Legacy in Concrete: The Truman Presidency Transforms America's Environment." In *Harry's Farewell: Interpreting and Teaching the Truman Presidency.* Ed. by Richard Kirkendall. Columbia: University of Missouri Press, 2004.

———. "'Powerless' No More: Postwar Judges and Pacific Northwest Hydroelectrification, 1946–1976." *Idaho Yesterdays* 45 (Winter 2001–2002): 11–26.

———. "Response to Edmund Russell and Arthur McEvoy." *Virginia Environmental Law Journal* 24, (2005): 389–394.

"California Pushes Clean Stream Drive." *Engineering News-Record*, February 1948, 221.

"California's Water Pollution Problem." *Stanford Law Review* 3 (1951): 649–666.

Callison, Charles. "The Real Value of Wildlife." *Missouri Conservationist*, November 1945, 4.

Coggins, George Cameron. "Private Rights to Public Natural Resources." *Twelfth Inaugural Lecture*, University of Kansas (12 December 1984).

"Congress Holds the Key." *Outdoor America*, March 1948, 7–8.

"Conservationists at the Barricades." *Fortune*, February 1970, 144–151.

Dant, Sara. "Making Wilderness Work: Frank Church and the American Wilderness Movement." *Pacific Historical Review* 77 (2008): 257–272.

Davis, Kenneth and Walter Gelhorn. "Present at the Creation: Regulatory Reform before 1946." *Administrative Law Review* 38 (Fall 1986): 511–533.

Davis, Kenneth Culp. "Standing to Challenge and to Enforce Administrative Action." *Columbia Law Review* 49 (June 1949): 759–815.

———. "Fiftieth Anniversary of the Administrative Procedure Act." *Administrative Law Review* 48 (Summer 1996): 307–398.

Douglas, William O. "Stare Decisis." *Columbia Law Review* 49 (June 1949): 735–758.

Ewert, Sara Dant. "The Evolution of an Environmentalist: Senator Frank Church and the Hells Canyon Controversy." *Montana: The Magazine of Western History* 51 (Spring 2001): 36–51.

Foster, Charles H. W. "Counsel for the Concerned." In *Law and the Environment* . Ed. by Malcolm F. Baldwin and James K. Page, Jr. New York: The Conservation Foundation, 1970.

Garrison, Lloyd K. "Willard Hurst: A Tribute." *Wisconsin Law Review* (1980): 1095–1097.

Gibbs, Nancy. "Global Warming." *Time*, 24 September 2007, 17.

Glicksman, Robert, and George Cameron Coggins. "Federal Recreational Land Policy: The Rise and Decline of the Land and Water Conservation Fund." *Columbia Journal of Environmental Law* 9 (1984): 125–161.

Gordon, Robert W. "J. Willard Hurst and the Common Law Tradition in American Legal Historiography." *Law and Society* 10 (Fall 1975): 9–55.

Graff, James. "Fight for the Top of the World." *Time* (1 October 2007), 28–36.

Graul, J. C. "Pennsylvania's Clean Streams Program." *Public Works*, February 1949, 28–30.

Halle, Louis J., Jr. "Gabrielson." *Audubon Magazine* 48 (May–June 1946), 140–144.

Harrop, Froma. "Candidates are Silent as City Sprawl Explodes." *Omaha World-Herald*, 16 August 2004, 7B.

Heilner, Van Campen. "The First 60 Years of *Field and Stream*." *Field and Stream*, November 1955, 87.

Herndon, G. B. "Can We Expect Good Fishing in Big, Man-Made Lakes?" *Missouri Conservationist*, March 1946, 4.

Jenkins, Willis, and Jon Cannon. "Introduction to Environmental Letters, Environmental Law: A Cross-Disciplinary Conference Exploring the Impact of the Humanities on Environmental Law." *Virginia Environmental Law Journal* 24, 3 (Fall 2005): i–iii, 231–394.

Kennedy, Harold W.. and Andrew O. Porter. "Air Pollution: Its Control and Abatement." *Vanderbilt Law Review* 8 (1955): 854–877.

Koch, Charles H., Jr. "James Landis: The Administrative Process." *Administrative Law Review* 48 (Summer 1996): 419–433.

Landis, James M. "The Administrative Process: The Third Decade." *American Bar Association Journal* 47 (February 1961): 135–139.

Laubach, John L., Jr., and Sanford Mark Lampl. "Stream Pollution and the Allegheny County Sanitary Authority." *University of Pittsburgh Law Review* 10 (1949): 345–363.

Lazarus, Richard J. "Human Nature, the Laws of Nature, and the Nature of Environmental Law." *Virginia Environmental Law Journal* 24, 3 (Fall 2005): 231–262.

"Los Angeles Smog." *Steel*, 23 February 1955, 48.

Main, Jeremy. "Conservationists at the Barricades." *Fortune*, February 1970, 144–151.

Myers, Gwynne B. "Water Pollution Control." *Ohio State Law Journal* 12 (1951): 376–380.

Nathanson, Nathaniel L. "The Administrative World of Felix Frankfurter." *Yale Law Journal* 60 (1957): 240–265.

Nixon, Richard M., and Edmund Muskie. "A Statement from President Nixon and Senator Muskie." *Fortune* (February 1970): 92–93.

"Pollution Abatement Laws." *Engineering News-Record*, September 1949, 22–23.

Rodgers, William H., Jr. "Industrial Water Pollution and the Refuse Act: A Second Chance for Water Quality." *University of Pennsylvania Law Review* 101 (April 1971): 761–822.

————. "The Persistent Problem of the Persistent Pesticides: A Lesson in Environmental Law." *Columbia Law Review* 70 (April 1970): 567–611.

Rome, Adam. "'Give Earth a Chance': The Environmental Movement and the Sixties." *Journal of American History* 90 (September 2003): 525–554.

Russell, Edmund. "Nicking the Thin Edge of the Wedge: What History Suggests about the Environmental Law of War." *Virginia Environmental Law Journal* 24, 3 (2005): 377–388.

————. " 'Speaking of Annihilation': Mobilizing for War against Human and Insect Enemies." *Journal of American History* 82 (March 1996): 1505–1529.

Schwartz, Bernard. "The Administrative Procedure Act in Operation." *New York University Law Review* 29 (June 1954): 1173–1264.

————. "The Administrative World of Mr. Justice Frankfurter." *Yale Law Journal* 59 (June 1950): 1228–1265.

————. "A Decade of Administrative Law: 1942–1951." *Michigan Law Review* 51 (April 1953): 791–862.

Shapiro, Sidney A., and Robert L. Glicksman. "Congress, the Supreme Court, and the Quiet Revolution in Administrative Law." *Duke Law Journal* 1988 (November 1988): 819–878.

Sive, David. "Some Thoughts of an Environmental Lawyer in the Wilderness of Administrative Law." *Columbia Law Review* 70 (1970): 612–651.

Smith, W. B. "Note: Statutory Treatment of Industrial Stream Pollution." *George Washington Law Review* 24 (1955): 302–319.

"Smog Fighters." *Chemical Engineering*, October 1948, 114.

Sowards, Adam. "William O. Douglas' Wilderness Politics: Public Protest and Committees of Correspondence in the Pacific Northwest." *Western Historical Quarterly* 37 (2006): 21–42.

Stephens, E. Sydney. "Where Are We and What Time Is It?" In *Transactions of the 11th North American Wildlife Conference.* Washington, D.C.: American Wildlife Institute, 1946.

Stine, Jeffrey K. "Natural Resources and Environmental Policy." In *The Reagan Presidency: Pragmatic Conservatism and Its Legacies.* Ed. by W. Elliot Brownlee and Hugh Davis Graham. Lawrence: University Press of Kansas, 2003.

"Symposium 1999: Land Use in the 21st Century—The Next Frontier for Environmental Law." *William and Mary Environmental Law and Policy Review* 23, 3 (Fall 1999).

Titus, Harold. Conservation. *Field and Stream*, (October 1951), 36; (February 1952), 16; (June 1952), 27; (April 1953), 36; (November 1953), 32; (May 1954), 33; (January

1956), 25; (September 1956), 18; (September 1957), 38; (November 1957), 48; January 1958), 52; (September 1960), 40; (May 1961), 36.

———. "A Sixty-Year Fight Continues." *Field and Stream* (November 1955), 68.

"Toughest Air Pollution Problem Yet Tackled." *Engineering News-Record*, 1955, 33.

Trueblood, Ted. "Must the Salmon River Die?" *Field and Stream*, October 1960, 10–12.

Tulenko, Paul. "The Federal-Aid Wildlife Program in Missouri." *Missouri Conservationist*, July 1946, 4.

———. "Back the Robertson Bill." *Missouri Conservationist* 7 (November 1946), i.

Twain, Mark. "The Gorky Incident (1901)." In *Letters From the Earth*. Ed. by Bernard DeVoto. Greenwich, Conn.: Fawcett Crest, 1962.

Wagner, Seymour C. "Notes: Statutory Stream Pollution Control." *University of Pennsylvania Law Review* 100 (1951): 225–241.

"Waltonians! Here Are Your Goals!" *Outdoor America*, April 1949, 6–7.

White, Richard. "'Are You an Environmentalist or Do You Work for a Living?': Work and Nature." In *Uncommon Ground: Rethinking the Human Place in Nature*. Ed. by William Cronon. New York: W. W. Norton, 1996.

BOOKS

Ambrose, Stephen E. *Eisenhower*, 2 vols. New York: Simon & Schuster, 1983, 1984.

American Bar Association. *Annual Report: 1970* and *Annual Report: 1971*.

Andrews, Richard N. L. *Managing the Environment, Managing Ourselves: A History of American Environmental Policy*. New Haven, Conn.: Yale University Press, 1999.

Ashby, Leroy, and Rod Gramer. *Fighting the Odds: The Life of Senator Frank Church*. Pullman: Washington State University Press, 1994.

Ashworth, William. *Hells Canyon: The Deepest Gorge on Earth*. New York: Hawthorn Books, 1977.

Badger, Anthony J. *The New Deal: The Depression Years, 1933–1940*. New York: Hill & Wang, 1989.

Baker, Leonard. *Brandeis and Frankfurter: A Dual Bibliography*. New York: Harper and Row, 1984.

Baldwin, Malcolm F., and James K. Page, Jr., eds. *Law and the Environment*. New York: Conservation Foundation, 1970.

Berger, Carl. *B29: The Superfortress*. New York: Ballantine Books, 1970.

Berry, Mary Frances. *Stability, Security, and Continuity: Mr. Justice Burton and Decision-Making in the Supreme Court, 1945–1958*. Westport, Conn.: Greenwood Press, 1978.

Brinkley, Alan, et al. *American History: A Survey*, 8th ed. New York: McGraw-Hill, 1991.

———. *Liberalism and its Discontents*. Cambridge, Mass.: Harvard University Press, 1998.

Brooks, Karl Boyd. *Public Power, Private Dams: The Hells Canyon High Dam Controversy.* Seattle: University of Washington Press, 2006.

Carlisle, Rodney P., and Joan M. Zenzen. *Supplying the Nuclear Arsenal: American Production Reactors, 1942–1992.* Baltimore: Johns Hopkins University Press, 1996.

Carson, Rachel. *Silent Spring.* Boston: Houghton Mifflin, 1994.

Carter, Dale, ed. *Cracking the Ike Age: Aspects of Fifties America.* Aarhus, Denmark: Aarhus University Press, 1992.

Cawley, R. McGreggor. *Federal Lands, Western Anger: The Sagebrush Rebellion and Environmental Politics.* Lawrence: University Press of Kansas, 1993.

Chafe, William H. *The Unfinished Journey: America since World War II,* 6th ed. New York: Oxford University Press, 2007.

Chafe, William H., Harvard Sitkoff, and Beth Bailey, eds. *A History of Our Time: Readings on Postwar America,* 7th ed. New York: Oxford University Press, 2008.

Coggins, George, Charles F. Wilkinson, and John D. Leshy. *Federal Public Lands and Resources Law,* 3d ed. Mineola, N.Y.: Foundation Press, 1993.

Cohen, Lizabeth. *A Consumer's Republic: The Politics of Mass Consumption in Postwar America.* New York: Knopf, 2003.

Cone, Joseph, and Sandy Ridlington, eds. *The Northwest Salmon Crisis: A Documentary History.* Corvallis: Oregon State University Press, 1996.

Congressional Quarterly. *Congress and the Nation: A Review of Government and Politics in the Postwar Years, 1945–1964.* Washington, D.C.: CQ Press, 1965.

Cronon, William, ed. *Uncommon Ground: Rethinking the Human Place in Nature.* New York: W. W. Norton, 1996.

Cunningham, William P., and Barbara Woodworth Saigo. *Environmental Science: A Global Concern,* 5th ed. Boston: WCB/McGraw-Hill, 1999.

Deverell, William, and Greg Hise, eds. *Land of Sunshine: An Environmental History of Metropolitan Los Angeles.* Pittsburgh: University of Pittsburgh Press, 2005.

Dewey, Scott Hamilton. *Don't Breathe the Air: Air Pollution and U.S. Environmental Politics, 1945–1970.* College Station: Texas A&M University Press, 2000.

Douglas, William O. *The Court Years, 1939–1975: The Autobiography of William O. Douglas.* New York: Random House, 1980.

———. *The Douglas Letters: Selections from the Private Papers of William O. Douglas.* Ed. by Melvin I. Urofsky. Bethesda, Md.: Adler & Adler, 1987.

——— *Go East, Young Man: The Early Years: The Autobiography of William O. Douglas.* New York: Random House, 1974.

Eisenhower, Dwight D. *The White House Years: Mandate for Change, 1953–1956.* Garden City, N.Y.: Doubleday, 1963.

———. *The White House Years: Waging Peace, 1956–1961.* Garden City, N.Y.: Doubleday, 1965.

Environmental Action, eds. *Earth Tool Kit.* New York: Pocket Books, 1971.

Fein, Michael R. *Paving the Way: New York Road Building and the American State, 1880–1956.* Lawrence: University Press of Kansas, 2008.

Findley, Roger W., and Daniel A. Farber. *Environmental Law in a Nutshell,* 5th ed. St. Paul, Minn.: West Group, 2000.

Ford, James L. C. *Magazines for the Millions: The Story of Specialized Publications.* Carbondale: Southern Illinois University Press, 1969.

Fox, Stephen. *John Muir and His Legacy: The American Conservation Movement.* Madison: University of Wisconsin Press, 1985.

Frankfurter, Felix. *From the Diaries of Felix Frankfurter.* Ed. by Joseph P. Lash. New York: W. W. Norton, 1975.

Fraser, Steve, and Gary Gerstle, eds. *The Rise and Fall of the New Deal Order, 1930–1980.* Princeton, N.J.: Princeton University Press, 1989.

Freyfogle, Eric T. *Bounded People, Boundless Lands: Envisioning a New Land Ethic.* Washington, D.C.: Island Press, 1998.

———. *The Land We Share: Private Property and the Common Good.* Washington, D.C.: Island Press/Shearwater Books, 2003.

Friedman, Lawrence M. *A History of American Law.* New York: Simon & Schuster, 1973.

Fuller, Lon L., and Melvin Aron Eisenberg, eds. *Basic Contract Law,* 3d ed. St. Paul, Minn.: West Publishing, 1972.

Gottlieb, Robert. *Forcing the Spring: The Transformation of the American Environmental Movement.* Washington, D.C.: Island Press, 1993.

Grad, Frank P., ed. *Environmental Law: Sources and Problems.* New York: Matthew Bender, 1971.

Gray, Oscar S., ed. *Cases and Materials on Environmental Law.* Washington, D.C.: BNA, 1970.

Hackett, A. P., and J. H. Burke. *80 Years of Best Sellers, 1895–1975.* New York: R. R. Bowker, 1977.

Hall, Kermit L., and Peter Karsten. *The Magic Mirror: Law in American History,* 2d ed. New York: Oxford University Press, 2009.

Harvey, Mark W. T. *A Symbol of Wilderness: Echo Park and the American Conservation Movement.* Seattle: University of Washington Press, 2004.

———. *Wilderness Forever: Howard Zahniser and the Path to the Wilderness Act.* Seattle: University of Washington Press, 2005.

Hays, Samuel P. *A History of Environmental Politics since 1945.* Pittsburgh: University of Pittsburgh Press, 2000.

Hays, Samuel P., and Barbara Hays. *Beauty, Health, and Permanence: Environmental Politics in the United States, 1955–1985*. New York: Cambridge University Press, 1987.

Hirt, Paul. *A Conspiracy of Optimism: Management of the National Forests since World War Two*. Lincoln: University of Nebraska Press, 1994.

Horowitz, Daniel. *Vance Packard and American Social Criticism*. Chapel Hill: University of North Carolina Press, 1994.

Hurst, J. Willard. *The Growth of American Law: The Law Makers*. Boston: Little, Brown, 1950.

———. *Law and the Conditions of Freedom in the Nineteenth-Century United States*. Madison: University of Wisconsin Press, 1956.

———. *Law and Economic Growth: The Legal History of the Lumber Industry in Wisconsin, 1836–1915*. Cambridge, Mass.: Belknap Press of Harvard University, 1964.

———. *Law and Social Process in United States History*. Ann Arbor: University of Michigan Press, 1960.

Jaffee, Louis L., and Laurence H. Tribe, eds. *Environmental Protection*. Chicago: Bracton Press, 1971.

Kaufman, Robert G. *Henry M. Jackson: A Life in Politics*. Seattle: University of Washington Press, 2000.

Keats, John C. *The Crack in the Picture Window*. Boston: Houghton Mifflin, 1956.

———. *The Insolent Chariots*. New York: Fawcett Crest, 1959.

Kieran, John, *A Natural History of New York City*. 1959. New York: Fordham University Press, 1982.

Kirkendall, Richard S., ed. *Harry's Farewell: Interpreting and Teaching the Truman Presidency*. Columbia: University of Missouri Press, 2004.

Krier, James E., and Edmund Ursin. *Pollution and Policy: A Case Essay on California and Federal Experience with Motor Vehicle Air Pollution, 1940–1975*. Berkeley: University of California Press, 1977.

Kubasek, Nancy K., and Gary S. Silverman. *Environmental Law*, 5th ed. Upper Saddle River, N.J.: Pearson/Prentice Hall, 2005.

Landau, Norman J., and Paul D. Rheingold. *The Environmental Law Handbook*. New York: Ballantine Books/Friends of the Earth, 1971.

Lazarus, Richard J. *The Making of Environmental Law*. Chicago: University of Chicago Press, 2004.

Lear, Linda J. *Rachel Carson: Witness for Nature*. New York: Henry Holt, 1997.

Leopold, Aldo. *A Sand County Almanac*. New York: Oxford University Press, 1949. Reissued with *Essays on Conservation from Round River*. New York: Oxford University Press, 1966.

Leuchtenburg, William E. *Franklin D. Roosevelt and the New Deal, 1932–1940*. New York: Harper Colophon, 1963.

———. *The Supreme Court Reborn: The Constitutional Revolution in the Age of Roosevelt*. New York: Oxford University Press, 1995.

Lewis, Michael, ed. *American Wilderness: A New History*. New York: Oxford University Press, 2007.

Lewis, Peter. *The Fifties*. Philadelphia: J. B. Lippincott, 1978.

Lichtenstein, Nelson. *State of the Unions: A Century of American Labor*. Princeton, N.J.: Princeton University Press, 2002.

Lytle, Mark Hamilton. *The Gentle Subversive: Rachel Carson, Silent Spring, and the Rise of the Environmental Movement*. New York: Oxford University Press, 2007.

Magoc, Chris J. *Environmental Issues in American History: A Reference Guide with Primary Documents*. Westport, Conn.: Greenwood Press, 2006.

Marsh, Kevin. *Drawing Lines in the Forest: Wilderness in the Pacific Northwest*. Seattle: University of Washington Press, 2007.

May, Elaine Tyler. *Homeward Bound: American Families in the Cold War Era*, rev. ed. New York: Basic Books, 1999.

May, Lary, ed. *Recasting America: Culture and Politics in the Age of the Cold War*. Chicago: University of Chicago Press, 1989.

McCullough, David. *Truman*. New York: Simon & Schuster, 1992.

McEvoy, Arthur. *The Fisherman's Problem: Ecology and Law in the California Fisheries, 1850–1980*. New York: Cambridge University Press, 1986.

Meine, Curt. *Aldo Leopold: His Life and Work*. Madison: University of Wisconsin Press, 1988.

Merrill, Karen R. *Public Lands and Political Meaning: Ranchers, the Government, and the Property between Them*. Berkeley: University of California Press, 2002.

Milazzo, Paul Charles. *Unlikely Environmentalists: Congress and Clean Water, 1945–1972*. Lawrence: University Press of Kansas, 2006.

Mott, Frank Luther. *A History of American Magazines*, vol. IV. Cambridge, Mass: Harvard University Press, 1957.

Nash, Roderick. *Wilderness and the American Mind*, 4th ed. New Haven, Conn.: Yale University Press, 2001.

Neil, J. M. *To the White Clouds: Idaho's Conservation Saga*. Pullman: Washington State University Press, 2005.

Opie, John. *Nature's Nation: An Environmental History of the United States*. Ft. Worth, Tex.: Harcourt Brace, 1998.

Palmer, Tim. *Endangered Rivers and the Conservation Movement*, 2d ed. Lanham, Md.: Rowman & Littlefield, 2004.

Pells, Richard H. *The Liberal Mind in a Conservative Age: American Intellectuals in the 1940s and 1950s.* New York: Harper & Row, 1985.

Percival, Robert V., Alan S. Miller, Christopher H. Schroeder, and James P. Leape. *Environmental Regulation: Law, Science, and Policy.* Boston: Little, Brown, 1992.

Phillips, Sarah T. *This Land, This Nation: Conservation, Rural America, and the New Deal.* New York: Cambridge University Press, 2007.

Potter, David Morris. *People of Plenty: Economic Abundance and the American Character.* Chicago: University of Chicago Press, 1954.

Reiger, John F. *American Sportsmen and the Origins of Conservation,* rev. ed. Norman: University of Oklahoma Press, 1986.

Richardson, Elmo. *Dams, Parks, and Politics: Resource Development and Preservation in the Truman-Eisenhower Era.* Lexington: University of Kentucky Press, 1973.

Rodgers, William H., Jr. *Handbook on Environmental Law.* St. Paul, Minn.: West Publishing, 1977.

Rome, Adam. *The Bulldozer in the Countryside: Suburban Sprawl and the Rise of American Environmentalism.* New York: Cambridge University Press, 2001.

Rothman, Hal K. *The Greening of a Nation? Environmentalism in the United States since 1945.* Ft. Worth, Tex.: Harcourt Brace, 1998.

Russell, Edmund. *War and Nature: Fighting Humans and Insects with Chemicals from World War I to Silent Spring.* New York: Cambridge University Press, 2001.

Salzman, James, and Barton H. Thompson, Jr. *Environmental Law and Policy,* 2d ed. New York: Foundation Press, 2007.

Sax, Joseph L. *Defending the Environment: A Strategy for Citizen Action.* 1970; New York: Alfred A. Knopf, 1971.

Smylie, Robert E. *Governor Smylie Remembers.* Moscow: University of Idaho Press, 1999.

Sowards, Adam. *Environmental Justice: William O. Douglas and American Conservation.* Corvallis: Oregon State University Press, forthcoming 2009.

Speth, James Gustave. *Red Sky at Morning: America and the Crisis of the Global Environment.* New Haven, Conn.: Yale University Press, 2004.

Stapilus, Randy. *Paradox Politics: People and Power in Idaho.* Boise, Idaho: Ridenbaugh Press, 1988.

Steinberg, Ted. *Down to Earth: Nature's Role in American History.* New York: Oxford University Press, 2002.

———. *Slide Mountain, or the Folly of Owning Nature.* Berkeley: University of California Press, 1995.

Stensvaag, John-Mark, ed. *Materials on Environmental Law.* St. Paul, Minn.: West Group, 1999.

Stoll, Steven. *U.S. Environmentalism since 1945: A Brief History with Documents*. Boston: Bedford/St. Martin's, 2007.

Stone, Irving. *Earl Warren: A Great American Story*. New York: Prentice-Hall, 1948.

Sutter, Paul. *Driven Wild: How the Fight Against Automobiles Launched the Modern Wilderness Movement*. Seattle: University of Washington Press, 2002.

Talbot, Allen R. *Power along the Hudson*. New York: Dutton, 1972.

Taylor, Joseph E., III. *Making Salmon: An Environmental History of the Northwest Fisheries Crisis*. Seattle: University of Washington Press, 1999.

Thorson, John E. *River of Promise, River of Peril: The Politics of Managing the Missouri River*. Lawrence: University Press of Kansas, 1994.

Train, Russell E. *A Memoir*. Washington, D.C.: [privately printed], 2000.

Vaughan, Ray. *Essentials of Environmental Law*. Rockville, Md.: Government Institutes, 1994.

Vig, Norman J., and Michael E. Kraft, eds. *Environmental Policy in the 1980s: Reagan's New Agenda*. Washington, D.C.: CQ Press, 1984.

———. *Environmental Policy in the 1990s*. Washington, D.C.: CQ Press, 1997.

White, G. Edward. *The American Judicial Tradition: Profiles of Leading American Judges*, 3d ed. New York: Oxford University Press, 2007.

———. *Earl Warren: A Public Life*. New York: Oxford University Press, 1982.

White, Richard. *The Organic Machine: The Remaking of the Columbia River*. New York: Hill & Wang, 1995.

Wilson, Sloan. *The Man in the Gray Flannel Suit*. New York: Arbor House, 1983.

Worster, Donald. *Dust Bowl: The Southern Plains in the 1930s*. New York: Oxford University Press, 2004.

———, ed. *The Ends of the Earth: Perspectives on Modern Environmental History*. New York: Cambridge University Press, 1988.

INDEX